## From the Reviews:

"This is a tremendous book, hugely entertaining as prose and terrible unnerving. Tenenbom is a wild writer, a real wiseass, terribly funny, sarcastic, engaging, powerful, accusatory, judgmental, good!" -*National Review*

"It is a stunner! It's funny, it's darkly funny, it's nervous-making funny!" -*WABC*

"An alarming account of anti-Semitism." -*Haaretz*

"Exposes the roots of anti-Ser ... biting humor." -*Report* (Austria)

"So chatty and engaging an ... s hard to put down. Tenenbom is bril...

"Thank you for exposing the myth that German anti-Semitism is a thing of the past."
-Rabbi Marvin Hier (founder & dean Simon Wiesenthal Center)

"Alternately grim and hilarious account of a six-month journey."
-*FrontPage*

"An eye-opening exposé." –*Ami Magazine*

"A revealing investigation." -*Jewish Telegraph*

"Rare wit. I couldn't put it down." -*Winnipeg Jewish Review*

"To understand Germans, one has to learn their language and live with them -- or read Tenenbom's book." -*Asia Times*

"Courageous, funny, outrageously absurd."
-*Der Spiegel* (Germany)

• • •

Tuvia Tenenbom is a political dramatist and journalist. His articles
and essays have been published in newspapers including *Die Zeit*
of Germany, *Corriere della Sera* of Italy, and *Yedioth Ahronoth* of
Israel as well as on various internet sites. Tuvia, who holds
advanced degrees in both fine arts and science, is also the founder
and artistic director of The Jewish Theater of New York.

# I Sleep in Hitler's Room

THE UNCENSORED VERSION

# I Sleep in Hitler's Room

---

*An American Jew Visits Germany*

## Tuvia Tenenbom

The Jewish Theater of New York Incorporated

New York, NY

**I Sleep in Hitler's Room**
Tuvia Tenenbom

This book is published thanks to generous funding by
Michael Steinhardt.

Edited by
Nicolas Frankovich

Photos by
Isi Tenenbom

Published in association with
The Jewish Theater of New York

Printed in the United States of America

ISBN 978-0-9839399-0-0

This book is dedicated to my wife, Isi Tenenbom,
who joined me along for the ride,
snapped close to 2,000 photos along the way,
lovingly comforted me when the going was tough,
and shared in the laughter when it was all done.

The Germans, I am apt to believe, derive their original from no other people.

—*Tacitus*

If my theory of relativity is proven successful, Germany will claim me as a German and France will declare that I am a citizen of the world. Should my theory prove untrue, France will say that I am a German and Germany will declare that I am a Jew.

—*Albert Einstein*

# Contents

## Acknowledgments and Thanks

My debt of gratitude to the many people, institutions, and companies for their help during the different stages of my journey:

The people of *Die Zeit* who guided me as I started out:
Helmut Schmidt, former chancellor of Germany; Giovanni di Lorenzo, editor in chief; Dr. Christof Siemes, culture reporter; Peter Kümmel, chief drama critic; Jens Jessen, culture editor; Evelyn Finger, Belief & Doubt editor.

Stanislaw Tillich, prime minister of Saxony; Kai Diekmann, editor in chief of the most-read European daily, *Bild*; the popular comedian and pianist Helge Schneider; Adolf Sauerland, mayor of Duisburg; the journalist and activist Peter Scholl-Latour—to name just a few.

The various tourist-information offices around the country who facilitated my free stay in hotels and eateries; the directors and managers of institutions who personally accompanied me into their treasures; the managers of the luxurious Steigenberger Frankfurter Hof in Frankfurt, Excelsior Hotel Ernst in Cologne, and Hotel Elephant in Weimar, among others; various leading politicians and activists of the right, left, and center; celebrated leaders of culture; various economists; bosses of industry, including Volkswagen and Mercedes; priests, pastors, rabbis, and heroin addicts; high-school students who warmly welcomed me into their classes and life; the Turkish community of Marxloh, including the imam of Germany's biggest mosque. Thanks go also to all those in between, including Germany's poor and forlorn in cities and farms across the land, as well as its richest on the island of Sylt. And for the many, too many to mention, who gracefully opened for me the door to their homes and the gate to their souls.

Deserving special mention are Michael Eberth, who fought and still fights for this book, for his loyalty and boundless intelligence, and Isa Lowy, my mother-in-law, who was—and is—always there for me.

From Rowohlt's publicity campaign for this book before it was censored.

Original title in German:
**Ich bin Deutschland:** Eine Entdeckungsreise

## Author's Notes

Events in this book span 2009 through 2011.

Journey in Germany: May through September 2010.

Not all people interviewed, or cities visited, have made it to this book. Those who are in this book are fair representations of those met and interviewed.

Order of appearance is chronological, unless otherwise stated. Specific date, day, hour, minute, or second not mentioned. This is not a work of fiction.

When used in interviews, quotation marks in this book indicate exact quotes by interviewees.

Interviews contained herein were recorded, filmed, or done in the presence of at least one witness. When none of these conditions existed, relevant pages were approved by the source before publication. On the occasions when interviewees requested their authorization before publication, their written authorizations were properly secured. In addition, supporting evidentiary materials were accumulated. Email correspondence, when applicable, was preserved. Nearly two thousand pictures were taken.

# Table of Locations

# Preface

This book was scheduled to be in German bookstores in April of 2011. It never got there.

It was advertised by Rowohlt, one of the biggest and most powerful publishing companies in Germany, as an up-and-coming title on its 2011 list, as a best seller.

It never got there, best seller or not.

Alexander Fest, head of Rowohlt, made sure of that. This book, he told me, would be published only if I agreed to tone it down. He had a plan, a simple plan: Cut or change the most revealing parts. Why? Well, there are things that are better kept secret. No, he didn't phrase it like that. He used harsher words. Words like "Your book is deplorably undercomplex [*sic*] and uninformed." What was so bad about it?

The answer came soon enough. I was presented with a version of the manuscript reflecting cuts and changes throughout, and only if I agreed with their "edited" version would they publish the book. Most of the edits had to do with German anti-Semitism, which this book uncovers. Accounts of it were fully cut from their edited version. Also cut were passages of certain interviews where respondents betrayed their anti-Semitism and were now transformed into philo-Semites by the stroke of a pen.

Other times Mr. Fest showed a creative streak. In a few instances where this book had the word *Jews* in it, he demanded that it be changed to *Israel*. It's not nice to show that there are Germans who hate Jews, but Israel is a different story; that's political and the Israelis, after all, are known to be bad people.

What he did was not make the book "overcomplex" or "informed." What he did was pure censorship, fit for an Iranian publisher under the ayatollahs. He steamed when I said this, but he didn't change his mind.

Discussions with Mr. Fest, or with those he charged with the task of negotiating with me in his company, lasted for months. Usually, he employed the worst conduct that this writer has ever witnessed in a professional context. Verbal abuse was a staple in his dealings, as he and his cadre of followers seemed to cherish every opportunity to get ugly and, at times, descend to anti-Semitism. I am, so I was told at one point, a "Jewish hysteric," like the "patron saint of all of them, Woody Allen."

Yes, Jews are "hysteric."

As time went by I was screamed at, constantly lied to, and spoken about in the most degrading terms. When I tried to meet Mr. Fest he would hide and say he's not in Germany and won't be any time soon. As time passed, I was not allowed to speak to anyone in the company, and if I called no one talked to me. Only emails. Abusive emails, to be exact. I was the Degenerate Jew, the "hysteric," treated like a slave by the Master Race.

It didn't start that way. The book in front of you was actually accepted by Rowohlt. My editor, the one who commissioned me to write it and followed its development, told me that "it's even better than I expected." She asked for no changes and demanded no cuts. All she wanted was to see it printed.

But Mr. Fest didn't.

Lawyers, outside editors, various literary agents and fellow journalists tried to intervene. Some tried to change Mr. Fest's mind, others tried to find different German publishers.

All failed.

No German publisher, I was told privately, would publish a book that paints Germans as anti-Semitic. It has nothing to do with truth; it has everything to do with image. Germans are a tribe, I was told, and the tribe will protect itself. This is something I am not used to. Walk into any American bookstore and you will find quite a number of books that are fiercely anti-American, and no one is protesting or raising any objections. This, after all, is the essence of free speech. But Germany, obviously, is not America.

Personally, I didn't want to believe it. Month after month and week after week, I tried to mend the fences, but, like everyone else, I too failed. Time passed, lies piled up, and nothing changed for the better.

This does not mean that I stop trying. Even as I write these words, I continue to identify and approach likely German publishers. Recently I entered negotiations with another of Germany's top publishers. They are "eager" to publish the book, they tell me, and I hope that they will follow through. Time passes, but hope springs eternal.

The passage of time, though painful and exhausting, proved a blessing in disguise, as it offered the benefit of hindsight. It is better indeed to look at events with a more rounded view that only time can afford.

Events described in this book are timelier today than they were last year. A demonstration in Hamburg, as recounted in these pages, provides a striking similarity to the demonstrations in the Middle East and North Africa: In both cases the younger generations rebel against their elders and demand a revolution. Can a demonstration in Hamburg better illustrate the demonstrations taking place in the Middle East today? I believe so. There's something in the spirit of youth, be it for good reasons or bad, that calls for rebellion; and there's something in the spirit of man, for better or worse, that if allowed to wreak havoc he or she will do so. Additionally, it illustrates the power of the crowd and its psychology and of mass mentality. Similarly, with respect to the Israeli–Palestinian conflict, the issue of Gaza and flotillas as told in this book grants us a better understanding of what is happening today and will happen in the years ahead.

The Muslim world, also covered and uncovered here, is the first chapter of a long story and sure to be followed by many others. The relationship between the Christian and Jewish worlds, methodically described below, is another example of the turmoil within us that is certain to affect us now and far into the future.

But we are affected not by war and politics alone; social phenomena make their mark as well. The birth of the iPad, for example, not only finds its way into this book but has had on our lives an impact that so far has been lasting. Then there are natural disasters, which no less than war or politics or social change deepens our understanding of the world over time. The volcanic ash cloud that hovered over our heads and plagued European skies in 2010, and which is discussed below, shares similarities with the subterranean eruption that led eventually to the nuclear disaster in Japan in 2011. In both cases we the people are players in a game of nature that we know almost nothing about.

But, truth be told, this is not why this book is presented to you today. These observations, as interesting as they may be, do not warrant the sweat that bringing this book to life exacted.

What drives me to see to it that this book is published can be summed up in one word: America. In the present political atmosphere, where for many of us human rights have attained the level almost of a religion, we can benefit from a reality check. Germany today is one of the most powerful economic powers in the world, a country that has bought many of our assets, including most of the American publishing industry—a country that exerts vast influence on us, a country that prides itself on having the best record of preserving human rights, a country that deems itself the best of democracies, a country many in America hold in highest regard and emulate, a country that this year reached the top of the Mainly Positive Influence chart in a BBC poll of "Countries' Influence"—and yet, this is a country that has not changed since Hitler's days in power. No, of course: Hitler does not rule Germany today, the Nazi party is outlawed, and Germany no longer exterminates Jews or gays. But Hitler, let us not forget, did not create the Holocaust, he simply operated in a social environment that invited it. The people were ready. Hitler, an Austrian nobody, stirred the pot of hate that had preceded him and his unsold paintings. The peoples' hearts were with him, as they are today. The hate for the Jew then, and the hate of the Jew today, as described in this book, is the same exact hate.

Yes, I know, it's a horrible thing to say, to accuse a whole nation of racism. But as horrible as it is to say this of a people, it's manifold more horrible to find out that this is the truth. I wish, from the bottom of my heart, that it were not the case, that the people of Germany, people I've always liked, were not what I found them to be.

Mr. Fest is just an example. There are many others like him. And you know it only when they get caught. People who have read Mr. Fest's emails came out of the woodwork to share some little secrets with me. His messages, they say, point to a "Herrenrasse" (master race) mentality. They explain that he is a man who grew up in a household sympathetic to the Nazis. The late Joachim Fest, Alexander's famous father, who served as an editor of infamous Nazi architect Albert Speer and wrote the biography of Adolf Hitler in which he hardly even mentioned the Holocaust, was indeed a controversial figure.

Some prominent Jews of the time, such as author Jurek Becker (author of the novel on which the movie versions were based, *Jakob der Lügner*, starring Armin Mueller-Stahl, and many years later, in the United States, *Jakob the Liar*, starring Robin Williams), would never accept an invitation to Mr. Joachim Fest's home. Jurek refused to shake Joachim's hand when both happened to be attending the same events; it was not, he said, a gesture of goodwill he would exchange with a Nazi.

But enough of Mr. Alexander Fest. He is, sadly, not the exception. I know because I witnessed many Fests.

As I write these lines, the Middle East is boiling over across many borders: Tunisia, Egypt, Libya, Bahrain, Syria, Yemen . . . as people demand the right to free speech. The West, ever eager to show its commitment to human rights, spares no bomb to kill those who stand in the way. It goes without saying that Arabs must pay with their lives to have free speech but Germans can suppress it and not lose a dime. Why are the Germans allowed to be pathetic censors while Arabs are forced to tell the truth? Who gave us in the West the right to kill others who are not really any worse than us?

Toward the end of correcting this injustice, in this book I tell the story of Germany today in the clearest, simplest, and most honest and straightforward way possible.

No. Not all people in Germany are bad. There are exceptions, but sadly not many. Yes, there are good people in Germany too, great men and women whom I'm proud to consider my friends. They inspire me, they challenge me, and I know I can trust them to be by my side if ever I need them. And indeed, it is also for their sake, in the name of my love for them, that I make this book public. No hate in a people will be extinguished if allowed to burn unchecked, no racism in a nation will disappear if allowed to be irrigated with the rain of silence, no German will survive the poison around him if the iron gate of censorship protects it and no Jew will survive if he keeps silent.

This is the history of humanity. This is the story of democracy. This is the essence of this book.

When I set out to travel the land of Germany, I didn't think for one moment that it would end up as it did. In the worst of my nightmares I never imagined that the word *Jew* would be on the minds of so many people. What I hoped for when I started the journey through the Fatherland was "lots of fun." Nobody ever warned me that Germany was a horrible place for a Jew. Nobody ever told me that I would finally understand why the Holocaust started there and nowhere else. Nobody prepared me for a gas chamber.

But luck, or misfortune, contributed to an interesting alignment of the stars when finally I arrived there. The deadly saga of the continuous hate between Israelis and Palestinians, coupled with the global financial crisis, happened to coincide with the World Cup, the one occasion when Germans feel quite comfortable about raising their national flag everywhere and repeatedly screaming

"Deutschland" at the top of their lungs with utmost pleasure. It was against this background that many people were willing to reveal, with no fear, what is normally hidden in the deepest corners of their being. Israelis, they confidently told me, are "Nazis." Jews, they said, are responsible for the global financial crisis. Who, they asked, controls the global markets? The Jews!

The following pages tell of the people I met and what they said to me. Not all of it is about Jews. Some of it is about hotels, cars, tattoos, restaurants, churches, beer, heroin, soccer, gays and straights, financial markets and hot dogs. But "the Jew" creeps in every few pages. If the Germans have one obsession, it is "Jews." They can't stop talking, or thinking, of The Jew. I am thankful to each one of them for letting me inside their hearts and souls, and for allowing themselves to open for me the doors into their lives. Elated by their soccer aspirations, they were generous in their sharing. They were dreaming of winning the world title, and they felt safe to unveil what lurks inside them. I am not the message, nor do I want to be. All I am is the messenger. This book is not about me; it is about the people. It is not about the past, it is about the future of America and of the West.

Let truth stand.

Fall 2011, New York City

Note: A German version of this book, under the title "Allein unter Deutschen," is published by Suhrkamp Verlag, Berlin.

Date of Publication: December 10, 2012

## Introduction

My original plan for 2010 was to spend the summer among the Hamas in Gaza. I was supposed to be there the year before, but in 2009 it didn't work out. First the Palestinians said "Welcome!" and the Israelis said they wouldn't let me cross the border. Then, by the time the Israelis finally changed their mind, the Palestinians changed theirs as well. It's normal over there. This year I decided not to ask anybody and just show up, giving nobody a chance to play games.

I was totally ready. I even made sure that I had with me the private telephone numbers of leading figures in Hamas. They are the people who would help me, a good German, in case I got into trouble once I was on the other side of the border.

Am I German? Not really. But whenever I'm in an Arab territory I am in the habit of telling everybody that I'm German. No, this has nothing to do with philosophy or politics; it has to do with life. The other day, in Jordan, I asked one of my hosts what he would do if I were a Jew. He didn't hesitate for a second and told me he would kill me on the spot. So I learned my lesson, and since that day I am German.

My Arab friends, Christian and Muslim alike, love me for this. "You are good people," they tell me. "What you [Germans] did to the Jews was good."

There's one little problem in all this: I am not German. I come, if I may share this with you, from a Holocaust-surviving family. Most of my family, that of my father and that of my mother, died in the war. By German order. My father fled Europe as a baby, and my mother survived a concentration camp, what the Germans call KZ. I wonder what they would say if they saw me walking around, calling myself German.

What does it mean to be German, anyway?

I've tried on occasion to figure this out. It so happens that I'm a journalist, and one of the newspapers I frequently write for is the German *Die Zeit*, arguably the most prestigious of German media. It is through this paper that I've made an acquaintance with some German journalists, all very fine people, but those who can help me to understand what being "German" means are few. Yes, I also

1

happen to be a political dramatist, and this brought me to Germany a few times when my plays were produced there. But, again, the number of people I met was too small to make me grasp the "German mentality," if such exists. Yet no matter what, one thing I know: Germany might have killed my ancestors, but it saves my life. It's my little German "complex," I guess.

I think of this complex today as a German lady by the name of Julia who contacts me. She is from Rowohlt Verlag, one of the biggest publishing companies in Germany. She asks if I would like to come to Germany, travel around the country a few months, and write a book about my experiences. She tries to make it sound exciting, by telling me that she's not looking for a research book or a travel guide. No, not that. What she's looking for, she says, is a book of First Impressions. My first impressions. All up to me. My thoughts. A Jew from New York visiting Germany.

For quite some time now, perhaps as a result of my saying "I'm German" so often, I have had this little dream of buying a house in Berlin one day. A German like me, won't you agree, should live in the capital. And if I accept Julia's offer, which will require of me an extended stay of a few months there, I might get a sense of what it truly means to live in Germany—

Hi Julia, I'm coming.

•••

## Chapter 1

### Do You Like Diet Coke with Ice? You Are an American Capitalist!

My office is in midtown Manhattan, just opposite Penn Station, a place where many tourists stroll by. And in preparation for my upcoming tour, I make it my business to schmooze with some German tourists; maybe they can teach me a thing or two about their culture.

In general, Europeans are more political than Americans. They love to talk and argue politics, and Germans in particular are no different. I like it. I sit down to talk with a couple of German tourists. They teach me something very interesting today: "We [meaning Germans] are capitalists by force, unwilling capitalists, while you [Americans] are willing capitalists." They love and hate America. They love the Beatles, they tell me. I don't bother to remind them that the Beatles weren't Americans. Why should I? They love the Americans they meet, they also tell me. And they love New York. Just LOVE it. They are very much against Capitalism. Capitalism is bad. But beer is good. I order Diet Coke with ice, they order beer. They look at my ice and say, "Very American!" For them if you order Coke with ice you are an American. And this is the second thing I learn today, who I am: An American. Not a German, an Arab, or Jew. An American. Good to know.

•••

My ticket paid for, suitcases at the ready, and three hours before my flight is scheduled for departure, the booking agency calls. "Don't go to the airport," they say. "Your flight has been cancelled." Cancelled? Yes. Some stupid mountain erupted in Iceland, sending ash clouds above Europe. I thought we were done with ash clouds in the skies of Europe after the last war, but it turns out that this is different: This one is very dangerous for planes. Or something like that; I'm no engineer. All I know is this: There's an ash cloud standing between me and Europe, between the

Capitalists and the Unwilling Capitalists. And the airspace of Europe is half grounded. I rebook a flight for three days later, taking whatever ticket I can find that gets me over to Europe. Cost: $917. It's about a hundred dollars more than the one cancelled, but that's OK. A few hours later, this same ticket gets a little more expensive. Capitalism, you might call it. Lufthansa will be happy to take me to the same destination for $9,800. But Lufthansa is German, so that's probably not capitalism.

•••

## Chapter 2

### In Rome They Know: The "Oldest Jews" Eat Bacon and Clams

Three days later, my plane takes off. I beat the ash cloud. Members of my family got lost in the ashes of Europe, but I beat the ash cloud. I am an American hero. I will conquer Europe! Germany will lie at my feet like an open book. This is the plan, the immediate plan.

I am now in the belly of the plane. In four hours I land in Rome. From there I fly to Budapest. From Budapest, to Hamburg. A slightly circuitous route to Germany, but it's a sure way around the stupid clouds. Jews have been wandering thousands of years and we know the best and safest ways to do it. And yes, finally, this American hero, a world-traveling Jew, lands in Rome. Safely. Securely. On time. Perfect. I walk over to my next plane. I am at the gate. The plane is not. I am the only person at the gate. Everybody else, I soon discover, is on the other side of the airport. I go there. I am not a police surveyor and I don't really know how to count people, but my cautious estimate is that there are about ten to twenty million. I walk over and try to strike up a conversation with them. They would be glad to talk. Do I speak Italian? Yes, I am a professor of Latin.

Not one word, my dear!

And this American hero suddenly feels like an American soldier in Afghanistan. I am here, dying to get out of here, but I have no clue how to do it. The Jewish traveler in me suddenly spots an English-speaking individual. A young Gypsy. He's also going to Budapest, he tells me. Great! Thanks, my lucky stars! Can he show me the way to Budapest? Yes. Gladly. He takes me to a line. It's longer than the Great Wall of China. Better than an empty gate, wouldn't you say? How do you negotiate this kind of line? I ask him.

"You wait," he says.

How long?

"Three days," he informs me in perfect English. If I want I can join him where he sleeps the nights.

Where is it?

"Right here, on the floor. Didn't take shower for some time," he tells me, "but life's good." His girlfriend is with him.

Where?

"Somewhere here," he says, pointing at the millions. He leaves.

And somewhere in the middle of all this mess, I notice a plain little piece of paper, hanging from a thread above something that looks like a counter, with the word "Budapest" handwritten on it. That must be the place I have to go to. The Chinese wall, it turns out, is made of many little lines. I get to my line. An Italian man tells me that Budapest airport is closed but that it will reopen in the evening. He will get a seat for tonight, he tells me in confidence, because he knows people. "Do you know people?" he asks me.

What kind of people is he talking about?

"In the Industry."

Yes, of course. The CEO of Budapest airport is my twin brother, but the problem is that he's not aware of it yet. Would my new Italian friend be kind enough to pass this info to his contacts in the Industry? "You will have to pay," he tells me.

Cell phone in hand, my new consultant goes away, dialing numbers here and there. He doesn't have to stand on line. I do.

Rome is European, the thought comes into my head. Socialist, perhaps, or some form of it. Unwilling Capitalists, maybe. Like the Germans. Will be interesting to see, I comfort myself, the ways of the Unwilling. I will learn something, I tell my heart. It's actually good, I try to reason with myself, that I am lost here in the middle of China. I look and watch. Around and around. There are quite a few Americans in my line, I notice. All stuck in Holy Rome.

The hours pass, and I get closer to the little paper above the sort of counter. An Italian clerk sits behind the counter, handling the masses. The man takes credit cards and issues new tickets. The people here, mind you, have already paid for their flights. But those flights are gone. They either stay here with the Gypsy and his girlfriend until their airline resumes flying, or they fork over their dollars and euros on all kinds of combinations with other airlines. Rome is democratic. You choose.

After hours, my turn. The Italian clerk tells me that my airline is not flying but another one is, and he will gladly find me a ticket for an additional 500 euros. Tonight. But he has to check if the flight is available. If it's not, I can stick around in Rome, there's a two-star hotel next to the airport for 300 euros a night. Oh, he found a ticket. "For tonight. 500 Euros, please. It's available now." Great, Budapest airport is open! "Now," he says.

What does he mean?

"The airport is open now, tickets are 500 euros for an evening flight, but if the airport closes again you come tomorrow and we'll renegotiate a new flight."

Will that be free?

No! "For another 500 euros."

Another 500?

"Yes." This clerk only takes money, he doesn't give any back. These are the rules. "Here you buy tickets," he explains to me. "If I sell you a ticket and there is no flight, you go to the airline and complain. Not to me. Do you have suitcases? Do you want them with you? That's extra. Ten euros for every kilo. How many kilos you have?"

This is Europe and I had better adjust. But it's quite expensive to adjust. With my suitcases, that's about 1,000 euros. For a flight that I've already paid for.

This clerk has had it with me, I can see it on his face. He doesn't want to spend his time with New York Capitalists. No way. "If you don't want to spend the 500 every day," he notifies me, then "I could book you a flight for four days later."

Four days later?

Yes. "Nothing available before. All booked. Your airline has a flight tomorrow morning, and it would be free because it's the same airline, but that flight is booked. And everything is booked till four days later. What do you want?"

I am not sure of the exact meaning of *unwilling capitalism*, or *socialism*, or *social democraticism*, but I'm sure that I have to put a stop to today's lesson. I "accidentally" dangle my press card in front of his eyes, and sure as day he catches sight of it.

"I have one ticket only," he sternly says. "Only one! For tomorrow morning's flight. No charge. But only one. One. Do you want it? I can't give you more than one!"

Yes. I wanted to have all my concubines flying over with me, but I'll settle for this one ticket.

I find myself a four-star hotel in the center of Rome, next to the American embassy, for about a third of the cost of the two-star hotel by the airport. That's some kind of socialism, I guess. The hotel is very nice, and very good. Only problem is, I don't have my suitcases with me. I have no clothes, except for the ones I have on me.

I slept with them. Walked a lot with them. In short: they stink. I let the faucet go, soak everything I have, all my clothes, in the water. I feel great: I beat the system! My Jewish heritage won. At exactly this moment my cell phone rings. It's Alvaro, an Italian journalist.

"Would you like me to come over with my motorbike and I take you for a nightly tour of Rome?"

I take one look at my soaking wet clothes, and another look at my cell phone, and quickly decide. "I'm coming!"

I'm not going to spend the first night of my journey to Germany naked in a hotel room in Rome. Nope. Motorbike. Let the wind dry my clothes!

Alvaro is a fat man. I am a fat man. But his motorbike is stronger than Mussolini, and it carries us around Rome as if we were a couple of ants.

As he drives his bike with this wet man, in the midst of our night journey, Alvaro tells me that he's the one who got Israel's strongman Arik Sharon's last media interview before Mr. Sharon disappeared from the map. And then he says: "What happened to the Jews? How they changed!"

The Jews, don't you know, used to be good. Now they're horrible.

It slowly dawns on me: I'm not in America. This is as clear as the night. I've lived thirty years in New York and I've never heard such a line. No. Alvaro doesn't hate Jews. He loves them. Kind of. After the Vatican, he takes me on a tour of the "Oldest Jews." In Rome, he tells me, we have the Most Original Jews. "Would you like me to take you to the most Authentic Jewish Restaurant?"

Yes, I say. Let me sit in a warmer place with my wet clothes. I take a look at the menu: choices of bacon. Choices of clams.

Is Alvaro for real? Or did he lose his mind?

Or, maybe, I lost mine.

This is a different continent. Definitely. Who knows what waits for me in Germany. If this is the starting point, heaven knows where it will end.

Alvaro is a kind man. And an intellectual as well. He is as familiar with history and philosophy as I am with my Diet Coke. Yes, I know a little bit: I spent fifteen years in various universities. Still, I don't get one iota of his logic when he talks about Jews. I have no clue what he is saying. Not only about Jews, but about America as well. He found out, on his own, that the Twin Towers in New York were blown up by the American government. Yes, for real. He spends about an hour, very passionately, explaining to me all the details of how the Americans did it and why. He has all the info. He leaves me speechless: The man is either an idiot or a genius. It will take a battery of psychiatrists to decide. Not that this really matters: We're busy eating, and the food is delicious.

Once we finish the "Jewish food," Alvaro kindly prepares me for my journey:

"Catholics are corrupt. Germans are not. That's why Reformation started with Germans. Luther. A German. Germans are the most democratic."

Well, let's find out!

•••

9

## Chapter 3

### Landing in Germany: REVOLUTION! Marching with the Radical Left

I fly to Budapest the next day, stick around for a few days, and then fly to the Fatherland. Why do I write down these little details? It's called record keeping . . . In any case, Hamburg is where I land, the date being May 1. I am in Germany!

In America we have Labor Day, and that's in September. But I think May Day is better. The summer about to come, warmer weather in the offing. Good time to celebrate. I'm ready! I ask around where I could celebrate, and I'm told that the unions are having a "demo," meaning demonstration, and that the "Anarchists," folks of the radical left, are having a parade. Which would I like? In the United States, Labor Day is an excuse for establishments like Macy's to have sales, 40 to 70 percent off, for example. Here, I quickly learn, the people like to enjoy the outside. OK with me. I choose both. I have time.

I start with the unions. A union guy speaks from the stage, via loudspeakers, and the people around are either drinking, eating, having something to smoke, or all the above. Few seem to be listening. I spot one listener, a man holding a banner of the leftist party Die Linke with a hot red color that I really like. I want to have it for myself, so I go to him. He is anticapitalist, he tells me. It's his mission, he says, to "fight the people who only think about money," those hated capitalists.

Fair. It's his right. Germany is the most democratic nation, as the Italian Alvaro taught me, and in democracy you should be allowed to hate. No problem.

Well, one little problem: How do I get him to give me his banner?

Let me try talking him into it.

It looks nice, I say to him. I love the red. This is really a good red. Could I have it?

The anti-Capitalist seems happy that I like his flag. "You can get it on Die Linke's website for five to ten Euros," he says to me.

You are anticapitalist, right?

"Yes, right."

Truth is, what's ten euros between you and me? Not real money.

Bernard, an older man standing next to him, is a very passionate leftist, and very, very anticapitalist. What did the capitalists do to make him hate them so? "They want money!"

The union guy on the stage speaks loudly, almost screaming. What does he talk about? Well, money. People—workers, that is— should be getting more money. And more money. I ask Bernard if he supports this union guy.

He gets a bit upset with me. Of course he supports him, how stupid could I be! "People need to eat and they need money, can't you get it?!"

I ask Bernard to explain to me what's the difference between the union guy and the capitalists whom he hates so passionately. Don't they both want the same thing, money?

Now Bernard gets really upset with me. He demands to know who I am and what country I am from. After all, it must take a special country to create an idiot like me.

I am from Jordan, I tell him.

Hearing this, Bernard softens. He obviously likes Jordan. Jordan is not really a Capitalist country, is it? Hot weather and stuff, he muses with me.

Tell me, Bernard, what's your reason for living? What drives you?

I have no idea why I ask him this question. Just came to me. Like that.

What's surprising is the man's answers:

"Two things: Achieve peace. Fight the capitalists."

There may be a little paradox there, but I say nothing. This May first is his day and I shouldn't ruin it. Jordanians are hospitable people.

I check around a bit more, looking at the few stands in the area and trying to see if I can get something for free from these money-hater union folks, but no.

Time to parade!

A bunch of youngsters, holding a banner that says, "WEG MIT

(ARTICLE) §129" (away with Article 129), are standing by. I ask them what Article 129 is.

Some don't really know, and others say it's "something about prisoners."

What?

"Something about freedom."

Freedom of what?

"Freedom! Can't you get it?!"

I don't want to get anybody upset at me and so I shut up. Good Jordanian boy.

The parade hasn't started yet. It's going to take some time, obviously.

Luckily, time is a commodity I have.

These are no union people, these are youngsters. And these youngsters, so my impression is, share something extremely important with me: Like me, they also have time. Plenty of it.

As they prepare for the parade ahead, these young anticapitalists fill up their stomachs with fresh sliced fruits, ice creams, crepes, wursts, and beer. Some of them—don't ask me to explain this—drink beer and immediately vomit it out. Then they drink again. Life is a cycle, I guess. They buy more beer. And some of them buy more than one bottle at a shot. Why not? Money is no problem, it seems. They have it aplenty.

Nothing happens, except for drinking and drinking, and then some eating.

This is the Radical Left, I'm told. It would be interesting to know what the Radical Right is doing today. Buying less beer? More beer? Eating sliced-vegetable salads instead of the fruit salads? Who knows. I'll have to check it out. I write a note to myself: Join Radical Right.

Eating done, someone barks from a very loud loudspeaker: "Erster Mai!" (May first!) And the audience barks back, stomachs full. To be honest, I'm really lost. If these people came here to demonstrate, I don't see it. I must have been given the wrong info. This is not a demo parade, this is a party. Yes, must be.

As if to confirm my thoughts, young German men in black clothes and red flags start performing rap music. Well, kind of rap. If you come from New York and have seen the real thing in clubs, or in subway stations, you know this ain't no rap. Just young Germans trying to be black. But it's a party. Who cares?

Other youngsters, apparently excited by the sound, start yelling: REVOLUTION!

Is this a song as well? Who knows!

There are other players in attendance, I notice as I walk around, the only parader so far. The police. Oops. I got it wrong, obviously. This IS a demonstration.

The cops are getting ready, walking around leisurely, helmets in hand. Are you expecting trouble? I ask one of them.

"I don't hope for trouble," he answers in English. Good.

The rap music continues. More beer is consumed. Slowly something like a parade begins to take shape, finally. I march with them. Slogans fly, about international solidarity, peace, love, revolution, anticapitalism, equality, justice, and other great words. Some have slogans taped on their clothes as well, which read THE CITY IS OURS. A young man tapes another slogan on an electricity pole. What's this about? I ask him.

"This is about," he says proudly, "alcohol and lemonade."

Can you say that again?

"Alcohol and lemonade. Together."

Right. Is this why you are here, demonstrating?

"Yes."

Could you explain?

"It should be permitted."

Is it forbidden?

While this dialogue is going on, a fellow marcher chimes in. "It's about police brutality," he offers.

Not about lemonade?

"No! The lemonade part with the alcohol," he explains, "is just a play on words. But it's not about lemonade. Nobody here is marching about lemonade. No. No!"

So, is this about police brutality?

"Yes!"

OK. We're getting somewhere. The lemonade guy is giving in. Brutality? Brutality! I must admit that I don't get it. How did you get from lemonade to brutality, if you don't mind me asking you?

"Where you from?"

Jordan. Today I am Jordanian.

This man, too, likes Jordanians, and he gets patient with me, a stupid but lovable Arab. "Police here are brutal. They don't think for themselves. Only follow orders."

14

It's rainy and messy and I'd like to know how far we still have to go. I ask him if he knows where the parade is heading.

He doesn't know.

So where are you going?

"Where everybody's going."

Follow them?

"Yes."

Like the police, following orders?

He smiles. "Yes," he says. "I, too." He lights up a cigarette, drinks a bit more beer, and stares at me.

Jordanians are not that stupid after all.


We arrive at a place called Sternschanze, a place on the planet. Nothing special happens. More beer. And more beer. If you are not a capitalist, I conclude, you drink beer. Lots of it. "We are waiting for the night," somebody finally confides in me.

The night finally arrives. The kids, who have been drinking beer like camels for hours, decide they would like to have an extra bang for their money: pleasurable use of the empty beer bottles. Why not? They paid for it. They throw the bottles. Everywhere. On cops, at stores. Anything that moves or doesn't deserve an empty bottle. And then some stones. Or whatever. Anything that can hurt or kill. Right next to me I see a young man bleeding on the street, lying between two cars. Nobody cares. It's a war zone. A battle. And in this battle between the young beer drinkers who want lemonade and the police who don't, the latter seem the weaker. The police fight back with water-canon trucks but use them sporadically. Spritz and then stop. Spritz. Stop. But not only water, as they also use video cameras. This is something amazingly beautiful: The cops charge into the crowd with video cameras. Between the lemonaders and the cops, it's the cops who are afraid to go to jail. That's the way it works here, I guess. The cops here must document their "good behavior."

Bottles splinter at the landing next to me. I ask the lemonaders to explain to me why they are doing this. They tell me they believe in freedom, in peace, and in love.

I hope they don't fall in love with me. This is love with no limits. And as the night wears on, the lovers/lemonaders start using

15

explosives. Boom! Boom! Boom!

This is the first day of my journey into Germany, but I feel totally lost. I spend hours here and I understand NOTHING. The only thing I figured out so far is this: I am a witness to a battle between lemonaders and video-camera carriers, where either side can potentially end up in the hospital or in the graveyard. But I don't get it. Why can't these two sides drink and take pix together in peace? I must be missing something here. I urgently need to find myself someone who can explain it to me. Who might that be?

I leave this Boom! Boom! Boom! techno/rap concert and go to the train station. Problem: the trains do not operate. No taxis either. I have to use my feet, like Adam and Eve. Not exactly: The streets here are littered with broken glass, this is no Garden of Eden. How did we get from a fresh fruit salad to explosives?

I get to the apartment where I live in Hamburg in one piece. It's a student dorm, known here as WG (*Wohngemeinschaft*). Maybe I should ask them to explain to me what I've just seen. But before I open my mouth I take a closer look around: The place is full with empty beer bottles. Everywhere I look is beer. Must be hundreds of bottles. I probably shouldn't waste my time discussing anything with more drinkers. How these students get to study anything is beyond my capacity to comprehend.

Upstairs on the top floor lives an old lady, a woman who can hardly walk. Young German students congregate next to her apartment, drinking, smoking, and having sex. The old lady won't sleep tonight, the noise is simply unbearable. But the young students are having fun. Only that they don't call themselves "fun people," Like the Boom! rappers in Sternschanze, these students call themselves Anarchists too. And these anarchists want to change Germany. Because, as I work hard to understand, life is very hard here. There's no Freedom, they tell me. The only way I can explain it is this: German Authorities force these youngsters to drink, smoke, and have sex. All the time.

I don't know, I'm a tourist here.

•••

For the next few days I ponder this question: Why am I here? Without an advanced degree in psychiatry or some other related field, I stand no chance to understand anything. Why did I take this assignment? Maybe I should see a movie, I say to myself.

A poster for a movie at a theater called Abaton shows two gay Orthodox Jews in Israel. The movie is called *Du Sollst Nicht Lieben* (Thou shalt not love). They even have an explanatory note in the window, claiming that, according to the Talmud, homosexuality doesn't exist. I don't know who taught them this particular item, since this is simply not true. Maybe they got confused by remarks the Iranian president, Ahmadinejad, made in a speech at Columbia University in New York the other day, where he said that there were no homosexuals in Iran.

Perhaps I'm just too literal, perhaps there is depth here that is still lost on me. Maybe the anarchists are geniuses and I simply don't get it. German culture must be so sophisticated that it takes extra care and concentration to understand it. This also makes sense, doesn't it? Look at Mercedes, Audi, BMW. They're all

German.

Bearing this new discovery about Germany in mind, I go back to the Sternschanze neighborhood to find some of the demonstrators and have them explain to me why they did what they did a couple of nights ago.

I meet Ole, a young man, a kid, actually, next to a very ugly place called Rote Flora.

Do you know the Rote Flora? That's where young people with orange and blue hair jellied up in the form of knives stroll by. Know them? They are the ones who are dressed with torn leather jackets, dirty pants, piercings all over, and usually accompanied by big dogs and big bottles.

Ole is glad to share his life philosophy with me:

> A. He believes in peace.
> B. There should be no police to protect the state.
> C. Anarchy is good.
> D. Let the people decide.

Next to where we chat there's a handmade memorial to a leftist who died in the area. "*In stiller Trauer* . . . *Joe*" (In loving memory . . . Joe), it says on it.

How did he die?

"I don't know."

What would you do, if there were no police and you caught a murderer?

"Talk to him and try to make him repent in the hope that he won't do it again."

And if someone rapes a woman, what should be done with him?

"Same thing. The idea is that the people should decide, not the police."

Do you have a girlfriend?

"No."

Did you have one before?

"Yes."

Did you love her?

"Yes. Very much."

If I raped her, what would you have done to me?

"Kill you!"

Wait a second! Didn't you just say—

"But that's my girlfriend. It's different!"

Do you think you make sense?

"I have to go. I'm sorry. I don't have time."

I must figure these people out!

I venture inside the Rote Flora. Like its exterior, the walls inside the Rote Flora are covered with graffiti:

*No heißt NEIN* [No means NO]

No border, no nation

*Erst geschossen nie gedacht* . . . (Shoot first, think later . . .)

They must be fighting for something, only I'm not sure what it is or whether in fact they're fighting not for it but against it. This place looks like a stable, actually. I'm not saying that in a bad way; stables can be good. The graffiti is the only evidence that this place is inhabited by people, not horses. The people, all youngsters, are moving in and about the various graffiti-filled rooms, looking busy. The most common activity here is beer drinking and smoking. So I get a beer, light up, become like them, and start talking to them. A young man tells me how Those Nazis got

him the other day, beat the hell out of him, and how he almost, just almost, had to bid life goodbye. It's a miracle that he survived. They are dangerous, the Nazis, he tells me, and they lurk everywhere in this land.

That's what we are doing here. Fighting the damn Nazis.

There is a reason to life, I guess, beyond just fighting the police: Fighting the Nazis.

This weekend, Rote Flora and other institutions of the radical left in the area will celebrate the defeat of the Nazis. My luck, I came at a good time. The fight goes on: one day the police, another day the Nazis, and in between a few beers. It takes me about an hour to feel at home in the Rote Flora. The box office—yes, they have one—sits empty. Good place to be. I go there, sit on the dirty chair, and get ready to sell tickets. Youngsters come to me and ask what's the plan. God, if I only knew! I check the pile of postcards to get familiar. I should know, shouldn't I? I am the Box Office Manager, after all. Oh, here's something interesting, a postcard that reads: *HITLER KAPUTT!* What is this? Oh, yeah, a concert at the Rote Flora.

These kids, mama's milk still on their lips, are celebrating *HITLER KAPUTT!* What year am I in? What century?

I know I'm going to lose my mind in this Germany, long before I write a single line about it. A voice tells me: Forget the book! And in my mind I write a letter to my publisher.

> Dear Publisher:
> Get yourselves another idiot.

Then I write another one:

> Dear Unwilling Capitalists,
> I will do it only if you pay me one billion euros.

Then another one:

> Dear Friends,
>     I need a psychiatrist to accompany me 24 hours
> a day. Please supply at once.

My contract with my publisher (Rowohlt) is pretty short and quite simple. I write, they pay. But it has a clause there, stating that I cannot write anything obscene. I want to scream Fuck You! Only I can't. Not now. I am the box-office manager of the Rote Flora and I've got to behave.

Anybody for *HITLER KAPUTT!*?
A guy from Nigeria stops by.
"What's new, man?" he asks.
Just finished my beer, need another one, I say.
"How many would you like? I buy."
Give me a few.
Oh boy, I really lost it.
He goes out to buy me the beer.
I can tell I'm into trouble. How long can I fake it?
I better switch sides. Fast. Maybe I should get me some Nazis to protect me, before these kids start throwing empty bottles on my head.
I get off my box-office manager's chair and walk about. Where

can I see the Nazis? I ask the kids.

"Everywhere," they say.

Everywhere?

"Yes, everywhere."

I got that. Can they show me to just one, *bitte*? I don't really want to see many. One, two, three, or let's say four. That would be enough. Can anybody show me four?

"No."

Three?

"No."

Two?

"No."

I feel like Abraham of the Bible, bargaining with God over a few righteous men in Sodom.

Water, water, everywhere, nor any drop to drink, as Coleridge says in *The Rime of the Ancient Mariner*. Nazis, Nazis, everywhere, nor one for me to see.

They hide them, these leftists! They hide my Nazis. These kids want all the Nazis for themselves, I can see.

I run out of the building. Got to get me a Nazi that's all mine!

But where? How?

I walk about in the streets of Hamburg asking people to do me a favor, a big favor: Get me to a Nazi.

The mavens immediately volunteer. "You got to go to the East," they say. "Bavaria," say others. Many send me to Austria.

But I am in the north of Germany. Are there no Nazis in the north?

Of course not. Hamburg people cannot be Nazis. "We don't have Nazis in the north of Germany," proud Hamburgers like to tell me. Unless, that is, you meet people here who are not native Hamburgers, the ones who really don't care for the good name of Hamburg. "Yes," they tell me, the north-haters, "there are plenty of Nazis" around. Where? "You can start in Neumünster," they say, "and then keep going."

Neumünster. You heard of it? I never did, but it exists. Let's go!

•••

## Chapter 4

## Joining the Radical Right against the Jewish Devil

Starting point: Titanic. Part cafe, part club, and mainly a darts pub. Men and women, who all know each other and every two minutes "give five" to each other, keep throwing darts at about five dartboards. In between they drink beer, more beer, coffee, and more beer. Cappuccino. Beer and beer. Another cappuccino. Another beer. More beer. And one more beer. Then coffee. And a beer. In the two hours or so that I watch them I see one man hitting the bull's-eye one time. Usually, the closest they get to the target is somewhere between the double and triple ring, and often they get no closer than outside those. Like on the floor. These people are not going to be CIA assassins. But who cares? One coffee, two beers, *bitte*.

I think: The leftists, or radical leftists, have only beer. Beer and more beer. These people here make a combo, beer and coffee. Does this mean that they are Nazis, or neo-Nazis?

Well, could be. This is Germany. Anything goes here. Lemonade means left, so go figure. I don't know. I'm only a tourist. Can I get two coffees and one beer, *bitte*? I ask the waiter. Oh God, I hope I didn't make a mistake. Two coffees, one beer might mean something here. I hope it doesn't mean Jewish or something. That would be horrible. I mean, if they're Nazis.

Don't laugh. This is all serious business here.

"That's a dangerous place," people told me before I went to Neumünster. "You must be very careful. Please DON'T wear your red scarf! Red is left. Leave your scarf at home. Please!"

I laughed, and my red scarf was laughing with me. But now we are both pretty quiet, my red scarf and me.

Two coffees. Am I nuts?

Maybe I should order a bottle of Vodka, I hear myself talking to my own self . . . No, please don't! With your red scarf . . .!

I'm losing my mind, if I still have one. I'm not really sure.

While in Hamburg, I was told by the north-haters that there's a place called Club 88 in Neumünster. The number 88 stands for HH, *Heil Hitler*. The question is: Where the heck is it? Maybe these darts people know. I can ask them, can't I? Let's try:

Excuse me: Do you know how to get from here to Club 88?

Asking doesn't cost money. And if they are leftists, even if they have guns I shouldn't worry. These folks can't aim.

But the Titanic people, it turns out, don't think of shooting me. Don't even dream of it. They are very happy to help out. Club 88 is their kind of place. They gladly give me the directions. Great. I've hit the bull's-eye.

Club 88. Have you ever been there? From the outside it looks like a great place, full of promise. Problem is, it's closed. Its black doors do not respond to my attempts to open them. But Jews, let me tell you, couldn't survive thousands of years in exile if they didn't have patience. I have patience. And patience pays.

Frank, the owner of Club 88, drives by. He parks his car and says Hallo.

*Heil Hitler*. We are in business.

He opens the doors wide.

And more people come in. Devotees.

I tell my new friends that I'm a computer analyst from the United States and that both my parents are German. I was born in Germany, I explain to them, but my parents emigrated to America when I was one year old. My name is Tobias and I'm a perfect Aryan. I came to Germany to reconnect with my roots, and I'd love to have one of those Club 88 hats that they have in their club. They like what I say, I can see it in their eyes. I choose the hat in which I look the most stupid, practically retarded, and put it on my head.

So good to get in touch with your roots!

*Sieg Heil*, my friends. Wish our Leader, Adolf Hitler, were here to see me.

Frank takes a liking to me. This club is also a drinking joint. There are many sweet drinks here, not just beer. This is not the Rote Flora. Here they love sweet. Would I like the blue liquor? Very good, Frank says. Anything I want, on the house. As much as I want. Club 88 welcomes its lost child. Tobias. Me.

Frank, let me tell you, is friendly, sympathetic, always smiling, and a very welcoming man. I have no idea why the kids from the extremely dirty Rote Flora want to kill him. He is cleaner than God. And, as he talks to me, he keeps on cleaning every dirty spot he finds. Maybe that's why the leftists hate him and his friends.

Would I like an energy drink? Everything for the guest!

Most of my life, how sad, I lived outside the Fatherland. I missed much, obviously. Frank would be very glad to fill in the holes and gaps in my cultural upbringing. Would I like to know? Would I like to acquire knowledge?

Please teach me, my friend!

Frank takes his new task seriously. He brings the books in.

Here is a book about Jews. With pictures, illustrations, tables, and other scholarly stuff. This is a textbook, as they call it in America. This is not fiction. This is reality.

Here, he shows me, is the image of the Jewish Devil. *Jüdischen Teufel*. It's a stamp.

He explains: "The Jews, who control the world, stamp everything that belongs to them with this stamp. When you see this stamp, you know you are under total control of the Jews."

Does The Stamp remind me of anything? he asks.

Not really.

He takes out his German ID card, turns it to the back, and then turns it upside down. He puts the image next to the one in his book, titled, if I'm not mistaken, *Das Deutschland Protokoll*, and shows me the similarities between the image of the Jewish Devil and the image on the German ID card. Practically the same.

Could he interpret the image for me?

Gladly.

Two horns on top. Jews have horns, naturally. In middle-bottom there is a long nose, another Jewish natural feature, as is known worldwide.

Yes. The Jew controls Germany. And he also controls America, in case I wondered.

Let's leave the Jews for a moment. What does Frank think of Obama?

"Obama is a Nigger and he should go to Africa."

Frank comes back to the Jews, his real passion:

"Six million Jews did not die in World War II. It takes seventy-two minutes to gas and burn one person. How could you burn so many so fast? What I say now, if the police heard me, would cost me six years in prison."

OK, let's talk about Jews. What should we do with the Jews of today?

"Kill them!"

Turks are bad. Idiots. Or, as he calls them, "dumb Jews." Turks have no patience, can't calculate ahead of time. Not so the Jews. The Jews, who are the worst of creatures, they can stick it to you five years later. Just wait and see. "The Jews are the worst. There are millions of Jews in Germany."

How many millions?

"At least one million."

Let's hope, says Frank, that "the Nigger American president takes care of the Jews of Israel, who steal the water from the Palestinians, and stops those Jews once and for all."

Frank is well versed in politics. Knows everything. He tells me: "The German chancellor must always visit America in order to submit to the Allies. Still. This is a shame for Germany!"

What does he think of, let's say, Helmut Schmidt?

"He is good."

Is he a Jew?

"No."

I heard that he is.

"Really? *Scheiße!*" (Shit!)

The German Reich still exists, he instructs me, though it's not functioning because of America and the Allies, which are controlled by the Jews.

Frank now offers beer and brandy to his guest, free of charge. He continues to talk: "The German left is dumb, stupid. All they care for is porno and alcohol. They just want to consume alcohol. Very bad. And porno. Who provides the porno? Jews. The Jews, who consider themselves Children of God, used to sacrifice their own kids to their God. This is a known fact. Today, in keeping with their ancient custom, they take dolls and perform a sacrificial ritual. Yes. When George Bush was president, Jewish leaders performed such a ritual in the presence of President Bush and other world leaders. This ritual was filmed and is available on YouTube."

Where on YouTube?

Frank opens his laptop to show me the YouTube clip. It takes some time. Much time. He can't find the clip. Maybe a Jew from Berlin has blocked him. But don't worry. Frank has the clip on a DVD. In his house. Maybe I will come again.

"Did you see the Jew Michel Friedman? Easy to tell he is a Jew because of his hairstyle. Jews have a different hairstyle. It's a wavy hairstyle. That's the way the Jews have it. And Michel Friedman, a Jew, smokes all kinds of forbidden leaves as well."

I'm delighted it's so easy to recognize a Jew.

No, Frank is not looking for trouble, he explains. All he wants is peace and love. Unification of Germany, Austria, Denmark, and other countries is needed because they are one country, one people. It's important to unite and protect the white race. But not the Poles. And, by the way, for the sake of honest and true history, may it be known that "Germany never invaded Poland. It's a lie.

Honor of family, love of brother and sister, that's what's important. And getting rid of the Jews, once and for all. Those schemers, creatures who invented a story about some holocaust so that they could squeeze out of Germany billions of euros plus four submarines. And then, when they wanted more money, they bombed the World Trade Center and made America fight for them."

After the Jews, Frank's biggest enemy is the police, the German police. And, like the anarchists, he would like to see them gone. And like those on the left, all he's really wishing for is Peace and Love.

What is most striking about Frank is that he is really a very lovely and generous person. Before coming here, people warned me of the dangers awaiting me once I crossed the entrance door to Club 88. They see the neo-Nazis on TV and think they're beasts. Little do they know. Frank, like the other people in the club, is no mass murderer. Quite the opposite: He is kind and so very welcoming. He offers free drinks, maintains constant personal attention, and is always smiling.

He likes to sing sometimes. He sings for me a little song, a romantic tune. Let me share it with you: "We have crematoriums, and in each crematorium there's a little Jew . . ." He smiles as he sings it. He has a good voice, by the way.

And I think: Probably that's how my family was led to death.

With a song and a smile.

It's time to leave. Frank poses for a picture with me, the American computer analyst. We shake hands and we hug. "I love my people, I love my family, and I love my land," he says to me before I leave his place. "All I want is to protect them."

He's a Believer, like any churchgoer you'll meet on Sunday morning during prayer. Both want the best for their families, both are dedicated to their beliefs, and both, it strangely strikes me just now, believe in dead Jews.

We part ways, and I go back to Hamburg.

•••

## Chapter 5

## Mind: Meeting Germany's Elite. Conversations with Chancellor Helmut Schmidt and with the Chief Editor of Germany's Highbrow Newspaper

I walk around the streets of Hamburg and ask people if they are proud to be German. Obviously I have totally lost my mind. No way back. I am on the verge of becoming a Prophet, a Revolutionary, a Philosopher, or any other incurable disease walking on two.

Are you proud to be German?

No, no, no, no, no, no, no, no, come the answers. Not one yes.

I get into a conversation with a young woman who is married to a man who could be her grandpa. He used to be her professor, she tells me. Must be a great thinker to make her fall in love with him. I chat with the man. Are you proud to be German? I ask him. "No, of course not," he says. We talk a little bit more. He has a few glasses of beer, I have a few Cola Lights, which is what they call Diet Coke here. And then I whisper in his ear: "You are in a dark room, all by yourself, naked. It's a wonderful evening. An angel drops from heaven to serve you. And he asks you, the angel, 'Are you proud to be German?' What's your answer?"

"Yes, I am!" The Professor says loudly.

No wonder this attractive young lady fell in love with this ancient thinker.

Who are the Germans? No clue.

Is there something "German" beyond just passport and some internationally recognized borders? Oh, Yes. Just do me a favor, please, and don't ask me to tell you what it is. I really don't know. The only thing I can tell you is this: I'm busy. Very busy. I'm trying to find somebody who'll tell me that he or she is proud to be German. I don't know what I'm going to do when I find those people, kiss them or slap them, but I think it'll be good for my sanity.

A day later I meet Mathias. He's Proud to be East German, he says, but can't say Proud to be German. No way. West Germans, he tells me, drink much less alcohol than the eastern ones. I try to process it. What does he mean "less"? What happens in the east, heaven help me? They bathe in rivers made of beer? While enjoying his beer, he and his girlfriend, Evelyn, share with me their thoughts about the characteristics of the German: "Seriousness, order, unfriendliness, cleanliness." "That's why," they explain to me, "the radical left is dirty . . . a protest against the 'German.'"

I need to get myself a smart person, a human creature with a clear head, to get me out of the mess I find myself in. Or I'm leaving this country on the next flight out. Ash cloud or not. I'll pay Lufthansa $9,800 to fly me to Iceland. I don't care.

I settle for the oldest surviving German chancellor, His Honor Mr. Helmut Schmidt. The man is an icon in this country, I'm told. Works for me. It will take an icon to get me back on track.

I just open my mouth, and the Icon comments to me:

"Let me make a technical remark: I am ninety-one years old, my ears are already a hundred and one years. I understand one half of what you say. The other half I have to make up in my little computer up here, and it's neither from Apple nor from HP, it's from God and therefore it's working slowly. You're speaking much too quickly for me. Please speak slowly."

Very slowly, as slowly as I can, I enunciate my first question to him:

Former French president Valéry Giscard d'Estaing said at the time that your father's father was Jewish. Is that correct?

Hell knows why this is the first question I pose to him. As if this were my business. Or, as if I really care. But you can't stop a tongue once it starts.

The response?

"Yes."

And I go on, like a classical idiot:

You never said it to anybody before. Why?

"There was no reason to talk about it."

Well, you might call Mr. Schmidt an icon. But to me, don't laugh, he's a Jew. Certified. This interview, strange as it might sound to your ears, is going to be a conversation between two Jews. Two Jews talking.

And the First Jew, yours truly, asks the Second Jew, your icon:

Is there a national characteristic that makes a German German?

Second Jew thinks. It takes the Jew time to answer. After two thousand years of Exile, Jews learned to be patient. So I wait until my fellow Jew comes up with an answer. Sure as the Exile, he finally does:

"You could write a whole book on that."

Brilliant. The exact answer I was waiting for. We Jews understand each other. I patiently wait for him to elaborate.

Give a Jew time to elaborate and he takes it.

Mr. Second Jew talks to me about national language. About Literature. About Collective Memory. He tells me that nations tend to be proud of the good things in their history and that so are the Germans. "But the Germans have a series of events in their history that they are ashamed of. Take, for example, the Holocaust, one word hinting at a whole complex."

And they live it to this day.

"The Germans," he says, "are very cautious to form a judgment about the conflict between the Arabs and the Israelis, because they are afraid of being called anti-Semites."

Plain and clear he sums it up for the First Jew:

"The Holocaust is part of the cultural heritage of the Germans, and will remain so."

If you ever doubted whether this man was indeed a Jew, now you know for sure: A Certified Jew. Which, as is the custom between two Jews talking, brings me to ask him:

For how long will this remain part of the German heritage?

Jews, if you didn't know by now, answer questions by asking another question. And so, to keep tradition alive, the Other Jew asks:

"I'll give you an example: How long ago was it when the Jews of Jerusalem were exiled by Nebuchadnezzar?"

Two thousand years ago, I say.

No Jew ever accepts another Jew's response without correcting it. And so does Rabbi Helmut:

"Twenty-five hundred years. More than twenty-five hundred years."

Now I got the answer. If we, Jews, mourn two thousand five hundred years, let the Germans mourn at least as much. And to make sure I got it totally right, the Rabbi adds:

"The Holocaust will be remembered," by the Germans, for "at least as long. Hundreds of years, thousands of years—it will remain. I do hope that this foreseeable future fact will lead the Germans to be extremely cautious in order to prevent any hint of repeating" such crimes.

It is another custom of the Jews, in case you are not aware of it, to apply historical events to the present, and to mix past worries with current ones. So, I ask my Rabbi to explain to me the demos in Hamburg, the violence I saw on the streets.

The Rabbi, as is dictated by rabbinical tradition, starts by proclaiming humility. He says:

"It's not my subject to talk about, because I haven't been there, I don't know." And now that we got the Humility part down pat, the Rabbi—as is always the tradition—goes on to actually answer and Spread the Knowledge. He says: "But I've read in the newspapers that through the Internet they have organized people from all over the place to come to Hamburg just in order to have fun in using force. Quite a few of them are not Germans. Quite a few of them are of Turkish background. Some of them are what in former generations they have called anarchists. But not ideological anarchists. Just young people who would not accept any kind of authority. You see this in the outskirts of Paris, in some quarters in London. I don't think it's a specific German phenomenon. It has something to do with the electronic media. If you didn't have television, if you didn't have the Internet, it would have been much more difficult to organize such things."

My fellow Jew and myself, and perhaps you've figured it out on your own already, keep on smoking while talking. I am not really sure about the law in this country, if this behavior is legal or not, but one thing must be made clear right now: Nobody in Hamburg is going to stop two Smoking Jews. Forget it. If anybody is trying, they'll immediately be accused of anti-Semitism. No German needs this on his or her résumé.

And so, between smokes, I ask him:

Are you proud to be German?

"I have never expressed any pride about my culture."

Never?

"No."

Would he like to have been part of another culture?

"Also no."

And then, between one cigarette and another, as he prepares to bring the new cigarette to his lips while holding to soon-to-be-lit lighter, the Chain-Smoking Rabbi brags a bit about his younger years:

"I was tempted to emigrate to the US after the war. My uncle offered me a job in his factory, he offered me an empty house that belonged to him. It was real temptation," laments the Elder Smoking Jew. Alas, he did not accept the offer.

Why?

"Because I was a German."

This German rabbi is funny, I must say.

This calls for another cigarette.

When a Jew changes into a new cigarette, it is very important to remember, he must change the topic of the conversation as well.

Any comment about Angela Merkel? I ask my Smoking Partner.

Partner or not, Rabbi Schmidt refuses to comment, saying he has been out of politics for thirty years. But later on, when I ask how it feels to be an icon in today's Germany, he dismisses it by saying that the real reason for his being made into an icon "has to do with the fact that the government today is not so impressive as it used to be."

That's Rabbinical!

Helmut is a rare combination of scholar and politician, though I am not clear which part influences which part and which is his stronger side. Hard to say. Per our agreement, he is going to read these pages, having the right to strike words off it. This will offer me a better and deeper understanding of the man. Will he go back on anything he said? But whatever he chooses to do, one thing seems clear to me: He is a man who lives history and loves it. He impresses me as someone intimately familiar with history's often contradictory turns, extracting pleasure from minute details that others would prefer to ignore. He sits in a wheelchair, the years obviously taking their toll on him, but his mind seems to be sharp and ever alert. He enjoys his job at *Die Zeit* and speaks fondly of it. He says to me, of his paper, that "we're totally independent. Nobody tells us what we ought to print and what not." He takes pride in that.

As I am about to leave this Elder Jew, he comes back to the Arab–Israeli conflict. He tells me that his admiration goes to former Egyptian president Anwar Sadat but not to former Israeli president Menachem Begin.

He explains:

"If Moshe Dayan [Israel's Foreign Minister at the time] was the one signing the peace treaty with Anwar Sadat, there would have been lasting peace in the Middle East today. The ones who killed both Rabin and Sadat knew what they were doing." Helmut, the historian that he is, ends the interview with a rather interesting prediction: "The war in the Middle East today can turn into a war between Western civilization and the Islamic world. And in the end Israel will be only a minor player, if at all."

Somehow I feel, don't ask me why, that during his younger years this man did not go to the streets and threw empty bottles at people just for the fun of it.

As I leave the Second Jew behind me, I feel calmer. It feels to me that I start gaining my sanity. I'm not going to Iceland. Not yet. There is some logic to it all. There's a system here in Germany. Not everybody is stupid. It has to do with history, not just beer.

Maybe, just maybe, the reason everybody is drinking so much beer is that they want to forget the Holocaust. It's possible. Everything is possible. Maybe that's why I smoke cigarettes, because I want to forget Auschwitz.

You never know.

But I am a little bothered. What the Smoking Jew told me, that "quite a few of them are of Turkish background," I know for a fact to be totally wrong. Unlike him, I took part in the demos—and I didn't see one Turkish man or woman in the crowds.

Well, he claimed to have read this piece of info in the media.

And since I have time aplenty, I decide to check up on it.

How do you check out The Media? A good idea would be to pay a visit.

Question: Visit whom?

I heard, don't tell anybody I told you, that here in the North there's a smart media man, half Italian, half German, who answers to the name of Giovanni di Lorenzo. He is the editor in chief of *Die Zeit*.

I go to see him.

Since the age of eleven, he tells me, he has lived in Germany.

"In Italy I am the German, in Germany I am the Italian."

Unlike Rabbi Schmidt, this man is no Jew.

And so what are you, I ask him, a German or Italian?

"I can't answer this."

Obviously no Jew. Can't answer the question. Or ask another question in reply. He is half and half.

What's it like to be half and half? Well, let's hear him talk:

"My relationship to Italians is passionate. My relationship to Germans is more like a marriage relationship. Too much passion in a marriage can be deadly."

This is a high philosophical argument and a deep psychological observation. I need time to ponder it.

I decide to engage in small talk and so I ask him:

36

What is the German character?

I hope that he will wander about for half an hour about this and that, giving me ample time to ponder his previous statement. But, oh no! This half-and-half Chief goes on into ever higher, ever deeper fields of thoughts, and I am totally lost.

First he starts with his German half, saying the usual stuff that we are all the same, all equal, same color and same height. Then, after completely satisfying the German in him, he gets into his better half, the Italian.

Being German, he says, is a fear that every item of clothing you give to the laundry will come back damaged.

I love this! I start liking the man!

Let me tell you, and this is between us—I will deny it if you ever quote me: This is so me! This is one of my most intimate fears: The Laundry. No wonder that people, when they get really upset with me, call me "German!"

There's a German lurking in me. How did he get there? Maybe I was switched at birth in the hospital. You can laugh, but things like that happen.

Imagine if my Jewish friends find out that I'm actually German. That's all I need.

No. I'll remain in the closet. I will never come out, I swear.

I am so shocked, I ask the Chief to elaborate.

He does. Thank God that the editor in chief of *Die Zeit* has nothing better to do with his time than to explain to this closeted German the root cause of his most intimate fear.

It's a pathological fear of patina, of Schmutz, he says. That's "German."

He's talking about me, and he has no clue!

Oh God: It just dawns on me: Am I really German? This is all I need now. After living a life of a Jew, it so abruptly and violently turns out that I am a German!

Couldn't I be somebody else? I would kill to be an Italian. Irish. Even Albanian. But German? After being Jewish!

This is Hell. But I have nobody to blame. When you visit Half Italian / Half German, what good can you expect to come out of it? Only a fool like me, a man blind to the future, puts himself in such dangerous waters.

And this Mr. Half and Half, who, I am sure, clearly sees to my inner misery, suddenly finds much pleasure in belaboring this dumb issue.

"Years ago," says Mr. Half and Half, "a German minister had to resign because he wrote a letter of recommendation for his brother-in-law. As a half Italian I say this to you: An Italian minister would have resigned if he didn't do it. In Germany you have to resign because you did it."

Yes, stick it to me, Mister! What do you think, that I don't want to be an Italian, a full-blooded Italian? I'd kill to be Berlusconi. Why do you torture me?

I say this line in my heart but don't utter it with my lips. Never! Instead, like any average neurotic Jew you ever met, I say:

How could such a country, so enlightened, have descended that low in World War II?

I wonder if there ever was a man, or a woman, who raised such a stupid question in this venerable office of *Die Zeit* since the day it was built. When the day comes and I become the chief editor of *Die Zeit*, I guarantee you this: I'll throw out anyone who asks me questions like this. Lucky me, Half and Half is still the chief.

"I spoke with Helmut Schmidt the other day and we discussed it. He told me that he doesn't trust the Germans. And he's a former chancellor."

I have no idea how this answers my question, but the mere mention of this other Jew, Rabbi Helmut, makes me feel good and totally calms my nerves.

And now that I am relaxed, abruptly feeling Jewish again, I go on to ask Giovanni about the anarchists. Jews like to talk about all kinds of extremes. For one reason or another, this issue pleases them since the day they strolled out of Egypt.

"The anarchists became more and more similar to the people they fight," he says. "This is a constant that exists in all radical political movements. I don't believe in a genetic disposition of one people as opposed to others."

I am not sure I agree with him, but I'm equally not sure that I don't agree with him. Simply stated, and I'm quite sad about this, I am no gene scientist. True, I should have been a doctor, or at least a biologist, but I'm not. The only thing I know about genes is how to spell them: *g.e.n.e.s.* That's it. But I don't think it's proper that I profess my gene ignorance at this point in time. So I switch the topic. I tell Half and Half how well I was welcomed by the neo-Nazis. Don't ask me how this particular part of my new past suddenly jumps into my mind. I'm no psychiatrist either.

Half and Half seems surprised. His reaction comes in one word:

"Really?"

And then, since I am talking to Mr. Half and Half, I switch from the radical right to the radical left. Why not? I tell him of my observation that the radical left is dirty, as opposed to the Mr. Clean radical right. His response is: "Yes, it's true. But from the point of view of a leftist, which I am not, I'd like to say: Nobody is perfect."

Giovanni, if you really want to know, strikes me as a German in an Italian suit. In other words: German soul in an Italian body. He is charismatic, fully in control, and he rules over this journalistic empire with a smile. In clichéd, stereotypical terms: His command is Germanic, the delivery Italian. The man has a style. But there is another level to him, deeper yet, that you get to see only if he feels comfortable with you and lets you swim in the very inside of his being. He is the perfect host: Friendly, loving, funny, and a great storyteller. He has to get loose, but once he does he shines.

"If you want to know the difference between Germany and Italy it is this: My two-year-old daughter, when she wants to say *Yes*, she speaks in Italian, she says *Si*, always, even to Germans. But when she wants to say *No*, she says *Nein*, and only *Nein*, not *No*, even to Italians!"

How do you explain this?

Herr Giovanni bursts into laughter: "The sound of the language!"

There is a cliché, which you probably heard, that the favorite word in German is *verboten*. Is that correct? He says No. It's just that it fits the stereotype.

He normally reads papers such as the *New York Times / International Herald Tribune*, and "they say that Germany wants to separate itself from Europe and join with the Russians, to restore Apollo, and this is bullshit. They live outside of Germany, and they are in love with their stereotypes."

Speaking of the *Times* and the *Tribune* brings Giovanni into the realm of his favorite subject: Media.

"*Die Zeit* is the biggest newspaper after the *Bild Zeitung*!"

What makes *Die Zeit*?

"First of all, the Tradition; we have a really big tradition here. *Unser Heiligen* [our saints]. I've been here for five and a half years. We're trying to renew the paper, without betraying two things. One, we don't want to indoctrinate, we don't tell people what to think, only give them the possibilities by which they could form their own opinion. It's not the ideological approach. Second: we always refuse to be part of the zeitgeist, to follow the fad of the moment. It's a nice joke on words, no? *Zeitgeist*."

Church bells are heard from outside. A great opportunity for Giovanni to come up with a little story: "A couple of weeks ago a Jewish friend of mine was here, from Tel Aviv, and when he heard the church bells he said: 'Oh, the priest saw that a Jew is sitting here. "Sabotage!"'"

He goes to close the window, hysterically laughing as he moves in the room. Coming back, he says:

"When I started here I said: I respect the tradition of the house, but I'll break one tradition. The slogan at the time was: 'We make the newspaper that we like.' This would be our ruin, I said. Shit doesn't taste good just because millions of flies like it. I believe, I said, that we have to make a newspaper while keeping in mind what our readers want to read. We cannot do just what our little brains want. In five years we grew 60 percent."

Which is your strongest department and which is the weakest?

"Politics and arts are the strongest sections," he says, later adding: Economics, too.

But he conveniently forgets to say what's the weakest section.

As the old Jewish saying goes, "Only the fools tell everything."

Giovanni di Lorenzo is aware that I have a long journey ahead of me, and he wants to help. He shares with me what he deeply feels about Germany:

> Here, the people think they live in a country that doesn't work very well. But of all the countries that I saw, that I visited, I can say: This country is exemplary. This country was built on the ruin of the most terrible state in the history of humanity. Let us work together that this marvelous work done here endures. My grandfather was in a concentration camp, and when my grandmother talked about it she lowered her voice because she was afraid that her neighbors, former Nazis, would hear her. Thank God THAT Germany is over, those people dead. I know this country. I am married to Germany. There exist passions that are higher, but for a marriage it's ideal.

I bid Half and Half goodbye and then I remember: I forgot to ask him about the Turks. Foolish me. I write a note to myself: Visit the Turks before you are done with journey.

•••

## Chapter 6

## Money: Where German Engineering Meets Disney

Evelyn and Mathias, two of the nicest people I met in Hamburg, tell me that on the day of morrow they go to Autostadt. Doesn't sound very Turkish to me, but I like the sound of the name. *Autostadt.* I decide to join. Do you know Autostadt? It's in a place called Wolfsburg, and it's where Volkswagen showcases its cars.

My first stop at Autostadt is at the Ritz-Carlton Hotel. I get out of the car, light up a cigarette, and three employees jump to tell me that this is a no-smoking zone. They are nice. One of them comes with an ashtray, so that I won't lose my cigarette. But no more cigarettes, please, he tells me.

Enter hotel.

There's more than one door as you walk in, each one opened by another smiling employee. All employees smile here. My cynic self tells me that, for every smile I get from these young and handsome employees, somewhere along the way my wallet will get lighter. But I push away this horrible, negative thought. I choose to be positive and believe that these young and beautiful people really love me and that they smile at me only because I am really so very wonderful. I feel good. The staff of Ritz-Carlton is—how should I put it?—different. Each of them carries a little booklet called Service Values that contains the Twelve Commandments of Ritz-Carlton. It starts with "1. I build strong relationships and create Ritz-Carlton guests for life" and ends with "12. I am responsible for uncompromising levels of cleanliness and creating a safe and accident-free environment."

No. Not one of them smile at me because of some booklet. They smile at me because I am a natural Smile Maker. You just see me, look at me, and you love me.

Yeah!

I enter my glitzy room and I'm immediately welcomed by a big TV that begs to spoil me. Erotic films are here for me, if I want. On the screen is this sexy young lady, lying so suggestively, and smiling at me. Even TV ladies love me! Such a good feeling! The Ritz is also happy to allow me to use a bathrobe for my pleasure, free of charge. I can also buy this robe, if I want, for only 128 euros. A steal. Maybe I'll buy it, but later. I say good-bye to my Lover Lady on the screen and go out. I'll come back, Lover. I will see Autostadt and then come back. Will you wait for me, Love?

Autostadt, a German Disney, is plain gorgeous. Everything is glitzy, shiny, and you can't smoke on the street. VW cares about people, and smoking is bad for the health. Gas is good, but smoking is bad.

Angelique, one of the employees, takes me on a privately guided tour of the car-delivery system at Autostadt. Obviously many German clients elect to come here and pick out their car at the source.

First she shows me to the two glass silos, shining towers that house the Volkswagens delivered on location. Already today, 690 cars were delivered. It's a marvel to watch. A forklift picks the car from the belly of the silo, as you watch, to be handed to you in just a bit. It's like the delivery of a baby, the silo being the womb.

There's a whole spiel to follow. When you actually get your car, VW agents come by equipped with cameras. They take pictures of you, and whoever is with you, standing next to the new car. This picture-taking ceremony reminds me of a wedding. The buyer and the car, in sickness and in health.

What VW has done here is wonderful: creating a community of great shoppers, of lovable followers.

Don't laugh at me. It really works. Say what you want, this is definitely a love affair. Between the German buyer and his car.

Here's a family who drove 500 km to get their car at Autostadt.

They are very happy they came all the way up here. It's a special experience. They will even stay at the Ritz an extra day. Just decided. But "the wife is better than the car," says the hubby. "She is softer."

I'm starting to understand—starting!—what Unwilling Capitalism is all about. Maybe I'll convert. Won't you?

There's a wonderful proclamation on the wall in the Audi Pavilion:

> To us, *Vorsprung* [leading] is an inner drive. The innermost drive. *Vorsprung* is in our genes. *Vorsprung durch Technik* [leading through technology] . . . this is where superiority comes to bear.

It's *Vorsprung*. I like it much. I want to be German. Tuvia Schmidt.

On the first floor of Volkswagen GroupForum you can see the Level Green exhibition. it's something about how people of next generations will have a good life, provided we do our part. VW is here to show us how.

Another exhibition nearby is about irrigation and how to save water.

Next to every exhibition there's a well-dressed person, an employee whose job it is to explain to you all kinds of good things. I like the way they look: like they just came out of the shower. For us.

I'm surrounded by love.

I have a chat with one of these employees, René. "Volkswagen recognizes its responsibility for the world," he says to me, and that's why they expend human resources on water shortages across our planet.

The Jewish Irritating Voice in me shouts into my ears, There are two possibilities here: 1) The people who come here don't believe a word this René says, and 2) they believe him. If possibility no. 1 is correct, then VW must be the laughingstock of Germany. It doesn't look it. If possibility no. 2 is correct, the Germans are the most naïve of people on our planet.

Shut up, Irritating Voice! Listen to René, he's talking to you! It takes 150 liters of water for one orange, René continues to share with me, and VW wants to find ways how to improve the system.

Will Volkswagen also build an exhibition on world peace? I ask him.

Oh, that's difficult, says René. Oranges are easier. In Spain, for instance, they need only 15 liters of water per orange, because they concentrate the water just on the orange. Not in Africa, a very rich and corrupt place, which spends all its water . . .

The man goes on and on and on. Who taught him so much stuff?

Nothing here is about money, in case you wondered; it's all about goodness. Really. I, Tuvia Schmidt, know. I can read a map. VW is run by people who care for human integrity and equality; it's not really a car company, it's a church. There are many nuns and pastors in this church, all of them selfish-less volunteers.

Above them all is Otto F. Wachs, CEO of Autostadt. We sit down to chat about the Autostadt Charitable Organization and Culture Corporation.

He's fifteen years on the job and personally he drives a "very fast Audi."

He explains to me, the slow-to-get-it American: "Our people, Germans, are very driven on technical elements. We might not be as good as you are in communications, as you are in Silicon Valley."

I don't know what comes over me suddenly, probably temporary insanity. My face gets very ugly, like the faces of those fat American journalists, and I say to him something very nasty: I tell him to drop the mask, that I don't buy his employees' comments that VW cares about people, and that all this Level Green business smells to me like one big hypocrisy. Will he challenge me on this?

I need a psychiatrist, no doubt. Otto looks at me and says:

"You want a very open answer? We are selling cars. You won't believe how many cars we sell!"

Did he lose his mind as well? Is he saying what I hear him saying? Does he say that all those exhibitions are just a show?

"My purpose is to sell cars."

Insanity is contagious, I can see.

VW, he tells me, produces more than six million cars a year. In America, he explains to me, a car is about going "from point A to B." Not so in Germany. Most Germans buy cars because they like the product. "They are buying it not because they need it for the mobility factor, for going from A to B. Much different from your country."

Mercedes-Benz, he is proud to share with me, is the inventor of cars, and this makes the Germans proud.

There are other differences between Americans and Europeans:

"I remember this *60 Minutes* piece, on CBS, with the priest saying, 'My daughter was driven to death by this Audi in the garage, because my car accelerated by itself. I could do nothing, and I killed my own daughter.' *60 Minutes*, CBS.' So, we are out of business. Now I have to say something, because I was very open with you. You are a very open, democratic society. But in your country . . . your public, your media . . . Sometimes it's over-exhausting, how the media is reacting in your country."

The German media, he obviously believes, won't do this.

Good to know. If one day I get to own a car company and suddenly get bogged down with sudden acceleration problems, I'll move to Germany in a blink of an eye.

Otto is in a good mood today. He keeps on talking, sharing with me the idea of it all:

"Once you leave Autostadt you believe in VW . . . and you're more inclined to buy a VW."

We talk for a long time and then he accompanies me out. He tells me that as long as I am with him I can smoke, that no one will stop me. I try it out. He's right! I go back to the hotel. I'm tired. Doors open, smiles again. I get to my room. I can't see my TV Lady. She must be very upset with me. I lie on the bed. Where am

I going from here?

If I learned anything today it's this:

Socialism is about making money while talking about the environment. Capitalism is about losing money during massive recalls.

Is this true? I don't know anything anymore. Maybe I should go downstairs, take a chair with me, sit between doors, and have all those lovely ladies smile at me for hours.

I fall asleep dreaming of the Eternal Smiles by the Ritz-Carlton ladies and a big smile covers my face. Good to be a Ritz'er!

•••

## Chapter 7

### Faith: Catholics and Protestants Looking to Eat "Body of Christ" Together, Jews Stay Up the Night Looking to Eat Other Things

In Munich, a bird whispers in my ears on the morning after, they have something called *Kirchentag* (an ecclesiastical congress or, literally, "church day"). The Catholics and the Protestants of Germany are making peace, or something like that. I wasn't aware that there was a war, but what do I know? Not much; I'm just a tourist.

Thousands upon thousands of Germans are flocking to Munich; perhaps I should join. Following breakfast in the hotel I board the train south. I'm no Christian, but I'm fascinated with people who want to unite. I love unifications, it gives me a sense of warmth. Especially today do I need it. It's cloudy and rainy and the Ash Cloud keeps on traveling around the skies of Europe. The *Bild-Zeitung* declares that this is the coldest summer in one hundred years. People are complaining but still have hope that the German team will win the WM (World Cup), which is of course very important. The DB, the German train system, issues a Fan Card. I get one. It's cheaper for fans to travel in Germany. Twenty-five percent off for two months from today, and, every time the German team wins, I get another month of 25 percent off.

The streets of Munich are packed with praying people. I never knew there were so many religious people in Germany. Here's a group praying for Afghanistan.

Across the street is another group praying to Maria. Or the other way around—I get confused. Regina, a nice lady from Lübeck, recommends a special prayer meeting that's scheduled for tomorrow.

What's that?

"We will find out on which side of Jesus we will sit in Heaven."

Which side do you think you will sit on?

"I'll find out tomorrow."

I get excited. If I stick around long enough, I'll get a nice place in heaven. Maybe, just maybe, I could take with me the smiling lady from my Ritz-Carlton TV screen. I don't know if I should tell you, but I get a kick out of this whole heaven business. Regina of Lübeck will get Jesus, and I'll get Ms. Ritz.

I jog into a church, to learn more.

"You have a Jew accent," Manfred says to me as I arrive at the church's *Gute Nacht* (good night) Café, exactly at closing time. I get ready to leave but the fine people here won't let a Heaven Seeker disappear into the night. I'm given a slice of cake with fresh coffee, and Manfred sits down to talk with me.

He met some Jews from the Jewish state, he informs me, and I share an accent with them. Am I a Jew?

No, I am Polish. Today I decide to be Polish. I had enough of being Jordanian, enough of being German. I need a Change. Like Barack Obama.

Manfred: "O, God. The Israelis are quite aggressive. They close down the border so that other people don't get food, they starve the Palestinians of Gaza, they're very engaged militarily. They don't want peace, they want war."

Nicely put, but there's a little problem here: Gaza is sandwiched between Israel and Egypt. While the Israelis allow passage of some food and medicine into Gaza, the Egyptians do not allow anything through and keep their border with Gaza hermetically closed.

Does it bother you that Egypt closes the border even more than the Israelis do?

"I don't know why the Egyptians do it, so I can't make a judgment."

But, of course, he knows The Jews.

Maybe he even knows I'm no Pole. I feel exposed. I sit here, eating this delicious cake in Munich, while I starve the Palestinians in Gaza. Horrible man I am. I'll get no heaven. I won't sit next to Ms. Ritz up there. Horrible, horrible, horrible. A horrible Jew, that's all that I am. Tomorrow I'll go to confession.

But on the day of morrow, cruel man that I am, I walk immediately into an exhibition tent called Oasis of Temptation. Where else! My temptation source for today is an attractive lady by the name of Sister Jutta-Maria. A Smiling Nun. She had a boyfriend for two years and then decided she wanted more from the relationship, but the only way she could get it, she thought, was by marrying Jesus. That's Christ, Jesus Christ. She's five years a sister, and she's getting close to Jesus. In three years, that's the plan now, she will marry Him.

How does Jesus look?

"He's not Italian. He has a short beard and brown hair."

Is he a good kisser?

"Are you Catholic or Protestant?" She asks in reply.

Me? Protestant! American Protestant from New York.

No Jew, no Pole, no Jordanian, no German. I can't believe I

change my identity so often. Psychiatrists would say that I suffer from Arrested Development or something related. But I just like it. I was given one life to live, and I want many more. You can try it too, it's very uplifting.

Is Jesus a good kisser?

Here Sister gets more cautious. "He's not a, a, not a—"

Not what?

"You know, not a, how do you say it in English? I don't know. He is not a, you know."

Well, let's try to figure it out.

How will it happen? I ask her. Will Jesus come to your room in the cloister at night and say, "Hello, Sister Jutta. Here I am!"

"Jutta-Maria!" she corrects me. Her birth name is Jutta, true, but the Virgin appeared to her and told her that "she wanted to hear her name out loud every time people call me." So, she smiles, "I added the name Maria."

Good. Now, let's try to imagine the Courtship Scene: Jesus will come to your room in the cloister at night and say, "Hello, Sister Jutta-Maria. Here I am!" What will you do?

First, she tells me, she's going to check it out, make sure it's Him. Her father is a policeman and she's not just trusting everybody.

"Are you tempted?" she says, changing the subject.

Is she "starting" with me, does she want me to take her to my Ritz bedroom? No, no. She offers me chips. Chips, she says, are very tempting. She used to have two packs a week before she fell in love with Jesus. But today she craves it only once every two months. She lives in a cloister, and when temptation calls she goes to the Head Sis and tells her of the problem. And the Head Sister says, "I am happy to give you chips." But not always. Sometimes there are no chips. Stuff happens. Jutta-Maria offers me chocolate, which is Temptation number 2. That's the way she sees it.

I say, Thank you, I'll conquer Temptation today!

She looks at the Head Sister, sitting nearby, and asks if she could have the chocolate later.

Yes!

Sr. Jutta-Maria now explains some Hebrew to her American Protestant visitor.

"*Maria*," she says, "means *beloved of God* in Hebrew."

This American Protestant is very happy to study Judaism and Hebrew in Munich.

My journey into Germany ends up being a journey into Judaism.

Life is full of surprises!

Manfred should have seen how I conquered Temptation. He'd be proud of this Pole.


I'm in Munich's "*Messe*," which is a big convention center. This is one of the locations where thousands of German Christians, Catholic and Protestant, are attempting to get a bit closer.

Margot Kassman gives a speech a few feet away. Dressed in black, she reads her speech from prepared pages. The audience repeatedly applauds. Journalists and photojournalists mix in the crowd. Lots of media here. Some of the photojournalists take pix of other photojournalists.

She doesn't strike me as a charismatic person, but the folks here seem to be her followers. I know very little about her. She used to be a bishop or something and resigned after she was caught driving while "intoxicated," as they say in New York. I wonder what my Half and Half of Hamburg thinks of her! I can see him in his office, on the sixth floor of the *Die Zeit* building, laughing for hours!

It took Margot a lifetime to be given a bishopric, and a glass of wine or a mug of beer to lose it.

Come hither, Giovanni, and we'll walk the streets of Munich together, laughing until this city explodes!

At Margot's side, at a table just behind her, a bishop sits. A Greek Orthodox by the name of Constantin Miron, if I got his name right. He has a long beard, a big belly, and a ponytail. He picks his nose, looks around, and picks his nose again. She talks about the good all religions give to people, or something to that effect, and the Greek picks his nose. If I get her right, she says that we can all have hope if we don't bow down to the rules of the media— and the multitude of photojournalists click. Applause. Music. End. Very PC. The audience goes wild. Germans, it seems, like their leaders noncharismatic. Dry, passionless leaders drive the German soul and psyche to ever greater heights. The audience, Margot's followers, approach the podium with their digital cameras. They push and they shove. They want to take pix. Pix of the living God.

More and more of them are coming.

She gets off the podium, a short woman in black, and the multitude follow.

Something like a stampede develops. The people just can't say goodbye. They want more of her. And more. And more. To be near. One more pic. One more autograph. They beg to be near. They don't know yet on which side of Jesus they'll sit up there, but they know on which side of Margot they stand down here. They push their digital cameras on top of one another. Here's one offering a scarf to be signed. Margot apparently loves all nations and all religions, and graciously accepts the admiration of all.

Where is the nose-picking Greek guy? He's gone. He disappeared; no one even noticed. It's just Margot, the admirers, and the scarf. A Trinity. I stand next to her, amazed by the crowd. One day, who knows, this scarf will be exhibited in a place called

Turin-2, and millions will come to see the miracles of the scarf. And I, from my place in heaven, to the right of Ms. Ritz, will smile and say to the Lübeck woman who sits to the left of Jesus: I saw it when it all started, with my own eyes!

Only now, still on earth, I have to deal with an old lady here who has just stepped on my foot. Small price to pay for witnessing a big miracle in the making.

As I write this, and I'm getting used to it already, people stop next to me to look at my iPad, a device not yet available in Germany. They are friendly. They ask if they could watch me writing on it, and they would like to know some more details, if I don't mind their asking. None of these people, I am impressed, is thinking of this iPad in terms of "Let me play Games on it." No. They wonder, and truly admire, the technology they think is in it. I look at them, and the thought comes to my mind: I admire their admiration. I don't know of any other culture where its people are so excited about technology.

I remember the Apple Store in New York just a few weeks ago, when the iPad was first released. There were tremendously long lines outside the store. Inside, it felt like a sardine can. Everybody wanted to touch the iPad. And the moment the people-sardines got it into their hands, they played different games on it. The excitement was about the games. But this is not the attitude of the people here, these Germans. They want to know the technical stuff. No one asks me what games could I play on it. Here they ask questions like: Were you really typing on it? Is it easy? You can create files, not just . . . Can I see the keyboard? Can you write long documents as well? And then send them via email? Is it better than a computer?

Funny, but this is the thing that most impresses me at this *Kirchentag*. No, they are not like this only here. Same in Hamburg, same in Autostadt. Only that here I have groups of people stopping to watch this wonder in my hands. Amazing, these Germans. I am impressed. They yearn to learn, and I love my new teaching position.

Every human excitement has a limit, as you probably know, and, after a day full of spirituality for my soul, my stomach begs for a little attention as well.

I leave the *Messe* and go to the city. Right next to a very nice-looking church by the name of Frauenkirche, the Andechser am Dom restaurant smiles at me. I'm going to eat here.

Reiner, a Catholic man who sits across from me at the same table, shares his thoughts about the *Kirchentag*. He thinks it's good that the Catholics and the Protestants talk to each other, but nothing will change on the ground as long as the Catholic Church believes itself to be the only true church. No, he doesn't recommend that the Catholic Church change its view. If it did, the Church would dissolve. And then he says this long German word: *Alleinvertretungsanspruch*, which means in English: the "Only True Church." You wouldn't know what it means unless you're Catholic, or about to be. But it sounds nice in German in any case, doesn't it? I like it.

A very friendly blond comes over. She's the waitress. What would I like to eat? Well, what does she think is good? I'm in the mood to eat good food. We settle on a schnitzel. She smiles, I smile, she cracks a joke, I crack a joke, and Reiner is busy talking. Reiner thinks that Obama is the best American president ever since Roosevelt.

Why does he think that Obama is so good?

Well, Reiner is personally very impressed by Obama. For a black man, Reiner says, Obama is outstandingly smart. Obama, says Reiner, can talk for an hour and make no mistakes! That's an amazing thing for Reiner to digest, a black man who can perform like this! Obama fired the executives of Goldman Sachs, Reiner adds, and that was good. Reiner is against capitalists worldwide, and against wars as well. Obama wants to get out of Afghanistan, and that's good. Obama's Middle East policy is not good yet, because he can't do much due to "strong pressure from the American press, which is Jewish, and also because of the pressures from American financial institutions and American economists who are also Jewish." Can he name one American financial institution that pressures Obama on behalf of the Jews? Yes, Goldman Sachs. Lehman Brothers, by the way, was founded by American Jews from Germany.

It's interesting for me to hear because, frankly, I wasn't aware that I was so rich. I didn't know I owned so many financial institutions. When I'm back in New York I'm going to attend all the board meetings at Goldman Sachs. I'll also have to hire a financial advisor to handle all my media holdings.

Reiner is much smarter than me. He knows everything he owns: five hundred acres of land in a place called Ammersee.

Reiner is a true scholar. He knows not only about Jews but about women as well. Austrian women are preferable to Germans. The German women, he advises me, are emancipated—which is a minus. But don't misunderstand him: Those Austrian beauties are no dumb babes. They seem obedient but they know how to wrap their naïve husbands around their little obeying Austrian fingers!

Beware!

The schnitzel arrives. I taste it. It's excellent. Between you and me, I don't really care what Germans think about Jews. As long as I can enjoy their schnitzels, may they be blessed.

In due course the schnitzel plate is depleted, as the *Kirchentag* is slowly winding down in the other part of town. Where should a rich Jew like me go from here?

A thought comes to this Goldman Sachs stocks owner: Now that you have visited the Christians, why not go and visit your Jewish media-owning partners in the land?

I decide: Yes. We own so much together, we should know each other.

Where do you find Jews in Germany?

Maybe Berlin. That's the capital; rich Jews should be there.

•••

Coincidentally, the Jewish holiday of Shavuot is coming up. In the religious Jewish world it is believed that on this day the Ten Commandments were given to the Jews at Mt. Sinai. The tradition is to "receive" the Torah by staying up on Shavuot and studying all night long. Will be interesting to see how German Jews do this. Rich people like them, they must have fabulous ways of celebrating.

I decide to stay up all night and visit Jewish temples wherever I find them.

I get a local Jewish paper and check what's going on where. First, I go to the synagogue in Pestalozzi Street. The rabbi here is from Israel. Cantor as well. People speak Hebrew to each other. Am I in Israel? Not exactly. Forty Israeli tourists are in attendance, the security man, also an Israeli, tells me. Without them, there would be very few people here. An Israeli journalist who lives in Berlin tells me that he once thought of writing a book about German Jews but that there's not much to write. Whatever you might have read, he adds, bears no resemblance to reality.

I look at the writing on the wall, a memorial to the six million dead, as I listen to the cantor's prayer, praising God for protecting the Jews.

I start doubting my sanity. Again.

The temple is on the hidden side of a courtyard. This, a man bothers to tell me, dates back to Jewish history in Germany before the war. Jews hiding their faith.

I'm done here. Enough.

There's another Jewish temple in Berlin, the one with a golden dome on top, police barriers below, and German police patrolling around. I go there.

The rabbi here is a female rabbi, who goes by the name of

Rabba Gesa S. Ederberg. She's wearing a skullcap and she teaches obscure texts about cheese made by non-Jews. Here goes:

"Bithynischer Käse von Nichtjuden ist verboten, und zwar erstreckt sich das Verbot auch auf die Nutznießung—so Rabbi Meir; die Weisen sagen, das Verbot erstrecke sich nicht auf die Nutznießung. . . . Weil sie ihn durch das Lab von Aastieren gerinnen lassen." (Basically: All kinds of different forbidden cheeses . . .)

There are so many texts in the Talmud that make much more sense and are much more enlightening. Why has this rabba, which is supposedly the feminine form of *rabbi*, chosen this nonsensical text? Don't ask me.

I grew up in Judaism, and something here smells foreign to me. I can't put my finger on it. What could it be? Maybe they are converts, I say to myself. But I don't really know. So I ask the rabba: How many converts have you here? She says she doesn't know the number, only that "we have some." How much is "some"? Is it 20 percent, 50 percent? "I don't know," she utters sharply, clearly upset with me.

Well, when the Rabba doesn't know, who does! Her assistant. Sixty percent, she tells me, when I catch up with her. Sixty percent, Jewishly speaking, is around 96 percent.

Another class follows, this time by a visiting rabba, also with a skullcap. She teaches about the making of cheese. She puts up a big paper on the wall with all kinds of info on it like: Milk, 3.8 fat.

She proceeds to give a sermon about cottage cheese, milk, sour cream, and cheeses of all kinds.

And all I can think is: Obviously, these people are not my partners at Goldman Sachs!

There's a Chabad temple in Berlin as well. I go to visit them.

Chabad-Lubavitch, a Hasidic movement that considers itself to be "the most dynamic force in Jewish life today," is dedicating itself to the work of introducing their brand of Judaism to Jews the world over, including those living in Germany. The movement, missionary in style and deed, achieves this by sending "emissaries," usually from the United States, to different countries.

These emissaries, once assuming their position, have to establish on their own the financial resources for their newly created communities.

The emissary here, who is also the leader of the community, of course, is Rabbi Yehuda Teichtal. He tells me that "we didn't go to the German government and say: 'You burned our temples, now you build them.' We built this temple on our own." *We* is actually *he*. Raising 6.5 million euros, he built one of the most outstanding new temples in Germany today. This man, I soon realize, has more energy than the fastest ICE train in existence.

"The Jew has a special soul," he tells me.

Special what?

"Every Jew is born with a love of God."

How about converts?

"Converts are just like every Jew."

Would you mind if your son marries a German convert?

"This is personal already . . . I'd rather my son did not . . ."

Rabbi Yehuda is not a fool. The moment these words pass through his lips he realizes he should have watched his tongue. You don't say this to a journalist. He tries to correct himself, shooting his own feet while he goes on. I do him a favor and change the topic. I ask him what's his motto in life.

"Remembering the past is good, but we should do for the future."

As in the first temple I visited, the rabbi here, Rabbi Yehuda, is not a homegrown German Jew. He and his wife are imports from the United States and Israel.

Most people of his temple speak either Hebrew or Russian. I stick around and after a while find a man who's German-born—a hard task here. He talks to me about German Jewish life. He tells me that Rabba Gesa is a convert.

I feel bad that I asked her about converts.

But the man tells me not to worry. He's also a convert.

Yehuda invites me to have lunch with him later on. I say, OK. Why not? Let me see if Jews make better schnitzels.

"Jews make news!" one of the worshippers at the temple tells me, trying to explain why, to his mind, German media are anti-Semitic.

A prominent German Jewish journalist, who refuses to be identified by name, calls me while I'm at the temple. I tell him I'm going to Yehuda's for lunch. He says: "Didn't you have enough with the neo-Nazis you met in the north? Why meet more Nazis?" I tell this to Yehuda. He laughs. He feels he must have done something really good to upset the journalist so much.

One thing becomes imminently very clear to me: Once you have entered Yehuda's kingdom, you have left Germany. Or, at least, German Judaism.

His is something else. The root of this Hasidic dynasty is Russia. And it shows. The method used here to get people is American. You enter, you feel good. It's all for the customer. Rabba Gesa might be brainy, but she's boring. Rabbi Yehuda might be simplistic, meaning the way he talks to people, but he's full of life: huge charisma, tons of laughter, and very welcoming. I listen to him give a lesson, a world apart from Gesa's. He speaks about Mt. Sinai. Using the Biblical version of the story, he says: "One mountain full of smoke changed the nation and the world. Is it hard to believe, as the nonbelievers claim? Look at the smoke coming today from the ash cloud and threatening global travel . . .! Hard to believe, isn't it?" You can agree with him or not, but you understand what he's saying. You can call it simplicity, but you can also call it clarity. What's more, it comes with delicious food attached. Yes, Yehuda feeds his people, at the temple and in his house. The food served at this man's house will fit any five-star hotel anywhere. Yehuda, you see, is a master philosopher: When the belly of his guest is satisfied, everything told in the room becomes brilliantly logical.

Not only food. Yehuda supplies entertainment as well. Did you, for example, ever notice that ubiquitous, funny-looking *Polizeihäuschen*? Usually manned by two or three cops, this little police house can be found next to many Jewish organizations in Germany. You may have wondered why we need them, as I wondered when I was in Hamburg. Well, today I finally discovered why they exist.

Yehuda wants to show me his temple's mikveh, or ritual bath, which has "the most modern water technology in the world." Problem is, the place is closed now and it's dark inside. He has the keys, but for him to turn the lights on is not permitted on Jewish holidays. That's the law. Nor is it permitted for him to ask a nonreligious Jew to do this for him. That's where the cop, the German cop, comes in handy. Yehuda yells to his son to call in the cop. Son immediately gets the point of what emergency has transpired, and the German cop soon shows up. Now, according to Jewish law, as this rabbi observes, you can ask a gentile to do this kind of "work" for you but you can't be direct

"It's dark here," says the rabbi.

"Here?" asks the German cop.

"Yes, here."

"OK." The cop turns on the light and is ready to go.

Rabbi says, "It's dark here too," pointing to next door.

Cop says, "Here?"

Yehuda says, "Yes, here."

Cop is ready to go. But rabbi says, "It's dark there."

"There?" asks the policeman.

"Yes, there." The policeman turns on the light there and is ready to go.

But Yehuda is not finished: "Can you come with me more, it's dark inside too . . ." This goes on until all lights are up.

And Yehuda says to me: "You see these Roman baths?"

But I just can't stop laughing. It's really, really funny what transpired here. Go to Yehuda's on Sabbath and ask him to show you his mikveh. You have to witness this at least once in your life. It will make you healthy!

And then do as I did and accept his invitation for lunch at his house. You won't regret it. Many people show up. You'll think you've been invited by a king. There is more food here than the eye can take in. And drinks of every sort and kind you can imagine. All kosher, of course. And yes, the food here is superb.

Don't listen to him when he says to you: "On the Sabbath you can eat as much as you want and you will not gain an ounce!"

You'll gain a few pounds here, my dear, but it's worth it. You'll leave happy.

Sorry, you got to be a Jew to be invited here. This missionary group is working only within the Jewish community. If you're a gentile, go to Rabba Gesa.

# I Sleep in Hitler's Room

For the record: Yehuda denies owning Goldman Sachs.

Belly full, I feel I need to go somewhere to relax. A nice place with a view. Where should I go?

•••

## Chapter 8

**Vows: Honey, Let's Get Married Next to Where They Decided to Gas the Jews**

Haus Sanssouci, which in French means "without worry," is a hotel of three rooms. It is also a restaurant, with capacity for 259 people. With its beautiful surroundings, it is no wonder that this place functions as a wedding hall, mostly from March to September. "Every Friday and Saturday there's a minimum of at least one marriage ceremony. Sometimes I have five marriages in one day," says Michael, the headwaiter, who has worked here for eight years. "People come here because it's quiet and we serve typical and original German food. We specialize in liver from veal, German-style, with onion rings and apples and mash potatoes."

Haus Sanssouci, if you didn't already know, is in Wannsee. The villa next door to this wedding hall was selected by Nazi officials on January 20, 1942, for the infamous Wannsee Conference, where the final nail in the coffin of European Jewry was tightly secured into place. Today the place is a museum. How does it feel to have a Liver from Veal next to the Final Solution to the Jewish Problem?

"In Berlin you are reminded of this history every five meters. So, you know what it is, you understand it, but it's history. You just live here, and that's that. Every member of the German parliament has the right to bring members of his party to any of the places that are important to him. Many of them choose this location. And then they come to eat here."

Günter Bolle is the owner of Haus Sanssouci.

"My father bought this house in 1954 from a Jew who left for America."

How did a Jew get to own this place?

"I don't know."

Why establish a restaurant and a wedding hall next to a place where gassing of the Jews was fine-tuned?

"When my father bought the house he didn't know what this place was. No one knew. I didn't know. Nothing."

I'm not sure I get it. So I say to him:

64

I'm trying to understand the young couple who gets married here. How does it work? I mean, I'm trying to picture it. The bride says to her beloved: "Sweetie, I got a great idea! Let's get married right next to the Wannsee Conference. You know, the place with the Jews and the gas." Is that, more or less, how it works? Probably, right? How do you explain it?

"No one ever, up to this day, posed this question to me. Never happened!"

His gardener sits next to us. He feels he must come to Günter's defense. "And you killed the Indians!" he shouts at me. Well, what can I say in my defense? I try this: "I don't get married next to where I kill them."

The gardener, like the trees and the grass, keeps silent.

But not Günter. He likes to talk. "Everybody knows that the Jews control the American economy. But I make a good living in Germany."

I, president and CEO of Goldman Sachs, ask him: How come the Jews are so rich?

"Most of them are bankers. They were here like this in Germany, and they are like this in America. And whoever has the money has the power."

What makes the Jew so money smart?

"I don't know. It's their character. I admire what they do in Israel. They have good business sense. It's in them. They were always like this."

I order the liver meal. I eat. I don't know why I do this. Just got into me. If people here sit in this place and enjoy themselves, let me enjoy it too. Just so. And then, I don't know why, the picture of the Nazi officers and their meeting next door to me makes me want to meet them. To have a talk, them and me. Very strange, I know.

Problem is, they are dead. I think a bit about this little dilemma and then remember the name Ulrich Matthes, the actor who played Goebbels in the film *"Der Untergang"* (Downfall). I go to meet him, in another restaurant, one that he likes.

He says to me: "For ninety percent of the people I am the one who played Goebbels. But for me, I am much more of a theater actor, and my most important work is in theater. There must be some physical resemblance between me and Goebbels, but I don't want to look like him. It's difficult enough to play him."

People still ask you about that role?

"Just yesterday I was asked. It's six years ago!"

Why do they still ask?

"There is something erotic in it, to look through the keyhole, to see Hitler eat his noodles. There's still a fascination with Nazi figures. Not only in Germany."

Are Germans just like everybody else, or is there something that identifies them, something unique that's "German"?

"As an actor, I'll say that it's the language."

That's it?

"When I read Rudolf Höss, who wrote that he killed Jews and then played Schubert and had tears rolling down his face . . . that's German. In my depressive or melancholic moments I think that this quality of being romantic and cruel is a German characteristic."

This is scary. I'm leaving Berlin.

•••

## Chapter 9

## Wedding with Angels: An American Prophet Comes to Visit

I take the train to Hamburg. I heard that an "American prophet," one Mr. Patrick Holloran, has come to town, and I am going to see him. The church, in a suburb of Hamburg, is packed with German believers, young and old. They raise their hands high, American Evangelical-style, they sing, they speak in tongues, and they give the impression of being pretty content. The Prophet enters. A somewhat tall man with a ponytail, shirt over pants, sporting a big belly. All that's missing from this picture is a Harley-Davidson. He looks so much like one of those characters!

Anyway, he has no Harley-Davidson. At least not here. What he does have is pictures. He shows everybody pix of his family, kids and stuff. God, he says to whoever has ears, uses his daughter-in-law to bring people to Jesus Christ.

And now he presents a picture of his wife.

An angel came the other day, he says, and "took four tumors out of her." The German audience applauds. They trust this American prophet. No questions asked. I look at a man sitting next to me; he wears a getitonline.eu t-shirt.

The Prophet keeps showing more pix of his family. We have to know everybody. Too bad we can't see the angels in the pix, but they are there. Here's his daughter, and the angels usually appear to her, he says. No pix of them. His wife again. The Prophet's wife, the Prophet tells his German listeners, is a Messianic Jew. Important fact, I guess. The Germans look on intently at this American family. They love the Prophet's family. He tells them about his daughter's wedding, where, you guessed it, the angels showed up and participated in the dancing. Not only that, but seventy-two people accepted Christ on the spot. Applause. Amazing how the people here believe everything he says. The parents or grandparents of these people believed a short Austrian; they believe a tall American.

End of pix show. Time for the sermon.

"Money is good," he says, and adds, "New BMW is better than a 1972 Beetle."

"Jesus is my banker," he reveals. Would be great to know which stocks Jesus recommends. Maybe I should ask the Prophet in private.

I have no clue what this prophet, dressed with the worst of taste, really wants from my life. He speaks in English and is translated by a German pastor named Gaby. Gaby, a blond pastor, is doing well for herself. The area here, a cluster of buildings, belongs to her family. I met her a while ago, when I came to this country for a show that I had here. She told me then that the owner of Aldi, a German supermarket chain, is Jewish. How do you know? I asked her. Because "he's so rich, he must be Jewish."

The Prophet is doing well here. People with migraines come to him and he cures them, he tells the audience. How does he do it? He says to God, Take off their old helmets. God obliges and immediately their headaches are gone.

Time to read the Bible together. We are to read "Joshua, chapter 8, where Jesus Christ says . . ."

Wait a sec. How did Jesus get into Joshua?

Doesn't matter. Prophets know better.

Patrick had cancer, he tells his Willing Listeners, but he got rid of it. How? He yelled at the cancer, he screamed at it, "Die!" and it died. That's it. Done.

I have nothing to add.

Another hour or two, and a bunch of people stand on line, wishing to have a prayer moment with the Prophet. He could cure their ills and diseases, after all. I decide to wait as well. I want to interview this guy. My holdings at Goldman Sachs will forever increase in value if only I can get a direct line to my banker.

"There are three angels with you," the Prophet says unto me. "One of them with the head of a lion. You have much more influence than you know!"

Very good. But can we sit down and talk, a little interview, maybe? I ask him. "Not tonight," he says, "but tomorrow," right after his morning sermon.

I show up the morning of morrow but Gaby, who stands next to Patrick, says there will be no interview because "you didn't show up for the morning sermon."

Excuse me?

"I told you that you must come to the sermon!"

I have no clue what she's talking about, and why she gets involved to begin with. Maybe she was having a conversation with my angels and they promised her something, but I'm totally not aware of it. I ask the Prophet to speak for himself, since we've arranged this schedule together.

He's suddenly quiet, he can't speak.

Are we going to sit down and have the interview? He stares at me, this Prophet, his tongue stuck somewhere inside his mouth.

Say Yes or No, I say unto him, ordering him by the power of my three angels, including the lion-headed one, to answer me. "No," he says.

I order the angel with the lion's head to strike this liar of a prophet for making me come all the way down here for nothing and to immediately depart from this condemned man.

●●●

## Chapter 10

## Culture: A Comedian, a Western Sheikh, Museum Kids, Law Students, Jesus Christ, and King Ludwig

Once that dark prophet is out of my way, I feel a need for a comedian.

Horst Tomayer is my man. We meet at a café in Hamburg. The German character has a "visible tendency to obedience," he says to me. But I'm not interested in obedience. Are Germans funny? I ask him.

"No. Very little sense of humor. For humor you need brains, and the Germans don't have them."

Say it again!

"Since the existence of Germany the people here haven't had brains. Two world wars, the Holocaust . . . Where are the brains?!"

How can you say that? You guys have Mercedes, BMW, VW. They require brains—

"Technical know-how has nothing to do with wisdom."

The most stupid question I can ask Horst, after this introduction, is: Are you proud to be German? But guess what, I ask him exactly this question.

The man bursts into such a loud laughter that everybody in the café notices us, to put it mildly. When he finally gathers himself, you can hear him, pretty LOUD, saying: "Never!"

He is one of those rare leftists who staunchly hates Germany and as staunchly loves Israel. There are Germans like that. Very few, but there are.

On a serious note, he predicts that "if the euro falls, the national currency will replace the euro and nationalism will rise again."

He says that at such a time the Turkish people living in Germany will "maybe" be ordered to leave the country. The Jews, on the other hand, will "*ganz klar*" (obviously) be ordered out.

What's the difference between the Turk and the Jew?

"The Jew is easier to blame. That's thousands of years of history."

•••

I leave this affable Horst and go back to *Die Zeit*, to meet Jens Jessen, a culture editor. He tells me something I never knew:

"The middle and upper classes read the *Bild-Zeitung*."

Why do you write? Is it just because you like it or because you want to change people's minds?

"Yes, to change minds. That's the driving force, not the mere writing."

Why?

"My basic feeling in life is depression and anger. Normally, I am desperate. I feel there's so much stupidity and bad thinking. I feel like a desperate teacher."

Germans are not the only stupid people on the planet, but "being German makes the stupidity much heavier."

Why?

"Stupidity in Germany is much more dangerous."

Why?

"In culture there are patterns of behavior. My fear is that the totalitarian kind of thinking can come back, like Nazism. I feel the possibility, in little communities . . . There is no sense for diversity in German culture."

They need to obey, the Germans? Meaning, it's not just a cliché . . .?

"Right. Yes."

What's the root of this need?

"The wars between Catholics and the Protestants taught the German people that they have to be together in their little community in order to survive. I think this is the reason, I don't know for sure."

What is *Die Zeit* doing about this?

"Tries to teach people that you can have liberal discussions without fear. *Die Zeit* is part of a small club, four media organizations in Germany, that try to do this."

Four. Which is the best of the four?

"*Deutschlandfunk* [German radio/web] is the best."

In what?

"Everything."

What makes them so good?

"The quality, depth, subjects."

I wouldn't encounter this kind of talk in the United States. No *Time* editor will be so nice to *Newsweek*, or vice versa. No one at the *New York Times* will shy away, in my experience, from saying they are the best. Why can't you? Is it so hard to say, We are the best?

"Honor! It's not honorable to advertise yourself. Definitely not."

Is this a German quality?

Jens wouldn't fall into this little trap . . .

No, he says. Spain is the same. Jens also tells me that, after *Die Wende* (the fall of the Berlin Wall), idealism died in both the east and the west of Germany. Originality is gone, he says, and so is idealism. Everybody is Economically Correct, and nobody wants to lose his job. As he sees it, we live in the Age of Opportunism. The young people, he says by way of example, don't understand those who died in the fight against Hitler. They ask why those people didn't just save themselves.

I like Jens. He's a smart man, a thinker, a man of honor, and a real gentleman. You won't find many like him around anymore, if at all. God, or nature, whatever you believe in, doesn't manufacture any more Jenses. In today's world of journalism, most are very PC. Not so Jens. He couldn't care less. He's an idealist, a word that today is wholly despised. In today's journalism you don't write what you think, if you think at all; you write what sells. This is not Jens. He belongs to a different era, an era that exists in legends. Once upon a time, when journalists wrote honestly, there was a man by the name of Jens . . .

I sit next to Jens, and while I listen to him I feel as if I am in a different place. Not in Germany, and not in the West. The intellectual Western world today preaches only one thing: tolerance. That's all they have to sell. Everybody is wonderful, and that's it. All cultures are great, end of story. What they think, deep down, you can't really tell. Maybe, just a possibility, deep down they think nothing. Maybe deep down is just an empty hole. Tolerance is the code, the flag. And that's it.

But Jens tells you what he thinks. His words are harsh. He has no tolerance, not even of his own people. He believes. You can agree with him, or you can disagree with him, but at least you know what he thinks and where he stands. This is so not Western! I've been talking to quite a few people in this country for the last few days. I've asked them what it means to be German. For the most part, the intellectuals among them were upset with me for asking this question. "You Americans," some of them said, "like to generalize everything!" Intellectually speaking, this statement is one huge paradox. But let's leave it. What is interesting is this common thought of "We are all the same. All peoples are the same." That's all they know. If this is intellectualism, I am Bavarian.

Yeah. I feel like I'm in another place, in a different world. But where? No, not in Israel. That country is very Western-thinking as well. Shallow. I feel as if I'm in the Arab Middle East. This Jens makes me feel so. Maybe I *am* in the Middle East. Maybe this German-accented English speaker across the table from me is in reality a sheikh. Sheikh Jens bin Mustafa. I go often to the Middle East. I talk to the people there and I am delighted to listen to them. No, not because I agree with them or because I disagree with them. Has nothing to do with it. It's because they are not empty inside. They might have no "tolerance," but I still respect them. Tremendously. They have something they stand for. It's not empty inside. I have had many honest dialogues with the "intolerant" people of the East but to date not a single one with the "tolerant" people of the West. The reason is very simple: The tolerant people of the West are the most intolerant people you can imagine. They are so afraid that you will uncover the emptiness inside them that the moment you start arguing with them their first instinct is: Kill him!

That said, I feel depressed after leaving Sheikh Jens. I need time to think, to collect my thoughts. But not here, not in Hamburg. It's a beautiful city, Hamburg, but the atmosphere here, the human atmosphere, is a bit too cold for my taste. I'm not making a generalization. It's just what I feel.

I keep my thoughts to myself. I don't tell the natives what I think of them. It's too dangerous. Hamburgers are very emotional about their city. Mention the word *Elbe* and these cold people suddenly become very warm. A man can talk to you about his wife as if she were a tree, no emotions; but talk to him about the trees of Hamburg and he gets extremely romantic. Women are the same. I don't know how they do it.

Don't tell them I said it! Hamburg is the World Capital of Militant Bicyclists, and if they know I have some reservations about them they might kill me.

No, I'm not kidding. I was schlepping two suitcases the other day, and the bicyclists here were torturing me. On a narrow sidewalk, which could contain either me with my suitcases or a flying Hamburg militia, as I call them, the militia demanded first right of passage. I had to squeeze myself to a tree so that the militia could pass. Then another militia arrived. Same thing. There was nothing I could do. With their bicycles they are ticking human bombs. I had to stop walking so many times, more than the average man in Gaza during the Israeli bombardment of it some years back. And I was thinking to myself: Interesting how animalistic people can become if only they think that the law is on their side. Maybe we should send a delegation of these Militant Bicyclists to the Middle East. They will get peace going there in one day, maximum.

Anyway, right or wrong, I'm leaving. I am heading south. Guess where? To Munich. Again. I'd rather spend my time with Sister Jutta-Maria than with a screaming Hamburger militia.

•••

As I make my way to Munich I watch Al Jazeera TV. Thanks to my iPad, I can watch cable TV on the go. Al Jazeera has two TV stations, one in Arabic and one in English, and two websites, also in Arabic and in English. The English part and the Arabic part are diametrically opposed. The English one is moderate, more or less like the British BBC. The Arabic part is more extreme than Hamas. For whatever reason, which I'm not clear about, this fact remains a secret in the West. But this fact does not mean that Al Jazeera Arabic is not interesting. On the contrary, it's much more interesting than its English sibling. Here I can watch news I see nowhere else.

At this very moment they carry a live broadcast from some

74

flotilla that makes its way into Gaza from Turkey. Sheikh Raed Salah, of the Islamic Movement in Israel, is currently giving a little speech. As is his usual routine, he incites the crowd against Jews. Raed Salah can easily claim the title "Biggest Anti-Semite in the Muslim World." Or, being that he's an Arab, the Biggest Jew Hater. Raed, who previously accused Jews of mixing the blood of non-Jewish children into their breads, is getting a lot of applause here. The Turkish government wholeheartedly supports this flotilla and this Raed, but if I were Muslim I would sink the flotilla right now. These people make Muslims look like total idiots. They call themselves "peace activists" and "human-rights activists," but their peace is the peace of the cemetery. As a Saudi man in Riyadh told me two years ago, when I asked him if he thought that peace was possible: "Yes. As it says in this Holy Book, all Jews die and there be peace between all." He imagined a big Peace Cemetery, where all the Jews will be buried. "We don't fight cemeteries," he said, a big smile on his face.

The Israeli blockade of Gaza probably went too far, but the sinking of the flotilla makes total sense to me. What makes no sense to me is this: I can watch, live, on my little iPad, what happens at sea. Where are all the news organizations, with hundreds and thousands of reporters, to report it? I can't locate one news item about this.

I can't think too much about the Middle East now. After all, it was my decision to be in Germany now instead of in Palestine. I am here. A fact. And before I know it, I arrive in Munich.

No *Kirchentag* anymore, of course. The religious Germans are either gone or hiding somewhere. But the cultured people are here, all over. Let's visit them.

I go to the Deutsches Museum. Why not?

Come along with me, it's an interesting place. Here you can learn things. I do. For example, I never thought about it, but there's a reason why diesel is called "diesel." Something to do with Mr. Diesel, the German who changed the world. Impressive, I can't deny. I live and learn.

This museum, by the way, is arranged very well.

Look here, a table where the first atomic fission took place. That's something you won't find in my backyard.

In a section called Electric Power, a lecture/class is given in the dark. This includes a test, during which loud explosions are heard and following each of them the audience erupts in applause.

You walk around, look up and down and sideways in this fantastic museum and you cannot not love the Germans. Not only because it suddenly dawns on you all the contributions that Germans have made in technology over the years, but also the very way everything is arranged here. It's a marvel to watch. No science museum I have ever visited comes even close.

Here you also get a chance to see Germany's future, the little kids. Whenever I open my iPad, which has been available in Germany only since the end of last month, the kids come. Totally fascinated by it. They obviously don't have it yet, these kids, but they desire it tremendously. They want to know how it works! Where is the modem? The tech genes, so to speak, since we are in a science environment, don't disappoint.

Standing outside and seeing the people just going in and out is an amazing thing to behold: Children as young as two or three years old are here, and they love the place! This, to me, is the best and most powerful exhibition of all! I feel much better. I love these kids!

This is a cause for celebration. A *Leberkäse* (a delicious German meatloaf made with minced liver, eggs, and spices) is in order.

Admira of Bosnia, of the chain store Vinzenzmurr, is the one who prepares the *Leberkäse* for me. She has worked here for ten years, and she teaches me what she's learned about the German people:

"Men order Cola Zero; women, Cola Light; children, Mezzo Mix or Cola; older people, water without gas or Sprite."

That's a philosopher! I love it!

I'm in such a good mood that I go to see a play. It is is called *Rechnitz (Der Würgeengel)* (Rechnitz [The exterminating angel]), by the Nobel Prize winner Elfriede Jelinek. It's playing at the Schauspielhaus at the Münchner Kammerspiele. Performance starts at 20:00, intro at 19:15. Yes. Intro. You get an introduction beforehand, so you can understand the play. Can't a piece of art speak for itself?

Well, maybe not.

The introduction is given by Julia Lochte, chief dramaturge.

The play takes place in Rechnitz, Austria. It is about 180 Budapest Jews who were taken as forced labor and ordered to build the Südostwall. They were too weak to work and were executed in the last days of the war, in 1945, just before the Russians came.

Elfriede, whose father was Jewish, never uses the word *Jews* in the play. Instead she calls them "hollow men."

Helmut Schmidt is not the only Jew in the German-speaking world. Elfriede Jelinek is another one.

Watching the play, one notices that the theme is sex and death. A man masturbates, or rubs his crotch, with a woman's foot. Over and over. While characters talk of murder, mass graves, and other fun stuff, they also engage sexually. What's the point of it? I'm not sure. On the good side, this play has interesting undercurrents of humor. "I am proud to be German!" says one of the characters, "even though I am not German." On the other side, it's too banal. If it intends to portray the banality of evil, well, Hannah Arendt does a much better job of it in *Eichmann in Jerusalem*.

I meet Julia after the show, just to have a little chat. Over a glass of ice-cold Cola Light, I ask Julia why the characters are making out while they talk about death and murder.

"Obscenity of evil," says Julia.

I say nothing.

An interesting note:

The text of the play reads: "Schon die Kreuzritter wollten nach Palestina und sind im Gazastreifen angekommen." (The Crusaders wanted to go to Palestine and arrived in Gaza Strip). But today the actor added, "Sie sind wenigstens angekommen!" (But they at least arrived!) This in reference to today's news from the Middle East, that Israeli troops stormed ships intended to break the Israeli blockade of Gaza.

(The "Free Gaza Flotilla," organized by pro-Palestinian organizations and supported by a Turkish Islamic group, İHH, and by the Turkish government, consisted of six ships, all bound for Gaza. Israeli forces ordered them to change course and sail into the

Israeli port city of Ashdod. The activists refused, and the Israelis raided the largest of them, a Turkish passenger ship named *Mavi Marmara*. Nine people, all associated with İHH, were killed. The raid took place in international waters, and the account of the events is disputed. The activists say that they were carrying food and medicine, not weapons, to the blockaded Gazans and that as they were "performing the morning prayers, Israeli soldiers started shooting." But the Israeli side claims that the "demonstrators" onboard attacked its naval personnel "with live fire and light weaponry including knives and clubs.")

Meeting the actor in the restaurant, I ask him to explain his action. He does.

"I find what happened today a scandal, a catastrophe, a horror," says Andre Jung, who played the Exceptional Messenger. "What the Israeli army did. Entered a ship and murdered people who wanted to give food and medication to closed people."

When asked if he considered all the facts and that maybe there are two sides to the story, he says, "I don't have the time to read everything."

What am I going to say? Should I say, You have to know the facts before you come to judgment, especially before you make a public statement onstage? That would be a waste of my time, I guess.

Jossi Wieler is the director of this piece. He is Jewish, he has family in Israel, and he travels there occasionally. Does he support the improvisation that Mr. Jung interjected into his performance today?

Wieler wonders if he should answer this question, muses that he hopes his answer would not cause him trouble next time he comes to Israel, and then says that "on such a day, with such news, I support it. Artistically and politically."

Well, that's brave of him, no doubt.

If you hear or read about a German Jewish director shot to death in the dark of night in a Tel Aviv bar, now you know why.

Funny. No German worth his name who criticizes the Israeli handling of the Gaza flotilla is afraid that the Israelis will exact revenge. This thought is too low even for your average anti-Semite. But Jossi, the Jew, is Holier than Thou.

I look at Julia and ask her: Are you proud to be German?

"I am proud to be born in Hamburg," she says.

I ask Jossi: Are you proud to be Jewish? Give me a yes or a no.

Wow. The man wants to kill me. How dare I force him to give a yes or a no! How can one be so simplistic? If I go on like this, he tells me, "I will leave." Period. What am I, the *Bild-Zeitung*? My question was complex question and requires a very complex and long answer!

•••

It's a rainy day in Munich. I go to the university of Munich, the law department, trying to find me Germany's next generation. I'm interested to know if the future judges and legal brains of Germany agree with the Gaza actor . . . I approach the students.

What do you think of the Israeli response to the Gaza Flotilla?

David: "It's illegal."

Christof: "Against international law."

Christian: "It's an aggression by the Israelis."

A group of students, mostly female, walk by. I ask them as well, but they walk away, refusing to talk. One of them says, "I am not going to answer this!"

Peter Landau, professor of law, also walks by. He has no problem answering. "I was very angry," he says. "It was a big mistake. The Israelis were motivated by nationalism. They do damage to themselves. I hope Israel can be preserved as a state, but they have not behaved properly since the Yom Kippur War."

Since he uses the Hebrew name for the war, I ask him if he's Jewish.

"I have Jewish ancestors. But my father was baptized."

God, everybody is a Jew in Germany!

Why did the girls refuse to talk? I ask him.

"Because of the Holocaust, some are afraid to get into trouble if they speak their mind. But I am not."

Are you proud to be German?

"I accept being German, but I would be reluctant to be proud."

Two students walk by, one German and one Turkish. When

79

prompted, they say they did not hear anything about anything. Busy studying.

Then Johanna passes by. She says, "I feel disgust about what the Israelis did. I am stunned by the behavior of the Israelis. When I first heard it—I'd just come back from vacation—I felt, oh God, how could this happen?! How could the Israelis have done that?!"

Are you proud to be German?

"Most of the time."

What does it mean to be German?

"Always be on time, conscious of your duties, boring at times, not as open, utilizing the head more than the heart."

What's the best thing about being German?

"Being in the center of Europe, so that you can travel around."

We're outside, and students show up. It's smoking time! What's on their minds? What do they think of the sea story?

Alex: "Bad. Very bad. You can't shoot people like this!"

Sarah: "I can't understand how they shot them. What kind of iPad do you have? Is it with 3G or just wi-fi?"

Florian: "It's a shame."

Sarah: "I don't know why you need an iPad. What's wrong with a netbook?"

Are they proud to be German? I ask them.

All say they are. Interesting!

But, oops, not all of them got to express their thoughts about the sea story. Mark wants to have his say.

Mark: "It's very, very bad."

As more students gather near me, I ask if any of them has a different opinion.

No, says Alex. Not one of them.

Why is it, I ask them, that in a democratic society everybody has the same opinion? What happened to multiplicity of ideas? And what happened to law, which requires facts first. Do they have the facts? Did any of them take into account the Israelis' version, that they were attacked first?

No. None of them.

Why do they dismiss the Israeli side? Do they have proof that the Israelis lie? None has.

As future lawyers, and judges as well, how did they arrive at a conclusion before examining the facts? This is the law school, right? Could it be, I push on, that you came to the conclusion that Israel is guilty because, how to put it mildly, you don't like Israel, because they are Jews—?

Quiet. Silence. Time passes and no one talks. The cheerful young faces are now fallen. Should I take a picture of this sad image?

I repeat the question, push more aggressively for an answer.

Finally Alex gives in. "It is against international law, that's why we are against it."

Do you actually study international law?

"No."

So how do you know?

Silence.

No one volunteers to say anything anymore. It is Sarah who breaks the silence.

Sarah: "I went to the Apple store, I wanted to buy the iPad with the 3G, but they didn't have it anymore. Sold out. I would buy it if they had it, but they didn't."

Is it good to be German?

Yes, all say.

Will they raise the German flag?

Only at soccer games.

Why only then?

Sarah: "They will call us Nazis if we did it any other time."

And then there is Lenard, another student.

Lenard: "I saw on TV that there were some kind of weapons on board. And unless I have all the facts I cannot decide. That's what being a lawyer is, you need the facts first."

Are you proud to be German?

He laughs loudly. "Oh, no!"

•••

Michael Krüger, publisher for the German firm Carl Hanser Verlag, and André Schiffrin, publisher and founder of the American firm New Press, don't laugh. They are serious people. And both are heavy guns in the publishing industry.

André, formerly with Pantheon Books, and the man who helped introduce Foucault and Chomsky to the American reader, is giving a speech tonight at Seidlvilla, Schwabing, where I am at this very moment. André is to speak in English, and Michael is going to be the translator. Besides these two, many other heavyweights presently grace my company. "Top of the top," a man tells me, "of German culture is here tonight."

The program for this highly intellectual evening is about to start. We all sit down, and André is all ready to enlighten us with his wisdom and knowledge. He tells his esteemed audience that Condoleezza Rice, former US secretary of state, met the heads of major American TV networks before the invasion of Iraq and asked them not to show images of wounded soldiers on screen. They agreed. It is why, André explains, former US president George W. Bush was reelected to his second term, and this is why 75 percent of Americans at the time thought that Iraq had nuclear weapons. Returning the favor, continues André, the Bush Administration tried to repeal the law prohibiting owners of print media from also owning TV networks.

This story about major American TV networks is a major claim. In essence, it means that there is no real democracy in the United States and that even the "free media" are controlled by the US government. According to this telling, the United States is actually a dictatorial regime. Michael seems to enjoy every word of this, nodding his head as André speaks. The rest of the esteemed company here seems to be utterly excited as well. They hang on every syllable that comes out of André's mouth. They look as if they're licking his words.

I have heard this story before and tried to substantiate it, but all I could find were propaganda films that offered no proof. Maybe André will finally solve the puzzle for me. And so I catch up with him after the talk and ask him for the source of his claims.

André: "Nobody has ever asked me this before. I have mentioned it many times and was never asked to supply a source. You can check on Google."

A more specific source?

"Did you try Google?"

I did, long ago, but couldn't find anything substantive. Do you have a more specific source than just Google?

"No, I don't have a specific source."

Can you substantiate it in any other way?

"Why are you asking me this?!"

I happen to be a journalist and I need a source to—

"If you want me to quote a source, I can't."

There is not much of a difference between the intellectuals here and the simple people I met at the church in the suburbs of Hamburg. Both have an American Prophet whom they blindly follow. Why are both groups so drawn to American liars? I don't know. What I do know is that I need a break. Too many brainy people around me and I need something lighter. Any "lighter" Germans in the neighborhood? Can you recommend?

There is a place, or so I hear, a two-hour train ride from here, where in 1633 the townspeople vowed to put on a Passion play, depicting the Passion of Christ, once every ten years. They believed that if they did that they would be saved from a plague that struck the area at the time. They were saved indeed, according to the story, and the town has kept the vow ever since. It's playing this year. I can see it tomorrow. Hundreds of thousands from all over the world come to see it. Why not me? Besides, I love train rides, and this is a good excuse.

A note here: Many Germans tell me that the DB is almost never on time. Let me tell you: Wrong! The DB is one of the most efficient train systems in the world. It's highly sophisticated, fast, and on time. You can set your clock by it.

I am going to Oberammergau, to see the world-famous Passion play, the *Passionsfestspiele.*

•••

The ride reveals unbelievably gorgeous landscapes. Here's Starnberg, a beauty to behold. You can't take your eyes off it. The train keeps moving, and the beautiful landscapes just keep coming. For miles on end. Valleys lie naked between the mountains, as slivers of clouds dance between them in rising songs. Angels in the image of ponds and rivers mix with cows and deer that constantly reveal themselves to you in their full glory. So much greenery, in all shapes of the imagination, lie in front of your eager eyes, that they shame the beauty of the Quranic Paradise. I can't take my eyes off the endless seduction rising so abundantly all around my being. Captivatingly gorgeous churches, testimony to long history, slowly join in this chorus of magic majesty right in front of my eyes and whole body.

And I wonder: Beauty like this my eyes have never seen, riches like these my heart never has felt, images like these my mind has never experienced. Is this earth or heaven?

Lucky are the men, blessed are the women, whose fate and destiny it is to live in this part of the planet. For they have it all: the mystery of old, the technology of the future, and the best of the present.

Who are these people? The Germans.

I get up from my seat, gaze out and in, look at creatures near me, and I want to scream: With these treasures joining you, with this beauty your inheritance, Why, in goodness' name, did you ever engage in a war? What else, what more, did you want? Could a man ever aspire to more? Could a woman?

What were you thinking?

The Passion play starts. And before you know it, Adam and Eve appear, he has brown hair and she's blonde. And then Jesus enters Jerusalem, kids in tow. (Sister Jutta-Maria was right. Jesus is no Italian. He's German.) Hundreds of actors are onstage, and mostly they just stand there almost motionless. Too bad, because this makes the performance too static. Whoever directed this must have been sleeping during rehearsals. Otherwise I can't understand how he allowed this to happen. All the characters here speak in the same tone, Jesus included. This makes me conclude that not one of the hundreds of the players on the stage is a real actor. I'm sure these people have some talents, maybe even many talents, but acting is not one of them.

This production earned much publicity, including in the United States. This is due to the involvement of some Jewish organizations, such as the American Jewish Committee, in reshaping this production. While years ago (most recently in 1984) Jewish priests had horns on their heads, today Jesus is referred to as "Rabbi," and his followers wear skullcaps. Biblical verses, as well as some Jewish prayers, are spoken and sung in Hebrew by the adults and children of this German town. Interestingly, these German kids and their parents, all residents of this little village, pronounce Hebrew much better than most of the highest-paid American Jewish rabbis.

By making it obvious that Jesus, as well as his disciples, was Jewish, the organizers here have tried to move away from the historic anti-Semitic overtones that traditionally plagued the Passion play. And by concentrating on the life of Jesus and not only on his death—a tough job, as the sources for his life are limited—the organizers signaled a desire to correct a wrong of many centuries, that of emphasizing the "Jewish torturers of Christ," that in the past earned so many accolades in the anti-Semitic world. Adolf Hitler, the history books tell us, was very delighted to see the Passion play in the Oberammergau of his time.

But the story as unfolded here lacks drama, and the reason for the creation of a new religion is not understood. Especially in this version, sensitive to Jewish feeling, the story comes across more as that of a Jewish rabbi and his followers than of a new religion being formed.

Part 1, lasting a little over two and a half hours, ends. Now we, the crowd of about five thousand, are going for a three-hour break. Part 2, which will have to include the death of Jesus, will be interesting to watch. How PC could the people here make it? Most

importantly, how will the Jews and Pilate be portrayed? This, after all, is one of the most sensitive issues in the historic Christian–Jewish relations. How unwilling of a character will Pilate be in terms of the order he gives to kill Jesus? How demanding will the Jews be in wanting him dead?

Part 2 starts. And in part 2 all PC collapses. Pilate is shown as forced to kill Jesus by the Sanhedrin, the high council, and the priests. He's pissed off, he refuses, he screams, he does all he can. But the Jews are smarter, more conniving, and they gain the upper hand. The Let's-be-nice-to-the-Jews part of this production falls completely apart. Interestingly, Pilate seems here much more innocent than a normal reading of the New Testament would allow.

How could this happen? How could a production geared to be pro-Jewish end up anti-? I don't know. Maybe it's part and parcel of the New Testament. It was Paul, after all, who said (1 Thessalonians [2:14–15]) that "the Jews" killed Lord Jesus. The problem, of course, is that people tend to forget that early Christians were Jews who debated with each other. True: This production tries to illustrate the Jewishness of Jesus and his disciples. But are they successful? I sit down with Renate Frank, the sister of the Passion director, Christian Stückl. Renate, who is also one of the players, has long hair that she let grow specifically for this show. I ask her if Jesus was Jewish.

"I think Jesus was Jewish but I'm not sure."

What do you mean?

"I think that he grew up in a Jewish area, but I am not sure who he was."

Does it say anywhere in the New Testament that Jesus was Jewish?

"I am not sure. I didn't read it so thoroughly."

What Renate knows, she shares with me: There are 4,800 seats in the theater, and there are 104 performances in a season. Up to 800 people are on stage, and 2,000 work on the show. There are

5,000 people living in this town.

And she knows this:

"Everything in America has something to do with Jews."

The Passion play is playing until October 3. What will she do come October 4?

"Big haircut! On the third of October we will all cry. The whole day. Everything you do on that day, you do it for the last time. In the last Hallelujah all the gates of the theater open and the whole community comes to see the last Hallelujah. And you think: What's going to be in the next ten years? Maybe my parents won't be alive for the next Passion play. You see the old people and you think: They won't be next time around. And the young people, when you look at them, you say to yourself: What will be with them next time? Married? With children? Everybody is very emotional."

•••

I need to go to a place where nobody will mention the word *Jew* to me. Is there a place like that in Germany? Seek and you shall find, the saying goes. And I did. Schloss (castle) Hohenschwangau, the summer residence of King Maximilian, father to King Ludwig.

To stand here is to ride on a journey into Germany's past.

It is here that you get a clue, a hint, of how this society was formed.

I understand Rabbi Helmut Schmidt a little bit better now.

The arrangement of paintings here, the colors of the walls, the furnishings, everything--they testify not only to immaculate taste and riches but also to inherent order. There is a secret door in here as well for "hanky-panky" business, our guide says as we walk into one of the rooms, wearing a big smile on his face. This German man loves his historically corrupt leaders.

We walk upstairs. Teutonic images in bronze and naked babes painted on the walls tell part of the story of how this country originated. Wagner used to come here, played on a piano standing right here. And that's culture for you.

When the tour is done, I go to Schloss Neuschwanstein, the castle of King Ludwig II—at the same beautiful place known as

Schwangau.

What heritage the German people have! A dream world.

This palace was built in homage to Richard Wagner and his works, says the guide, a smiling Bavarian lady. The king was very devout, she tells the tourists, and she points to his private chapel, a nice little room with young blond ladies on painted glass and an old man. And there is also a reading corner, with a place for books, but no iPad. He also had a phone, our guide tells us, and he used it to communicate with the other castle, Hohenschwangau.

All in all, this palace is a beauty no words can accurately describe. This is what the people of Germany have inherited from their rulers. It now belongs to the people. The Jews' inheritance is the Wailing Wall. The Germans', Schloss Neuschwanstein.

But I'm not going to talk about it. I'm very happy no one mentioned the word *Jew* to me today.

I catch up with the guide at the end of the tour.

That phone you showed us, is it the first in history? I ask her, impressed by Ludwig and German technology.

"Yes, first. It was invented by Siemens. It's the first in the world."

A young man, who seems to be the janitor of the place, listens in and interrupts the lady: "No. The first to invent the phone was Bell, not us."

I write down what he says.

The lady looks at him and at me. Why are you writing this? she asks.

I am a journalist.

"You are not supposed to write anything," she says, turning at once from a smiling lady into a classic bitch. "This property belongs to the government, and everything I said, all the words I used, are government property and can NOT be used. I would like to see your press card!"

I show it to her.

"Did you come here as press? Did you tell the authorities—"

Yes, I did.

She shuts up. Since the "authorities" know, I can obviously use her Government Words.

This woman is more deranged than Mr. King Ludwig.

It's time to leave this German Government Property.

Not as easy a task as you might think.

Many steps take you down, and you must pass through two souvenir stores. No way out of it. This is something new to me, never seen this in the States. There are souvenir stores in America, but you are not forced to pass through them.

Well, this is not America. Here it's a different system. It's not Capitalism, it's Forced Capitalism. I get it.

I hold in my hands a timetable that I got in Munich from the DB, detailing the bus and train schedules from the castle back to Munich.

Let's try the buses; see if they arrive on time.

I'm happy to report to you my findings: Each of the buses arrives at their destinations on the minute. Exactly.

What a country!

•••

## Chapter 11

### How Many Millions of Euros Should Be Spent Per Fake Jew? When Did the "No Smoking" Policy Start? How Do You Wash Your Hands Using a Faucet?

I'm back in Munich. What should I do? Well, for one thing, I have to take care of my Goldman Sachs assets and my media holdings. Best thing, perhaps, would be to connect with other board members in town. Hence I go to the Jewish community, my business partners. The chief rabbi of the Jewish community in Munich, Rabbi Steven Langnas, welcomes me at the synagogue.

The rabbi is an "import" from the United States, but his family roots are Germanic. How do I know? He tells me. He also tells me, in case I ever wondered, that the congregation, an Orthodox community, has nine thousand members. I am delighted to know. Not only that, but soon I am going to be personally acquainted with this huge Jewish community. I can't wait. It's Friday night and time for the traditional Friday night services, to celebrate the coming Sabbath, in this beautiful Jewish center of Munich, a center that must have cost millions upon millions to build, and most likely was paid for by the German government. I'm not religious, but I'm excited to be here anyway. I start counting the nine thousand. Well, not really. The number of worshippers, including those who are tourists and guests from Israel and the United States: thirty-five. In other words, the place would be practically empty if not for the foreigners. For comparison: An average Orthodox temple in New York is full a on Friday night. What happened to the nine thousand? I'm not sure. When services are done, I go to the rabbi's home for dinner and some questioning.

The chief rabbi of Munich lives in an apartment building, on one of the top floors. On the Sabbath, Orthodox Jews are not permitted to use elevators or to turn on the lights, and unlike the likeable rabbi from Berlin, this Jew has no German policeman around here to do any "Goy" work. So we walk up the stairs in the dark. Not very funny, let me tell you. But we make it. The Jews crossed a sea in Egypt, they should be able to mount stairs in Germany.

Once we've made it, the rabbi, Steven, greets the angels at his home, as custom dictates. "Welcome, angels," he sings, to what sounds to me like a Germanic tune. "Bless me, Angels," he sings. Yes, another American clergyman with angels on his head. As if I didn't have enough with the "American prophet" in the north.

Do you believe in angels? I ask Steven.

"Yes, of course."

What do the angels do?

"They walk along with people, protecting them from disaster."

So how come there are car accidents?

"Because God sometimes overrules the angels."

If that's the case, can't God protect the people without angels?

"Of course he can!"

Then why do we need angels to start with?

"Do you want some Schnapps?"

Yes.

He pours and we drink, to our health and to the health of the nine-thousand-strong Jewish community. Not that this goes without comment. The rabbi's wife is not amused by any of this, and neither is she impressed. "Nine thousand?" she asks rhetorically. "You should ask how many of them are Jewish!"

And she doesn't stop there. She goes on:

"There's no future to Jewish life in Germany. This is a cursed country and no blessing will come out of it." Whatever her husband is doing here, she tells me brazenly, is "a huge waste of time." Interestingly, none of what she says is lost on her husband. "Did you get enough of what you need for your book?" he asks, so that his wife can hear his dissatisfaction with her comments . . .

I leave the Rabbi and his wife to decide on their own the future of Jewry in Germany.

I turn on the light in the stairways and then it suddenly dawns on me: I'm so empty-headed sometimes! I totally forgot to discuss with the rabbi our mutual holdings at Goldman Sachs!

•••

On the morning after, I meet Dr. Dieter and his wife, Juliane, in an outside café next to the English Garden, the "Central Park" of

Munich. Juliane talks about her teenage son, who "plays the music loud and says to me, his mom, 'If you don't like it, give me a house for myself.'" He is politically inclined and "he very strongly opposes Israel and identifies with the Palestinians."

This couple, a physician and his wife, feel shame when anyone raises the German flag. "I am a European," Dr. Dieter announces, "and proud of it. Europeans did much shit, too. But I am proud to be European still."

Neither faults their son. It's not his problem, they believe, but the problem of this country. The young people of Germany care about one thing only: The Bottle. Puberty strikes, and the youngsters get out of the house and buy drinks. The other day Dieter asked his son, How much do you drink outside? "Five beers," his son told him. Five?! "Yes."

Drinking among youth is not the only problem in Germany. "Germany is not running well," the doctor says. "Take the DB. Never on time."

I can't let this pass without comment. I say to him: You, Germans, are just a bunch of complainers who can't see how good they have it!

He's quiet. Takes a few moments to digest my accusation. Then, eyes looking down, he says: "Yes. We are people who are not satisfied with what we have achieved, critical about ourselves, and pessimistic. But Swiss trains are more punctual. "

Oh, you're so German!

"Probably . . ."


To the English Garden I go, to see people drinking beer from barrels. Something is wrong with this picture. People sit for hours, drinking more than camels. Others pass by, carrying bottles or mugs. It's not only the Bavarians, by the way. Every time I meet any German, a beer joins the conversation. Why is it? Is it genetic? Do the people of Germany suffer from a natural disorder, a catastrophic liquid deficiency, such that they just must keep on irrigating themselves? I should have discussed this with Dr. Dieter! Why can't I think in the moment?

Today is a beautiful day. It's sunny, it's warm, it's June. After a few rainy days, people seem to warmly embrace the Return of

Summer. Men in shorts and women in bikinis rush to grab the sun and get a little darker. Imagine if it were possible for darker-skinned people to leisurely lie down, just like these people here, but get whiter instead of darker. How many of them would take the opportunity?

It's obvious that I have nothing to do.

Until Z. shows up. He is from the Jewish community in Munich and he wants to get something off his chest. I raise no objection. He talks:

"The community buildings (the Jewish Center) cost about 70 million euros, most of the money comes from the German government. We told the government that we had nine thousand members, but that's not true. We don't, it's just on paper. We have at most five hundred people who are involved, not all of them Jews. But we wouldn't get 70 million if we told the truth. In the school system we don't have enough students either, not enough Jews. So we put in non-Jews and make them community members until the age of eighteen. When they're 18 we kick them out, because they're not Jews. That's what we do to get money. This is the way it goes. This is an Orthodox community.

"Do you know how many families we actually have? Somewhere between ten and fifteen. I don't have the exact number. Seventy million euros to build, plus you have to add all the money that it takes to maintain everything, for fifteen families at the most. That's how the Jewish community operates. All about money and then calling Germans anti-Semites. If you see anti-Semitism in Germany now, you know why. Wouldn't you be an anti-Semite if you saw people doing this? It's only about money. The Jewish communities in Germany are only about money, not just the community in Munich. Go to our synagogue and see how many people come, between thirty and forty, which includes ten security guards. Waste of money. Who needs this? It's a shame."

Z. gets up and leaves. He leaves me to ponder on my own.

Sad.

•••

But *Biergartens* are not places to be sad. These are places to have

93

fun, and I'm not one to break with tradition. Here is a group of black singers and musicians playing African music of some sort, and they do it really well. They hardly miss a beat, almost perfect. Some white folks gather around them and enthusiastically dance to the tunes. But their dance lacks grace, talent, and its rhythm—if one can use such a word here—is totally misplaced. Here's a white lady, a remarkably bad dancer, who keeps on laughing while she dances. I've seen this phenomenon before, but I still can't understood why bad dancers laugh as they jump up and down in no particular order. I look at this scene and a thought comes to my mind: So good to just watch the little things in life without occupying myself with Jews all the time! And so, I make up my mind: No more dealing with Jews. I got addicted and didn't notice. Well, I'm putting an end to this bad habit. Not one single word again about Jews. Jews have nothing to do with Germany; Germany is only beer and horrible white dancers. From now on I'll occupy my time looking at white ladies who jump on floors to no rhythm and at the men who drink beer next to them.

I stay in an apartment in a beautiful section of town, Kaulbach Street. No Jews here, as far as I can tell. No Nazis either, as far as I can see. And No Smoking is requested. Yes, that's what I've been told. Which for me, a smoker, is a huge problem. Should I smoke here anyway, since nobody can see me? Well, I'd rather not. I promised I wouldn't. But now, late at night, when all the Jews have already left my brain, my craving for a cigarette got me up from my deep sleep. What am I to do? I must smoke something! I dress up and go outside to puff with extreme joy. I walk the street slowly, looking right and watching left. On the third puff I see a poster with an image of Hasidic Jews. How did the Jews sneak into my beautiful non-Jewish street? Who let them in? I check closer, to make sure that my eyes don't betray me; but yes, these are Jews. Jews are the First Mountaineers, an explanation follows. What? Yes, this is what it really says. The poster is from the Alpine Museum, announcing an exhibition that will run through February of next year. Just after I made up my mind to get the Jews out of my head, they show up as mountaineers. Who needs this!

I smoke my rest and swear to forget the Jews anyway! Don't let one advertisement change my mind, I preach to myself. I finish my cigarette and go to sleep.

In the morning I've forgotten all about the Jew Mountaineers and decide to start the day afresh looking for new German faces, new German ideas, new German thinking, new German obsessions, new anything that's new German. But then I have a strong urge for something old, a cigarette. I go out to smoke. And instinctively take another direction, as far away from the Mountaineering Jews as possible.

Lighting up, I start walking at a leisurely pace. So good not to be bothered with the Jews! The "Germans" are enough for one man, believe you me.

My cigarettes are good. I light up one, then another one, walking as slow as the sun. I check the scenery around me. Here's an advertisement for the *Süddeutsche Zeitung*. This ad, which is glued to the wall, is a "permanent" ad, meaning it's there to stay. No rain can take it off. The ad shows a "model" front page of the *Süddeutsche Zeitung*. Obviously, this is intended to convince people to buy the paper. As if to say, If you buy our paper this is what you'll get. On top of the page there's an image of Japanese youngsters wearing traditional Bavarian clothes. Looks really cute! Under the Japanese there's a political article, a model article, I guess. The article says that Obama wants to force peace in the Middle East, that the Israelis are stubborn, and that the Palestinians are stuck. I puff and puff and digest the idea put in front of me by this ad: Buy our paper and we will give you cute Japanese, stubborn Israelis, and poor Palestinians. Not bad. Reason enough, I believe, to order a subscription for ten years minimum. And then it hits me: Jews again! Oh, heavens! I can't walk five steps here without those Stubborn Jews!

Calm down, Tuvia, I hear a voice saying to me. It's just this street. The rest of Munich is lovely and clean of Jewish obsessions. And so, to calm myself, I move on to another street. Can't allow "the Jews" to sneak into my head again. This other street has a bookstore. Let's see what they're selling today.

I window-shop. *History of Zionism*. Really? Yes. I try to ignore this, just a mistake. Let's see the other offerings. "Jewish cookbook." Jews all over. Why? I don't know. I smoke me another cigarette while pondering why Germans are so obsessed with Jews.

I decide, in spite of myself, to dig deeper into German–Jewish relations. But how do I do that? Maybe I should have gone to Palestine, as I initially planned, to talk to the Germans who go there to help the Palestinians, or to Israel to talk to the Germans who go there to help *them*? Wait a second: Why are Germans going to those places to begin with? Well, if the Germans go to the Middle East, let me muddle in their middle. Dachau, I hear, is not far from me. No plane is required; an S-bahn, that quick local train, will take me there even if those ash clouds come back.

•••

I arrive safely in Dachau.

First thing I encounter is the Appellplatz, the Roll Call ground. Here prisoners stood for at least an hour, motionless. The dead among the prisoners had to show up as well. Yeah. Fun place, isn't it? And that's not all: On the roof of the maintenance building, as shown in a photo of the original, the following was painted in white: "There is a path to freedom. Its milestones are: obedience, honesty, cleanliness, sobriety, hard work, discipline, sacrifice, truthfulness, love of thy Fatherland." Hannah Aerndt might call this the Banality of Evil, but to me it looks more like the Genius of Evil.

This KZ, the first built by the Nazis, is a dark place, just like the rest of them, the ones I have seen before. Here's where the killing was elevated into an art form: An exact, scientific, well-organized, cruel, orderly, clean operation. What was discovered here, a man who stands next to me tells me, as he refers to various brutal medical tests conducted on live humans here, "is used to this day by NASA." I keep on walking. The area I enter seems to be the main building, and here I notice, in stark black letters on one of the walls, a Nazi order: Smoking Prohibited. Then another one, in red: No Smoking. I'm not sure about the NASA thing, but this is something we do "use" today: No Smoking. Walk into the main train station of today's Munich and the most conspicuous of signs you see, more visible than Coca Cola's, is the No Smoking one.

To get a fresh perspective on the world of KZs, or *Konzentrationslager*, I entertain a thought in my head: to talk to one of the mavens, the folks who come here every day.

Which leads me to Rosi, a woman with old-style eyeglasses, who is one of the employees of this KZ. Would she be willing to talk to me? She says she cannot give me an interview because she is not allowed to do so. Is that it? Well, not exactly. She can, if I want, share with me her personal thoughts. This kind of interview is allowed. Fine with me, since this is exactly what I want.

Do you go home and think about this KZ?

"No. I have other problems to think of, like my car."

Do you think often about the horrors that happened here?

"In the beginning, when I started to work here, I had to learn about crematoriums and stuff like that. But now it's dealing with tourists and answering questions like, 'Where is the toilet?'"

Doing this job, did you learn something?

"Yes. I learned about other cultures and also about different groups in Germany, like farmers, Jews, and others."

Did you ever meet a Jew personally?

"No. I think they live in Munich, but I never met a Jew."

Did Germany, as a country, learn something from its past?

"Germany doesn't learn the lesson. Germany sells tanks and aircrafts to make wars even today."

What's your dream?

"I dream of summer. We didn't have sun this year, and I dream of going to the Bodensee and having sun. That's my dream."

•••

Besides Rosi and her colleagues, there are nuns in Dachau as well, 24/7. Welcome to Karmel Heilig Blut (Carmelite convent of the Holy Blood) Dachau.

The principle here is silence and prayer, or prayer via silence.

The nuns are supposed to pray in silence, let's see them.

Sadly, I am late.

The place seems empty, the nuns must have gone.

Maybe they're talking somewhere.

Oh, wait. There's a bookshop over yonder. Let's go in and check.

A nun is there. And a little book, more like a brochure: *Edith Stein: Die neue Heilige— Jüdin und Ordensfrau"* (The new saint, Jewess and nun.)

In this place of so many dead, why do they the need to sell a book about yet another dead Jew? Is this such big news

Why is it important to mention that Edith Stein is a Jew? I ask this of Theresa, the nun, who says with a smile, "Because the Mother of God was a Jew, because Jesus was a Jew, and all the Apostles were Jews, and if we remembered that in those days, the Holocaust would not have happened."

Did Pope Pius XII not know that the Mother of God was Jewish?

"Yes, yes, he knew."

So, what did you mean when you said—

Here comes a long reply, which I don't really get. Maybe silence would be better. I change the subject.

Were you ever married?

"No."

Ever in love?

She blushes, like a child.

So, was there love?

Yes . . . She had one love story, but the man died. That's it.

She came to this camp when she was twenty.

"When I just got my driver's license, I drove right here."

At twenty, your first desire is to go to Dachau??

"I wanted to find out about the human condition."

Why not go to a Biergarten?

"Because I had a sympathy with the Jews."

With the Jews. Why?

"Because the Jews are all united, all over the world the Jews are united. Religious or not, they all believe in one God."

God bless the German people. They teach me everything I have to know about Jews.

Wouldn't you have liked to have had children?

"I have many children, others' children. That's enough."

What's the future, what's after all this?

"After this life, I will be totally happy."

What will happen to you in the afterlife, up there? Describe it to me.

"I don't have a good imagination."

Do you think of it sometimes?

"Jesus said that it will be like a wedding, and I think that's what will happen there."

Not only does Sister Jutta-Maria of Munich dream of getting married to Jesus, Theresa does too. I imagine Heaven. Must be a fun place there. Muslim men are busy with their virgin brides and Christian nuns with Jesus. I wonder if Freud has an office up there as well. One day I should write a book about that.

Meanwhile, in this earthly life, Theresa has been in Dachau already for nineteen years.

How does it feel?

"I love this place. So many people died here and they got eternal life here. I am convinced that the people who were burned here now live with God."

What is God?

"Total forgiveness."

Is Adolf Hitler forgiven by God as well?

"Yes, I think so."

What did you have for breakfast today?

"Bread, jam, and muesli. On Sunday we get wurst as well and fruit. Between two and three we have coffee or tea."

What's for lunch?

"Wednesday and Friday, no meat. Today, turkey, schnitzel, and potato salad. Plus wine."

Supper?

"Cold food, but good."

Vacations?

"I haven't taken a vacation in the last nineteen years."

Theresa offers me orange juice and takes me on a tour of the place. She does this better than some real-estate agents I've met.

"Would you like to stay here tonight? It's only 25 euros. I have a room, I can show it to you, this is a room where a Jew usually stays when he comes by. An old Jew, over ninety years old. A survivor. He stays here. It's a small room, but very quiet. It has a backyard, and you can see the watchtower from the backyard."

That's a Room with a View. A stone's throw from the crematorium.

"You can stay one night, you can stay one week."

Yes, I will think about it. Life must be pretty good here if she hasn't taken a vacation in nineteen years.

"I wear a black veil," she tells me, as if I didn't notice. Definitely, Theresa could walk into an average mosque and no one would object. At least not on the grounds of Modesty.

"It took me six years to get the black veil. In the first years I could wear only the white veil, because I was studying, and I was not fully part of the order. Not totally. Today I am. A full member. A Carmelite."

Interesting what makes people happy. I, for one, wouldn't toil so many years for a black veil. If I wanted one, I would go to a store and buy it for a dollar or two. But, honestly, come to think of it, isn't life funny all over? In the average university, after six years of hard work you get a paper with letters on it that says something like "Master of Arts." Here at least you get something more useful: a veil. So, don't laugh at her!

"Here is the toilet," she shows me. "And if you decide to stay over, here's the showers."

Yes, maybe I should take a shower in Dachau. A good idea. Brilliant!

I leave Dachau, the KZ, but stick around the town. I want to meet the local people of Dachau. An average Dachau family, let's say.

And before I know it, I get my wish. I am invited to lunch with a local family.

They welcome me with open arms. Food is arranged on the table in the backyard. Herring, cheeses of all kinds and cold cuts of all sorts, filled peppers, various jams, and quite a few beverages. No Cola Light. Would I like multiple-vitamin drinks? Maybe soda? The lady of the house apologizes that the soda today is of the "little-gas" variety. If only they had known that an "American" would be coming, they would surely have had the strong-gas soda.

Yes, they have different levels of gas in their sodas here.

Sounds strange, I know, when you speak of gas in Dachau.

But she has ice for her American guest. Loads of it. Would I like? Little gas with ice.

Americans like ice in their sodas. Every German knows of this strange American habit, even in Dachau.

But enough about gas and ice. I didn't come to Dachau to learn about American gas and American ice. Let's listen to the people.

Else, the mom, came to Dachau in 1966, on June 1. Got to be exact: June 1. I love it!

We have a little chat.

Why Dachau?

"My husband worked in Munich and houses here were cheaper."

Did you and your husband know the history of the town before moving in?

"Yes."

Was it a consideration, a reason perhaps not to move in?

"No."

It would be reasonable to assume that a few of the people who lived here in 1966 lived here during the war as well. Did you ask them, talk to them about what happened here during the war?

"No."

Why not?

"We had other problems."

Do you regret not asking?

"No."

We are in Jürgen's house. Else's son, Jürgen is a lovely man. He had an encounter with Jesus Christ some years ago, he says, and was "born again." Bodily, though, he was born here, in Dachau.

At what age were you aware of the story of Dachau?

"Ten. When we learned history in school."

And until then you didn't know anything?

"No."

What did you feel when you first realized?

"I was shocked."

Can you describe this shock—like, what did you do?

"Nothing."

Did you go to papa and mama and say, Where the heck do we live?

"No."

Why not, if you were shocked?

"I don't know."

Do you know anyone here whose parents or grandparents were part of the Dachau operation?

"Only one lady, who's already dead."

Nobody else?

"No."

Did you ever ask around?

"No."

I have no idea why, but I get a little upset with this guy and I push him.

From the perspective of an outsider, it seems to me that you just don't want to know, that you don't fucking care, excuse my French. From a foreigner's perspective, this sounds horrible. Agree or disagree?

"Agree."

Anything to add?

"Years ago I was born again, and years ago I also realized that I have to protect the Apple of the Eye of God, the Jewish people. And I do my best."

But you still don't want to know who of your neighbors' families were involved in one way or another with Dachau KZ?

"No."

Why not?

"I focus on one thing."

Are you serious?

"What I am saying is that I want to look into the future and not think of the past."

Can you move forward if you don't know where you've come from?

No answer. He gives me the silence treatment. Maybe he's

actually a Carmelite. Go figure. Anything is possible in Dachau.

I don't know why, maybe it's all those watchtowers of Dachau that get to me, but I don't let this go by. I go on, try my best to squeeze out whatever is inside this man and have him lay it naked on the table, his table. I push harder, using his faith as a tool to get to him

You are a religious man. May I remind you that the Bible is full of stories, all with minute details . . .? For example: In Genesis you can read about this man who is the son of that man, who himself is the son of another man who is the . . . Is this correct?

"Yes, that's true."

But you still don't want to ask anybody anything, you want only to follow the Bible as your guiding light. Is that correct?

"Yes."

Here's the Bible, giving you an example of how to behave, but you refuse. True?

"Yes."

Why?

"I have no answer."

Don't you really?

"No."

Would you like to have an answer?

"I don't know."

Would you like to know?

"Maybe I don't want to know."

Why don't you want to know?

"This is the problem, yes."

And what is the solution?

Jürgen's eyes get wet. He breaks. The confident man that I met only half an hour ago is now a broken man whose parts lay naked in the backyard of his house.

"I look into the mirror and I don't want to see it."

Why?

"It's not a nice picture."

Give me a better answer.

"It's going to be me, staring at me from that mirror. And I don't want to see it!"

Those people are you?

103

"Yes."

Them?

"Yes."

They are you?

"Yes."

The Nazis.

"Yes."

It's hard to look at his face now, he looks like a criminal caught red-handed. His wife, Barbara, hugs me tight. Why is she hugging me? She should hug her husband! "Sorry," she says, "sorry. Sorry for what we did to your people. Sorry."

That's Germany. Reporting from Dachau, the town.

As I leave Dachau, this "motto" refuses to leave my head: "There is a path to freedom. Its milestones are: obedience, honesty, cleanliness, sobriety, hard work, discipline, sacrifice, truthfulness, love of thy Fatherland."

You really think, Rabbi Helmut Schmidt, that after twenty-five hundred years all this will be forgotten? It's not just the killing of people, Rabbi Helmut. It's the way it was done. Nobody, ever, will do a "better" job at murdering. Ever. Or as cynically.

Murderers, murderers everywhere,

Nor one murderer to see.

I need my Half and Half now, Giovanni di Lorenzo. We have things to discuss. But Giovanni is half a world away. He is in the north of our German planet, I am in the south.

•••

I opt, by practical necessity, to meet a Jew instead. Nine thousand in the Orthodox community of Munich, let me see one of them.

Jews, Jews, everywhere . . .

"Hard work" pays, and I get me a Jew: Jacques Cohen, of Cohen's Jüdisches restaurant. The famous Jewish restaurant, established in 1960.

Is there Jewish life here? I ask him.

"Bar mitzvah, bat mitzvah, so people can show off how much money they have, and that's about it."

Who are the people who come to eat at your restaurant?

"The goyim."

Why do they come here?

"They like Jewish food."

And the Jews?

"They go to McDonald's."

Jacques tells me that he loves Henryk Broder, the German Jewish journalist. "He is a Jew with no fear or shame, a Jew who says what he thinks." What makes him think of Henryk Broder eludes me. Jacques likes to spend time in his restaurant, pondering the big issues of life.

It's hard to be a Jew, he says, nobody loves the Jew anywhere. Worse is to be a Jewess, he considers, because on top of carrying the burden of being hated she also has so much work. But the worst, he abruptly adds, is Austria: more anti-Semites there than anywhere else.

What does it mean to be a Jew?

"Nobody ever asked me this question."

What is it?

"What do you mean 'What is it'?"

What does it mean to be a Jew—

"Religion. The religion."

Are you religious?

"No."

Are you Jewish?

"Yes. I am proud to be a Jew."

What is it?

"You break my head. I don't know."

Since most of his customers, he says, are not Jewish—though I don't see anyone around, Jew or not, as this place is totally empty—he feels the need to introduce them to basic Jewish ideas and customs. On the tables of his restaurant are cards explaining Jewish law and custom. For example, what is 'nonkosher wine.' Nonkosher wine, according to the cards, is a wine made from rotten fruits.

Really, Jacques?

"Yes."

I thought that nonkosher wine was wine that was touched by a non-Jew. That's the real deal, isn't it?

Well, Jacques is not so stupid to write stuff like that, no matter what kosher law says.

"I don't have to write everything," he muses.

Judaism, Munich-style.

Here's another card. It's a Combo Offer card. Go to the museum and eat Jewish food for a Special Price.

I don't feel like eating anything now, and so I go to the museum.

•••

I am at the Neue Pinakothek. I don't know what the name means, but the building looks cool. Not only that, but there's also a special tour today. It's called Traces of the Third Reich at the Pinakothek. The people here, I see, can't get over that period. Should I join them? Hey, why not? I'm a tourist, and tourists do things like this. Tourists and a tour call for a lecture, at least in this country. The lecturer today is an artistic-looking woman who tells of the bombardment of this museum during World War II. I hope she forgives me, but after Dachau I don't feel much sympathy. My fellow listeners, very fine Germans if one can judge by the way these people are dressed, don't share my feeling and seem very moved indeed by the tragic bombardment story. Yes, it would probably be better if I felt like them, at least I wouldn't be so bored now. I lose interest somewhere near the beginning of that Reich and get captivated instead by the paintings in front of me. Many Marys here, in case you've never been to this museum, one sexier than the other. If only the Jews knew how sexy they are—or were!

After the virgins come the warriors. Here's a painting called *The Entry of king Othon of Greece into Nauplia*, by Peter von Hess, dated 1835. Amazing details. Each person in the crowd is captured in a unique mood, every person's eye movement and bodily expression is gloriously detailed, and each of the ships, and every shape of stone and cloud, every instinct of animal and every detail of weather—all masterfully recorded.

And here's *The Park of an Italian Villa* by Oswald Achenbach, circa 1860. It looks like a simple painting, but it's bewitching. The shades and shadows the painter is playing with are just outstanding. You start looking at this painting and you become a prisoner of it.

Wait. Where is the Third Reich group?

Oh, here they are. Far from the Virgins and Warriors. They are in the private collection room of Reichsmarschall (Nazi Germany's highest military rank) Hermann Göring's. I join them and try to glean from the paintings a perspective into the man and his character. But then I realize, thanks to the guide here, that some of these paintings might actually have belonged to Jews. Too bad. I was just on the verge of creating an unbelievably genius theory that relates the connection between a man and his paintings, and this guide destroyed it all in one sentence!

Yes. As hard as it is to believe, Hermann was a little thief.

I leave the Nazis and the Jews and move on. Here is *View of Arles* by the poor Vincent van Gogh. He must have been in a good mood when he painted this one, using such lively colors and spirit. Not far from him is Claude Monet's *The Bridge at Argenteuil*. There's magic in it, especially his portrayal of the harshness of the industrial versus the softness of green grass.

I think I should become an Art Critic. For the life of me I can't draw a straight line, not to mention a circle, but I'm so good at Criticism! Really. I'm serious!

I'm getting so lost in my thoughts and writing that I fail to see the guard next to me. I think he doesn't like that I'm standing here and writing. Too many visitors stop to see my iPad. This creates unfair competition.

Where the heck are my Third Reichers?! Maybe they are in the restroom.

I go there, just in case.

Now, here's something interesting: instructions on how to wash your hands.

The leaders of this institution, and the government bureaucrats who finance it, have obviously concluded that Munich museumgoers are not well informed in the art of washing their hands after nature's call. People need instructions. Yes. Every restroom here has them. For those who, for religious reasons, don't read in restrooms, there's a big instruction sheet next to the faucets. There are many steps involved, in case you didn't know, when washing your hands. Put hands under running water, my dear, because otherwise the water won't come to you. Hard to understand? Here's an illustration of it. Yes, true. Under an image of running water, you have this instruction: Hold hands under running water. Image of soap, then: Rub your hands with soap for twenty to thirty seconds. Image of hands, then: Also between the fingers. Image of hands AND running water, then: Then rinse thoroughly. Image of hands and a paper tissue, then: Carefully dry hands.

The city of Munich, or the state of Bavaria, is of the opinion that Munich residents are certified idiots.

•••

I want to find out on my own.

Next to the magnificent Theatinerkirche (Theatiner Church) there's a little Biergarten. Here people come to drink beer, stare at the church, look at each other for hours on end, schmooze with no limit, or contemplate life while sipping this or that alcoholic beverage.

Werner is one of them, a handsome Bavarian man who sits and drinks his white wine all by himself. What is Werner thinking of all alone at this time of night? Love. What else! "Ten years ago I fell in love with a Jewish lady from America" who came to visit Munich. He showed her the town, they had a nice time, but nothing intimate happened. She went back. But when she got home, she found another woman in her bed. Her husband, that poor man, miscalculated when his wife would be back. But she didn't, and she divorced him and invited Werner to join her in her lonely bed. What a beautiful life awaited Werner! The Jewish lady, what a surprise, was a very rich lady. Like all Jews. She lived on Park Avenue. Where else? And then one day she threw a party. And she invited her friends. Jewish friends, of course. Rich, if you doubted. And one of them, a Jewish beauty straight out of *One Thousand and One Nights*, in his description of her, invited Werner to an exclusive restaurant. Jews do that sometimes. Werner couldn't refuse. You don't refuse beautiful Jewesses. It's not polite. And he got caught. How not! Those Jewish ladies, you've got to be careful. And that was the end of the romance.

Jewish ladies, Werner tells me, live on Park Avenue, and they are all irresistible.

Poor Werner. He could be living today on Park Avenue, with the rich Jewess, but instead he drinks wine by himself in Munich and schmoozes with a traveling male Jew.

"Old Jewish ladies," Werner informs this Jewish traveler, "paint their faces and look like little dolls."

Really?

"Yes." And "they all work in diamonds."

It's good to leave New York and come here, where I get to know more about where I come from. You need perspective in life.


Why is it, I'm really curious to know, that so many German people talk to me about Jews? Is it written somewhere on my forehead, Speak about Jews Unto Me?

True: It is not only Germans who have "Jews" on their minds. There are others. Only a few hours ago, thousands of miles away, the US veteran White House reporter Helen Thomas resigned after controversial comments she'd made earlier went public. Jews "should get the hell out of Palestine" and "go home" to their real homelands, such as Poland and Germany.

I am in Germany. Maybe I should get a passport.

Look there, across the street in this my homeland, on the left side of the venerated church, somebody painted the Star of David. Graffiti, you can call it. I've seen many of them in Lodz, Poland, my other homeland. There, the Star of David means, "You are a Jew!" As in, "You are a thief, You are an animal." And sometimes, next to the stars, you can find an "explanation": "Send the Jews to crematoriums," or "Juden Raus!" (Jews Out!)

What does the Star mean here? Werner's painted faces?

•••

As the sun finally rises in the skies of Munich, I am in the English Garden. I sip my fresh coffee and listen to the trees. The wind is blowing softly. Vote NEIN says a poster not far from me. Vote No to a total ban on smoking!

*Rauchen verboten* (Smoking prohibited), said the order in Dachau.

Many children and many teenagers soon fill the Garden. More youngsters than trees. And bicyclists are all over. But they are nice, they are not like the ones in Hamburg. Here they are not militants, here they are nice humans. They live and let live.

I light up a cigarette, sip my coffee, stare at the beautiful youngsters showing off their young skins, until one of them approaches me.

"May I ask you a few questions?" he asks.

Yes, why not.

He tells me that he is a film student at the University of Munich, and since I struck him as a native Bavarian he would like to interview me for his documentary.

Me? Native Bavarian? How did he find out?

"The way you look, the way you sit, the way you sip your morning coffee."

I started my journey as a Jordanian and now I am a Bavarian.

Not bad. Not bad. I am German! I'm so happy, I feel like getting up and screaming: Ich bin Deutschland!

His name is Jonas. He already made a film, and this is going to be his second one.

What was the first film about?

"Dachau."

Oh God, not that again!

Why Dachau?

"I worked at the KZ for four years."

You did. Why?

"It's important."

Is it?

"Yes."

Why? Did your family have any connection to it, to Dachau?

He looks at me, as if I've spoken Chinese.

I guess there's a reason why the Pinakothek museum instructs people in how to wash their hands. Munich people are a little, you know, slow, and they need some basic explanations! Yeah. I rephrase my question:

Do you know what your grandparents, for instance, did during the war? I mean, since you made a movie about the period and spent a few years at a concentration camp—?

Are you Jewish?

Now I'm offended. How can he call this native Bavarian "Jew"?!

Why would you think so?

"Because of the way you ask me the question."

Damn that Pinakothek Museum! Munich folks aren't that stupid after all!

Well, did you ask your grandparents?

"One time."

One time?

"Yes, one time I asked my grandmother."

One time you asked your grandma . . . what?

"I asked her who she voted for in 1933."

And what did she say?

"She said—she didn't answer, she asked a question. She said, 'Who should I have voted for, the Communists?!'"

And?

"That was it."

That was it?

"Yes."

You didn't ask any other questions?

"No. I was shocked. I couldn't ask anything. I couldn't."

Yes, here's how my morning goes. I prayed to have a Jew-free day. But no.

•••

Deeper inside the Garden a man sits drinking soda. His name is Dr. S. von Liebe, a surgeon. He is done with beer.

"Germany is rich," he says, "but the politics here are bad. You can never tell who's right and who's wrong, who's the truth teller and who's the liar. Look at the ash cloud. Someone told us that we couldn't have planes flying, no way. Then others said this is stupid, of course we can fly. How would I know who is honest and who

111

lies? German political parties fight with each other and you don't have the tools to decide who's right and who's wrong." That's the problem with Germany. Other than that it's good. America, on the other hand, is bad. "Big country, huge country, and it's busy with 'terror' and 'terrorists' all the time. Like Hitler with his Jews. He blamed the Jews, America blames the 'terrorists.' They want to control their people." He raises his voice, he's pissed off. He takes a pretzel, bites into it hard, to get more energy. "Why is America doing this?"

I really have no idea what he wants from my life.

Why are you so pissed off at the Americans?

"The Americans refuse to force the Israelis into conceding land to the Palestinians."

Did somebody put something in the doctor's soda? What's going on with him? Or better yet: What's going on with this country? They're more obsessed with Palestinians than Al Jazeera TV.

Why do you care about the Palestinians?

"Because I want peace in the world."

Do you care about Chechnya?

"What?"

Chechnya.

"What?"

Chechnya. You know, Russia and stuff.

"Oh, yes! Chechnya."

Do you care?

"Yes, I do. Certainly."

But you don't get emotional about Chechnya, obviously. Why not?

"Because, because the Middle East is more important!"

Why?

"Because that's where the religion is. Because of the religion! That's the basis of our—"

Are you religious?

"Me?"

Yes. You. Are you religious?

"Me? No!"

Dr. S. was born in 1945. What did his father do in the war? He

112

doesn't know. But one thing he knows for sure: He was not involved with the Nazis. How does he know? His father, he says, "was a womanizer and the only thing he cared about was women."

There you go. Bullets were flying, people were dying, and the man was fucking. "Never in my life," adds the doctor, "did I meet an anti-Semite in Germany. They are not here."

Where are they?

"In Austria."

Bavaria, my love, you drive me nuts!

•••

## Chapter 12

### Fast Cars in the Museum, Naked Statues for the Celibate, Poor People in a Posh Club, Cuba Is the Only Democracy, Stabbed Women Are Sexy, PhD in Push-Ups

I leave the Garden and go to BMW. When you've had "enough" of people, cars can function as a great replacement. Two ladies are at the info desk, welcoming me at the entrance of the BMW building in Munich. One is white, one is black. Very white and very black. Like on a piano. Very PC.

Excuse me, ladies. Do you have a BMW?

Silence.

I mean, you know, outside of the job. Do you drive a BMW?

"My husband," says the first, "has a BMW, but I have a VW." The second one musters the courage to answer as well. She, too, has two cars, one of each.

Well. We are all equal; cars too.

Once I cross the "piano," I find the motto of the company displayed on video screens at the entrance:

> To bring a design to life you need to believe in it.
> BMW design embodies what BMW stands for.
> We create . . . emotional pieces.
> Emotion drives perfection.

Emotional pieces?? Come on!

In an adjacent building there is this hall, it has only one car in it, with screens all around and one huge screen in the back.

And this line: "Who knew perfection could be that beautiful!"

It looks like a temple, where the car is the God. We, the visitors, are the worshippers.

I knew that Germany was never capitalistic. It's an extremely religious society, very devout.

All said, the BMW museum is less ambitious than Autostadt, but also less glaring and at many points more pleasing to the eye. In both cases, however, you must admire the genius of German design. Its beauty is captivating. And it's something I find in this country more and more: Amazing design and superb visuals. Everywhere. If it's set designs in theaters, sculptures and architecture in the main squares, or museums such as this one, German design screams to the sky in utter beauty. In a single word: Genius.

I move on to the Plant, where they also teach me a few things. Car manufactured here: Series 3. It takes 52 hours to manufacture a car, from start to finish, not including employee breaks. Cars completed per day in this plant: 900. Most Americans want their BMWs in white. Most Germans would rather have theirs in dark colors, such as deep blue. Of the 1,100 employees work here, 10 percent are female. But this last detail: I'm not sure why they need that many. If you happened to come by today and see them, you would agree with me. Here's one employee playing with his iPhone, checking emails. Here's one walking around with coffee. And there's another one having coffee. Hard life.

The robots here, on the other hand, don't take coffee breaks. These robots work like a team, and they are. It's science fiction minus the fiction. How a robot waits for another robot to finish a task before assuming its own task is amazing and amusing at the same time. And the more you look at them the more you get a liking to them, as if they were human, or pets.
Oh, doggie.

Soon these robots will form a union, demand robot rights, and declare their loyalty to the Palestinian people. I know.

A word about the cleanliness in this plant: You can lick the floor. Every millimeter of it. Seriously. How do they keep a place like this so clean? Who created these Germans? Couldn't be God, He's not that perfect.

I move on. Come along with me. Take a look at this section, where they paint the cars. I make more mess when I fill my fountain pen. And here we have cars. I'm talking *cars*. Not one, not two— hundreds of them. And the place is spic and span. How do these people achieve this? How do these Germans, excuse my French, accomplish their mission with such cleanliness?

Don't ask me why, but the image of Rote Flora has just infiltrated my head. Many faces has this Fatherland, not all of them the same. Or is it just the other side of the same coin?

I feel so clean, I'm about to vomit. I go outside, take a train, and ten minutes later I get off. A "demo" welcomes me. Where am I, in Hamburg? No, no. It's Munich still. University students are having a demonstration. What about? Tony, a student of politics, explains to me, in a long-winded speech, that this is a demo about fair politics, just financial practices, just law, socialism, equal opportunity, equal rights, and some other goodies.

What do you want, Tony? Talk to me! I like it short and simple.

"Not to pay tuition fees."

I like Tony and his bunch of drinking friends. Tomorrow, they say to me, they will have a big demo and they predict that five thousand will join at midday. Traffic will stop, and the government will learn a lesson.

And if not?

"We will take over the buildings of the university."

At midday the next day I come to witness the miracle, me and the Munich police. This demonstration, what in New York you'd call a party, is fun. Everybody is drinking, gallons of beer are poured. The most these students pay in tuition fees is 500 euro per semester. They way it looks to me, they spend this amount in a couple of days on beer. They should demonstrate against the beer companies, demand free beer. They desperately need a prayer, I think. And, as I'm in the neighborhood, I try to help. That yellow church, Theatinerkirche St. Kajetan, only a few minutes' walk from here, seems the perfect place. I volunteer to pray for them at the church.

Lovely place. Here's a Black Madonna, I think. Mother of God was black. Yeah.

The folks at Oberammergau made a huge mistake.

It happens.

Two old German ladies sit next to God's Mom. "Is this a Catholic church?" asks one of the other. The other lady shrugs, confused like her friend. They leave the church.

The old ladies gone, I'm left alone with some naked little angels. Quite a number of them, actually.

If I were a Catholic priest, a man denied marriage and sex, how would I react to all these little naked boys with little flowers on their penises? I'd probably become a pedophile. In the US of A, if you trade with images like these outside the Church, that's twenty-five hundred years in prison, minimum.

I try to converse with the Black Mama about the students and my Free Beer Program, but she doesn't speak Yiddish.

I try another church, Der Alter Peter. Maybe the Mother of God speaks Yiddish there. What a magnificent church! Unbelievable! Whatever the German government spent on the Jewish Center in Munich is peanuts compared with what the Christians got here. If I become a billionaire one day I'd like to buy this place.

There's a woman behind me and she's crying, bitterly. Why is she crying?

It's Prayer Time. People sit, people stand, over and again. I guess that's the way God likes it. T-Mobile wants your money to connect you, God wants you to exercise.

An old priest takes hosts and puts them in the people's mouths, as if they were infants. These hosts are supposedly the Body of Christ and the priest puts his body in your mouth, if you are

Catholic. Protestants are not welcomed to eat Christ. At the *Kirchentag* a few weeks ago in this very city, Protestants told me they were offended. I am not. It's OK with me if I don't eat him. My culinary taste is quite different.

I'd rather eat at Schumann's Bar. I was told that this is the place of the Beautiful and the Rich. Sounds more Godly to me than the host. God, after all, must love the rich and the beautiful, otherwise he wouldn't give them so much money and so much beauty. Right? Right. I leave the church to meet the beauties.

The first beauty I meet is Charles Schumann, the owner.

What's special about this bar?

"Nothing."

How did you get the name?

"I worked so many years. Not like the fucking Americans. Thirty years! I never wanted to be famous. Maybe I am famous now, but I didn't work for it. There are no bartenders in America; they are mixologists."

American bartenders are not the only people on his I Don't Like list. He has no respect for the cooks of Germany either. "There are no cooks today," he says derisively, "only food designers."

What do your clients get out of your thirty-year experience?

"Nothing. Schumann's now is too big."

Who are the average clients here?

"Everybody."

Poor too?

"Yes. The prices are low here."

I look around at the people; they are as poor as he is.

What's the philosophy behind a bar, what's the idea?

"To be your home, without having your wife tell you, 'Tomorrow we have to go to the cinema.' The barmen should not be too close to clients, I say this to my employees."

Why do people come to the bar?

"To forget everything."

These rich people are not happy?

"No. This is the mark of our time. We live in a very superficial world. Bars are too loud, including Schumann's, and people can hardly talk to each other. Most people come to watch people. They sit and watch, they look, and they feel good when they see nice-looking people. They get a vibration. Sometimes I do this in the afternoon. I sit outside and watch people walk by. And sometimes I say: I wish the world would drown."

Why?

"Because people behave so badly. And some of them are dressed so badly!"

What did you learn about human nature after thirty years of watching people in the bar?

"I am not a friend of humanity."

Explain, please.

"Very few people are not egotistical. I see how they act. They are not polite. They are not gentlemanly. They are badly dressed, without taste. All the same."

If you could choose to be of any nationality, which one would it be?

"Not German."

Why not?

"The Germans are too heavy. They don't know how to relax."

I just realize that I forgot to pray for my students. Oh gosh. But there's no time for remorse now. Charles invites me for lunch in the court outside. I must accept. You can't refuse lunch.

I'm happy I accepted. It is here that I get the real taste of Schumann's Bar. First, it's Charles. He's involved in everything. He knows his clientele and greets them personally. If he missed them when they came in, he pinches their faces later as he walks by their table. He enjoys waiting on people and he is constantly at it. The rule of not getting too close doesn't apply to him. The food, moderately priced, is superb. And unlike Cohen's, this restaurant is full. Actually, this is not a restaurant, nor is it a bar. This is a club. A club for a certain class of people. And he, King Charles the First, rules over every detail. Not a table empty, not a glass unused. Ages ago it was King Ludwig who ruled here, but now it's Charles. And King Charles I rules that I won't drink Coke. Wine is better. White wine, not a dark cola. I obey. King Charles pinches my face. I become a full-fledged citizen. Proud to be Schumannist.

# I Sleep in Hitler's Room

The *Rucola-Kartoffel-Salat mit Pulpo* travels from my mouth to my belly express, as every part in between says Thank You for the delight. The *Hacksteak mit Spitzkohl* is every bit satisfying. But the best on this hot day is the drink to close the stomach. This is made of lillet lacanau—mixed with Campari, much ice, and a tiny rind of orange on top—that mesmerizes your sense of smell as you drink it. "I am a bottle," says Charles to me, "and I gravitate these ingredients into me." The man is a poet.

Suddenly I remember the students. Again. I promised that I'd participate in their demo. I must go! But before I go, Charles has something to tell me:

"There is one thing I can't teach my employees, the ability to spot the interesting people walking into the bar. This I do, and I

befriend them."

He certainly does.

I go to my students. I, too, demonstrate. Not a very hard job. All it takes is beer. I spot two new young students, whom I didn't see before.

They are Kerem and Lisa, and they sit aimlessly watching people passing by. He is an atheist Muslim, she is an atheist Christian. Both are sworn communists. They want Germany to be a communist state. "Communism is good," they say in unison. "People should decide for themselves and not the politicians."

They've known each other for many years, these two twenty-something youngsters, and that's why "we cannot become a couple." Never. But they are good friends and they share the same values. They both visited Cuba. Cuba is good. Heaven on earth. They saw it with their own eyes. "Cuba is really democratic, not like Germany. In Cuba the people decide, in Germany it's the corrupt politicians who decide for us. In Cuba, if the politicians are corrupt, people go to the polls and throw them out. Did it ever happen in Germany? Can you vote out corrupt politicians in the middle of their term? In Cuba you can."

The interesting thing is that both Kerem and Lisa are sober.

I leave Munich.

•••

Let the train take me. Where to? Nürnberg. Nice name.

It's 75 euros to Nürnberg unless, that is, you want to pay only 10. The price of train tickets in Germany is very complex. In order to figure this out you need twenty years of chess-playing experience before buying your first ticket. Or, luck be on your side, be a native of this land. For this particular trip: You can buy a normal ticket—that's if your papa is Charles Schumann—or a "Bayren Ticket," if he isn't.

I arrive in Nürnberg after midnight and immediately thank Allah for the Arabs. No, not because I changed my mind about going to Palestine. Has nothing to do with *those* Arabs. Everything has to do with the Arabs here. You see, there's a law in this town, routinely enforced by the local police, which calls for owners of restaurants and cafés to close the outside portions of their businesses by midnight. But the Iraqi owner of the Turkish restaurant here, so touched that I spoke to him in Arabic—"He speaks my tongue," he says to a young German lady, his eyes shining with pleasure and delight—that he keeps a couple of chairs and a table outside for me to enjoy. And the food he prepares for me, I must say, is heavenly. He also introduces me to a sweet Turkish concoction, which is 100 percent nonnatural but really good. I eat and drink while I enjoy the view across the street from me: St. Klara.

This church was originally built in 1273, the sign says, was destroyed in 1945 and reconstructed by 1953. A characteristically German story, I might add. The sight of the church causes me to be a little philosophical: There is a reason for madness in this land. As I travel from city to city in this big country, my eyes encounter a repeated image: destroyed properties of past millennia reconstructed in recent years. Hundreds of years of history, their history, was wiped out in one cloudy day, courtesy of World War II. This story of loss, no doubt, will stay with the people here for eternity. Wherever they live—south of Germany, north of Germany, east, or west—World War II's mark of Cain will never disappear. Their old buildings, their pride, had to be reconstructed.

I go to my hotel, the Drei Raben (Three ravens), which is a theme hotel.

It's time to sleep. I've been thinking too much today. I check my surroundings. In my room there's a wooden box, with a knob that I can press. I do so and a child's voice speaks. He tells the story of this hotel in 1945, how it caught fire and burned down. He is talking about the Allied bombardment of Nürnberg.

I guess now I can have a good night's sleep. That's the intention, no?

When I get up in the morning, I meet Daniela Hüttinger, the owner.

She tells me of the events in 1945. Her father tried to quench the fire but did not succeed. Only the first floor survived. They left the city immediately thereafter and came back after the war.

"My father told me the story many, many times."

What else did he tell you about the war?

"There were dead bodies all over the streets."

Did he tell you why this happened?

"No."

Nothing?

"He told me that his father was not part of the Nazi party."

That's all?

"Yes."

All?

"He was a simple hotel owner, he was not a student, he was not a critical person."

I see—

"My grandmother was half Jewish, maybe you should write this, this might be interesting. When one day the Nazis came around to investigate the family, because the grandfather was listening to a foreign radio station, he yelled at them, he was an actor, you know: 'I will call Julius Streicher [the famous publisher of the Nazi weekly *Der Stürmer*], what do you want from me!'

And they left."

Slowly, slowly I realize that this country has more Jews than Israel. From Rabbi Helmut Schmidt down. Except, maybe, for Half and Half. But I say nothing to Daniela; can't hurt a fellow Jew. Instead I ask her: Why "Three Ravens"?

"My father, when asked by guests, used to tell a story: There was a gallows near the city station ages ago, and ravens were flying over, seeing it all, and afterward they came to this building, went to the chimney, and told the story of what they had seen."

This city has an interesting history, and some nice stories too.

"When I lose an eyelash," she says, relaxing, "I make a wish. The wish is that it stays the way it is, because I am very happy. Because life is perfect. I am happy with life, despite being German."

Hard to be German. Yes. One day you wake up and your city, Nürnberg, is bombed.

But enough of that period. Enough of the Nazis. I don't want to hear about Nazis anymore, I don't want to think of them, I don't want to read about them. Nothing. Enough is enough. I didn't come to Nürnberg for its Nazi history. I came to see the train. Yeah. I was told that the first train that ever ran is stationed here. A German friend told me and I am here to see it.

But Daniela says I should go to the Documentation Center Nazi Party Rally Grounds Museum. Wow, this is a long name for a museum. I tell Daniela that I've finished my chapter with Nazis, that for me it's over. But she is not impressed. "You must go," the Jewess orders me, shaking her head. "You must!"

Jewish women can get very tough. You better obey them.

That's how I find myself listening to Göring testifying.

He is asked: Did you know about the mass murder of Jews?

No, he did not. The man had no clue. Didn't see, didn't hear. This is one of his last comments on earth, his last will and testament to the German nation. He didn't know. Total news to him. Nobody told him. Nobody knew, especially him.

Like Daniela's father.

Let me run out of this place!

To the DB museum, right now! Trains are better than Nazis.

Let me see the First Train Ever!

First train, says the DB man standing at the info desk of the DB museum, was in Manchester, in 1824. The first one in Germany was in 1835, and that one was the world's fifth. In this museum you can see a 1953 replica of a train built in 1935, which itself is a replica. The original was sold in parts in 1851 to a textile factory in Augsburg.

He says, he knows.

There you go. I came to Nürnberg for nothing.

But kill me, I am not leaving. I made the trip, am here already, so let me see trains. Original. Replicas. Whatever. Every ancient church in this country is also a replica. Big deal.

First things first: At the entrance to this museum there is a welcome sign, on shiny glass. The DB welcomes you. Me. In many languages, including two Semitic ones. The Welcome in Hebrew, interestingly, has three mistakes in it. This could be a Guinness record, I believe. Some of the letters don't even belong here.

How could the DB make so many mistakes in one "Welcome"?!

Well, I'm the last one who should complain. I paid only 10 euros for my ticket to Nürnberg. The "Welcome" in Arabic, by the way, is well written. Not one mistake.
I guess Arab tourists buy the 75-euro tickets.

That must be the reason. After all, the Germans, as far as I know, know very much about Israel, the Jews, and everything in between. So how can they make such a huge mistake? Because I bought the cheap ticket. Makes total sense.

Hey, look here! It's the train car of King Ludwig. What a beauty! I would love to be a king. And here is the Adler train, the replica of the replica. I don't know about you, but I think this train puts DB's new ICE (Intercity Express) trains to shame. What an eye-catcher! Yes, the new trains ride faster, but the old ones were such beauties! No wonder they were slower—nobody ever wanted to get off! Not just the trains themselves, the stations as well. Look at the Centralbahnhof (Central station) sign, at the end of the Adler line. They have a drawing of a station. Amazingly well done, my Germans! Has great depth to it, looks real. Better than some paintings in the best of museums. Sorry. I keep on staring at it. Sit next to it. It is alive. Really good!

I keep on going, delighted like a cat with fresh cream.

Oh no! Without warning I arrive at the Deutsche Reichsbahn (Third Reich's train) section. The Nazis again! I run out. Enough with the Nazis. Get over it already!

•••

I go to the Frauenkirche, I still owe a prayer for the Munich students.

There is a huge poster inside, announcing a big event in the church. Something about a pogrom. What kind of pogrom? Against Jews. Jews again? Yes. When did the pogrom take place? In 1349.

Can't leave the Jews alone. Ever.

I've had enough with the Jews. I'm walking out.

I am looking for a Leberkäse. But what I find instead is the Way of Human Rights, a thirty-pillar memorial. Poor Germans. People shove the World War II period in their faces every opportunity that comes by. Those people, what irony, are the Germans themselves—in this case, the Germanisches Nationalmuseum, which commissioned this memorial.

I hear there's a torture chamber under the Rathaus (city hall). Maybe I should go and visit it. Seems like a good break from all this Holocaust business. But the chamber is closed. What I find instead is Mr. Amano, of the Amano jewelry store. Amano, a Sri Lankan, came to Germany thirty years ago. Today he has two stores in the old city and is "sitting pretty."

We are in a coffee shop next to one of his stores. People are watching the start of the WM (World Cup) on the big TV screen, but Amano is not interested. He tells me that he loves the Germans.

What makes them so good?

"They think a lot."

And he likes that. He also likes that his German clients make him rich.

"Do you know what was the first sentence I ever spoke in German?" he asks me.

No.

"Why are you so serious?"
And what was the response?
"They got even more serious."
He shares with me the facts of his life, which is his business:
"Ninety-nine percent of the people who buy in my store are men. Mostly repeat clients. Some men buy for more than one woman. If a man says to me, 'Give me three rings and three necklaces and make sure they're not the same color,' I know he has more than one woman. The most expensive items that men buy are for their girlfriends. The wives get the cheaper jewelry. My clientele is made up of doctors, lawyers, businessmen, and industrialists. Most of my clients are Germans, but sometimes I have Arabs and Turks. They always ask for a discount!"

And then he adds: "Abrahamic religions are crazy. There's no difference between Christians, Muslims, or Jews. I'm not religious. I'm a Buddhist and I follow Buddha's teachings."

Why do you follow him, if you're not religious?
"Because he's smart."
And Nietzsche is not?
"He was a sad man, a negative man."
Are there no more happy smarts, other than Buddha?
Here Amano gets lost.
"What would you like to drink?" he asks. "It's on me."
On the street nearby is a truck with a sign of the State Theater Nürnberg and a picture of a woman stabbing herself with a knife, blood dripping on her white dress. In other parts of the world this

image could serve as an icon of the local mental hospital. Here it is for the locals, the normal people.

I go back to the train station and board the next train out.

•••

In Lichtenfels station, the train makes a long stop. I get off for a few minutes and look around. Graffiti all over. "Multi-Kulti nein Danke." "Frei Sozial und National." (No to Multiculturalism. Free, Socialist, and National [far-right battle cries]).

Where am I going?

To a *Turnfest* in Coburg, at Castle Ehrenburg. There, I'm told, they celebrate one hundred fifty years of the *Deutscher Turnverein*. I have no clue what it is, but hopefully I'll find out. When I get there, the first thing I find is Joachim Herrmann, the Bavarian minister of the interior. A funny, tall man with the voice of a cantor.

What does it mean to be Bavarian? I ask him.

Sometimes I ask questions that are not very intelligent. Happily for me, Joachim doesn't mind. He's a politician and will answer any question you come up with.

"A thousand-year-old history," he says. "And self-consciousness. Bavarians feel that they are the special, beautiful part of Germany."

I am not sure I really understand. I tell him that.

"We are more conscious of our tradition than other parts of Germany are. We are also more religious than the rest of Germany."

How about beer? Do Bavarians drink more beer than the rest of the Germans do?

"Maybe a little more."

Personally, how much do you drink?

"Not much."

And on holidays?

"Never more than two *masses*." (Mass, or maß, is a glass of beer containing one liter.)

Now that I know all, I just shut up. Nothing else pops into my head. This is a situation that in journalism school they teach you to avoid at all cost, but life is not a university. Luckily, my man goes on.

"In Bavaria we love our country."

You display the flag higher than the other Germans do?

"The Bavarian flag."

How about the German flag?

"During soccer games."

"The German flag," I repeat, as if I won't be able to sleep tonight unless I know all the details about raising and displaying the German flag.

Are you proud of the German flag?

"We are proud of our Bavarian flag."

This man is certainly a qualified politician. He can't answer a question straight.

Would you like to be the German chancellor one day?

"No. I want to stay in Bavaria."

Me too. At least in this place. There are so many sandwiches on the tables all around, all looking so delicious, and each smiling at me, begging that I let them into my mouth.

I came here because Christof, a man I truly respect and trust, told me that in Coburg they have a *Turnfest*, which, he explained to me, was a gym competition.

It sounded bizarre and I said: Yes, I'll go. I never heard about gym competitions before. Soccer, yeah. I understand soccer: You raise the German flag and you feel good. But what is a gym competition? It sounded good. I hadn't been to the gym for about a decade and I feel guilty about it. Maybe I'd feel better in that department if I went to a gym competition. I'd stay a few hours in Coburg, see people do push-ups, and get over the guilt.

Nobody told me there was going to be food!

Nobody but nobody told me there were going to be two hours of speeches as well. I thought *Turnfest* was about push-ups. Does *push-up* in Germany mean *speech*?

A professor of sports is speaking. A sports professor? What are my Germans going to invent next, doctor of soccer?

I am so amazed that I just keep eating. I gain between five and seven kilos. Is there a weight professor around?

Before I become an elephant, I find me a man who can explain to me where I am. Dr. Reinhard Ganten it is. He's a former lawyer for Germany's ministry of justice, and now he's the president of the *Akademischer Turnbund*.

Responding to my emergency call, the doctor will be glad to explain to me the idea of the *Turnverein* and the whole *Turnen* thing. "Sport is competition," he says. "But *Turnen* is a controlled movements of your body."

He's seventy years old and "my mind works perfectly, because, I think this is because I have always done sports, from the age of three or four."

Is this something uniquely German? I ask him, biting into a German salami.

"Doing different sports, all at the same time, in order to get control of your body, and to know which muscles to use, I think this is German."

For days and nights I have been denying myself sleep as I have been poring over the question, What is German? And this man has known the answer exactly, for seventy years and counting!

He knows more stuff:

"The *Turnfest*, the original one a hundred fifty years ago, helped create this nation. The duke of Coburg allowed people from different areas to come to his dukedom for the *Turnfest*, something other kings and dukes at the time did not permit in their areas of control. This created a sense of unity among the people, the people who would later make up Germany. In fact, the founder of the *Turn* movement, Friedrich Ludwig Jahn, established it so that people would be fit to fight foreign occupiers and serve as protectors of the homeland. Today there are about twenty thousand clubs of the DTB (*Deutscher Turner-Bund*), and there are five million members."

Praised be Jahn. Yes, I know, he's the guy who once wrote that the Jews, among others, are "Germany's misfortune." But I'm not going to raise the issue. I want this day to be a day free of Jews, Nazis, or any other sensitive creatures.

I talk to a few more people, men in suits and ladies in evening dresses, and they confirm to me that this *Turnen* makes for the soul of this country, the very essence of Germany. The DTB logo, the *Turnerkreuz*, they explain to me, "has four *F*s, which stand for

*Frisch, Fromm, Fröhlich, Frei ist die deutsche Turnerei.*" Can they say it in English? I ask them. They can, only they give me different translations of it. I let it go.

But don't spend too much time on this, for here comes the real thing: "It's not just sports or exercises," one of them explains to me elegantly, "it's a *Verein*. When I meet people I use the form *SIE* ["you," the more respectful form], when I meet members of the club, even for the first time, I use *DU* ["you" as it's used among friends]. It's like a family. And that's uniquely German."

Get it? Here we are introduced to a new concept: *Verein*. What is it? Asked to explain this word, everyone here would agree that *Verein* is German, very German. What is *Verein*? Each person gives me a different translation: Club. Union. Association. Group. In short: Hard to translate. Something German. *Verein*.

Like a good and learned scientist, I rush to meet the sports professor, in order to have an intellectual conversation between a push-up analyst and a salami-sandwich expert. Her name is Prof. Dr. Gudrun Doll-Tepper.

Tell me, Doctor, where did you get your degree?

"Freie Universität, Berlin."

Could you help me? I have a big problem here. Could you please describe *Turnen* for me?

Yes, she can.

"*Turnen* is practicing physical activity with particular equipment. Like an iron bar."

Sounds to me like the average American gym. Is it?

"Gyms as we see know them today use equipment developed in Germany two hundred years ago!"

Got to have a PhD to know this stuff.

In the big hall of Castle Ehrenburg, somebody has just put up a huge sign:

Wir sehen uns vom 18. bis 25. Mai 2013.
[See you May 18–25, 2013.]

That's planning, baby! I don't know where I'll be tomorrow, but these people already know where they'll be two years from now!

But no time to marvel at this phenomenon. There's a sports

show at 19:00. Local teens, adults, and children are to show off their gymnastic skills. About one thousand people are expected to show up for the event, as I'm told.

I join the crowd. What a happy bunch! Everybody seems to know everybody here.

The stage is ready. The gym players come with the one tool they have: their bodies. They do push-ups, they do fitness exercises, they work out, and the audience roars in applause.

As Charles Schumann said to me: People watching people. I wonder if ravens also like to watch other ravens.

•••

## Chapter 13

### The Germans Love their Soccer Team and the Mercedes Boss Loves his Mama

A German I met in New York the other day has invited me to visit him in Tübingen when I'm in Germany. I am now in Germany and it's three hours from here to Tübingen on the regional train. Should I go or not? Well, I have nothing better to do today. So, let's go!

I love the regional trains. Especially the one I've just boarded. It's the old style, the one on which you can pull down the windows and let the fresh air of summer greet your face. Love it. Love it. Love it.

Happy like a child, I sit down and lower the window. Can't wait for the ride to start. There aren't many people in this car, about five altogether, and I can stretch. Fat people like to stretch.

The train is moving! The air is rushing in! I'm in heaven!

And then, immediately, there is a German Invasion.

First, a thirty-year old woman approaches. She asks me, in German-accented English, to please pull up the window. "There is too much draft!" she says. How did she know I speak English? She must have been trained in the German secret service. She's so tough, so demanding, that I think it's not really worth it to start World War III just for this. I offer a compromise: half opened, half closed. She says nothing and so I assume she agrees, and I close it halfway. One and one-half minutes later another German lady approaches. This one looks to be in her early twenties, fit and healthy, beautiful and athletic. She wants me to close the window because, she says, "it's too cold." Where was she born, in the Sahara Desert? Today is one of the hottest days of the year. What's happening with her? She demands that I comply with her order.

I try the 50 percent formula again. She leaves, saying nothing. I pull up the window. Now I have it open only one quarter of the way. You would think everybody would be happy by now. No!

An older man, seems to be in his mid-sixties, approaches me. "Why are you doing this?!" he raises his voice at me.

*Lebensraum*, I tell him.

It is a peaceful ride from here on.

132

World War III, when it starts, will start in Germany on a regional train. On a nice summer day, on a train from Nürnberg to Tübingen. All because of a window.

Somewhere between Nürnberg and Stuttgart, groups of people board. A group here, a group there. Young drinkers, for the most part. I watch them closely, diligently planning my war strategy in case they attack me for my one-quarter open window. They don't act as individuals, these people. There's something strange about them, though I can't really tell what. It feels to me that it's not a collection of individuals here; it's more like a unit that has its own energy and rules, like a herd of sheep or a flock of birds. Here's a group of men going to a concert, all of them wearing black T-shirts, and here's another group of people, young men all as well, who discuss "tits" for over an hour and continuously drink beer.

A thought comes to me: These people, the Germans, my Germans, are group people. *Extreme* group people. Strangely, the young drinking creatures on this train hand me a key to a world I have been trying to understand for quite some time: The world of the German. Yes, how could I be so stupid: This is the *Verein* thing! They are "group" people, the Germans. They are clinging to each other, thinking with each other, and are each other. Whatever this means.

Yes!

Be they students in Munich, worshippers in churches, intellectuals in various disciplines, artists in various media, residents of the same villages: This is a *Verein* Country.

It's as if something's opened in my brain suddenly, giving me insight into much of what I witnessed in this land during my journey so far. Namely: Germans move together, walk together, celebrate together, act together, and think together.

Even in the media world, which is probably one of the most advanced in German society, they have those conferences, so they can think together.

Maybe Germany's national symbol should be a lamb, not an eagle. I'm not trying to put anybody down; lambs are nice too. I like lambs. I really do.

•••

I am in Tübingen. Good-bye Bavaria, hello Baden-Württemberg.

Tübingen has a church—sorry for bringing up churches again—that could be well categorized as philo-Semitic. It is known for, among other things, its dedication to the remembrance of the Holocaust. One of their activities, to cite an example, is the conducting of marches (*Marsch des Lebens*) in various locations in Germany in order to commemorate the Marches of Death, a Nazi practice that claimed thousands upon thousands of lives toward the end of World War II.

Don't think that their emphasis on remembrance of the Holocaust is causing them to be a sad bunch of people. The opposite is true, if today is a fair example. They dance and they sing and they move and they shake for almost three hours and they don't seem to get either tired or exhausted. Not a bit.

Yes, it's another *Verein*.

The style here is very much American Evangelical. They jump in place, very cheerful, happy shmappy, they move and shake their bodies the way yeshiva students do in Israel. It's not every day that you get to see German blonds shaking like ultra-Orthodox Jews. An interesting sight. The lyrics go something like: "Today is today, I don't worry about tomorrow. Thank you, Lord." Most of the people here are in their twenties and thirties. Pretty young bunch.

They also have a bookstore here, where they sell such titles as *How Children Learn to Believe*. On the stage, the flags of three nations are proudly displayed: Germany's, Israel's, and the United States'. This pretty much says it all: These people are not from Cuba.

Time for a little sermon. The Pastor talks at length against Western media, attacking the media's criticism of Israel on the issue of the flotilla to Gaza. Tomorrow, he says, a delegation from the church will go to Israel, where they have rented an apartment for two weeks. What will they do there? Pray for the protection of Israel. He'll be going as well.

At the entrance gate of this church, known as TOS, there is a sign proclaiming in big letters, "FREE!" Meaning, I assume, come in and it won't cost you a dime. Yet, money is raised here, via passing of the hat. Music follows. Happy people like to sing. Then, following the music, the pastor gives a speech about the high cost of the apartment in Israel. He urges the worshippers to help. Music comes up again. He leaves the stage. The worshippers, many of them, now come up to the stage and lay down euro notes, creating a nice Euro pile. Many twenties and fifties.

The pastor comes up again.

God, says the pastor, told him to go to Israel and pray to Him from there.

I don't get it, really. If God and this pastor are already talking with each other, if there's already a connection, why is God telling this pastor to go to Israel and pray to Him from there? If I talk to somebody on the phone and he tells me to go to Japan and finish the conversation from there, I'll hang up.

I decide that I need to talk to this pastor eye-to-eye and see how he explains all this to me. His name is Jobst Bittner, and we sit down after the service for a quiet face-to-face interview. He tells me that his father was in North Africa during the war but that as a young man "he was strongly for Hitler. My mom was part of Bund Deutscher Mädchen" (or BDM, the female branch of Hitler Youth). I ask him if he knows why God is telling him to go to Israel instead of finishing the talk in Germany.

It takes him about an hour of talking and he still hasn't given me an answer. I ask him what's the problem, why can't he give me a straight answer. He tells me to look for Jesus. I tell him to look for Muhammad. And that's, more or less, where we end up.

He seems to be a guy driven to do good for his country and willing to spare no effort, but I don't get him. I conclude: My Germans are sometimes extremely complex, no matter what their political views.

The soccer match between Germany and Australia is about to begin and the church offers a "Public Viewing" of it. My Germans want to see the game in a group. I join. And as the German team keeps scoring, the Jew-loving church goes wild. They sing:

Allee, allee, allee, allee. Eine strasse, viele baeume, ja das ist eine allee.
Wir wollen Tore sehen wir wollen Tore sehen, wir wollen, wir wollen Tore sehen.
Einer geht noch, einer geht noch rein, zwei wären besser drei

müssen's sein.

[basically: We want more goals.]

It's 2–0 to Germany in the first half. The crowd is elated. Beer time. All Germans drink beer. Left, right, center. Doesn't matter. And then it's the second half. The German team keeps doing well and TOS fans keep screaming. Lines include: "Das war elegant!" and "Die Deutschen sind perfect!" (The Germans are perfect!) Flags suddenly appear as from nowhere; obviously the people here have been carrying flags in their bags just in case their team wins. Some paint their faces with the colors of the German flag. Others paint other parts of their bodies in the flag's colors. Kisses, hugs, very loud sounds. My Germans are happy.

I leave them happy and walk to the town square.

Looks like a party, or an orgy, is going on. Drivers honk their horns all over, so happy are they. People dance in the marketplace after midnight. They have huge flags, my Germans. They kiss their fellow Germans. They dance wildly. The game ended 4–0 for the German team, and my Germans just can't be any prouder. Some flags are much bigger, longer, and wider than their carriers. They want to cover themselves, and whoever is around them, with the flag.

Extreme people, my Germans, and they love their country. Deeply. They scream. From the top of their lungs, "Deutschland! Deutschland! Deutschland!" Over and over. They jump, and jump, and jump. Here's one jumping over a traffic light. Three cops are watching, laughing. They are part of the happy crowd. Strangers hug and kiss each other, over and over again. Happy bunch, the Germans. Look at the size of the flag over there: fits two king-size beds.

It's good to be German!

I go to bed and sleep calmly. When my Germans feel good, I feel good as well.

•••

Once I'm on my feet again I go to meet Bruno Gebhart-Pietzsch, owner of a store that sells fair-trade coffee, fair-handled tea, philosophy books, bio drinks, and CDs such as *Kinder der Sonne* (Children of the sun). Bruno is also a member of the city council, representing the Green Party.

The Greens in the Rathaus of Tübingen are 35 percent, the largest percentage in the country, Bruno says proudly.

Who are more beautiful, Swabian women or Bavarian? I ask him.

The man is shocked, he simply cannot believe that what his ears have just heard is true. He's stunned by the question.

A man, dressed like a member of the British Parliament, enters the store. He works in the library of the university, where one of the students left an empty bottle on the table. He has a question: Would Bruno like to have it?

I have a question: Is he trying to sell the bottle?

No, no! It's just that empty bottles shouldn't be thrown away. They must be properly recycled.

Righteous people, my Germans, and pretty extreme. Where else, on this planet, would you find people who care so much about an empty bottle, carrying it all over until they find a Green man who would know what to do with it? Germany!

To be honest, this righteousness starts scaring me. Righteous people can turn into animals in a second. Blind were the people who couldn't see Nazism coming during the Weimar Republic. It wasn't the bad economy that turned the country to Nazism; it was the Weimar people and their righteousness.

I know. How do I know? I've met many righteous people in my life. Not only Germans. Not one righteous man or woman ever "disappointed" me. When I stood in their way they turned into beasts in a matter of seconds.

Yes, many a historian would disagree with me on this. But I spent years studying German history, especially the Third Reich era, and this is my conclusion. I might be wrong, but that the others might be wrong is equally true.

Whichever it is, I write a note in my head: must go to Weimar.

I am not done with Bruno.

I ask my main man, Bruno: Who is smarter, the Swabians or the Bavarians?

Bruno, a PC man, won't even entertain the thought of

answering this.

You are very PC, I say to him. Were you always like this?

"I used to be Catholic but became very disappointed with it as I grew up."

Is this store your new church?

He laughs, nods his head. Then says: "Maybe."

Outside Bruno's store is a tent for Ärzte ohne Grenzen (Doctors Without Borders). Righteous people as well. This is a city of the righteous, I soon see. Here I see Georg, a young man who sells donation subscriptions. You can, for example, authorize the No-Border doctors to take 10 or 160 euros from your bank account once a month. Jobst sells you eternity with God, Georg sells you righteousness with man. And the people of Tübingen buy.

How much are you getting paid to stand here, Georg?

"I do it because I believe it!"

How much, man? Give me a number!

"Five hundred fifty euros a week."

My interviews done for the day, at least as far as I know, I walk about smoking my cigarettes. Done with one pack, I try to dispose of my empty cigarette box in the garbage can. But it's not an easy task in this town, as I soon learn, when a local woman catches me in the act and sternly reminds me that anything that has a plastic cover, like my empty cigarette box, must be taken out, together with the silver wrapper inside, and be disposed of in the YELLOW bin, BITTE! You cannot put the whole empty box in one bin, just like that. She stands next to me to watch me comply. I must first separate the parts of the empty box. Yes.

I'll NEVER live in Tübingen!

The Nazi Lady is leaving, and another woman is making her way in, a Muslim lady.

She is interesting. Really.

Did you ever see a woman with a burka making a call on her cell phone? You must take a look at this one. It's a very complex operation, let me tell you, and it takes quite a few steps: Move the veil so that it doesn't stick to your face but don't reveal your face, look at numbers but don't let light from outside in, click on the numbers but don't let anybody see your fingers, then move the phone to your covered ears and make sure all the black textile doesn't get in the way. Say Hallo, but don't raise your voice. Men might get tempted.

Finished the call? Good.

Now, do you know where to store your cell phone? In your bra! But don't let anybody catch you doing this. Breasts are very tempting and it's a major crime to tempt men.

This woman must have a PhD in Burka Cell Calling from the Free University, Berlin. Otherwise, I don't know how she could follow all these steps so flawlessly.

There's a Talmudic question that I entertain at the moment. What is the law if you live in the Black Forest, very deep inside it, in its darkest and blackest point: Should you still wear a burka, or are the trees good enough, are they sufficient covering? I should go to the Black Forest and examine the place before I issue a ruling.

I sit at a café next to the Rathaus, order myself a dark, black Cola Zero, and ponder this question in total seriousness. As I sip my Zero, I notice another Muslim woman passing by. But she's wearing a hijab, and her face is showing. She is walking a few steps behind her husband, the boss. She's all in black, he's with a short white shirt and sandals. While she's sweating, he's having a good time.

I interviewed one of these ladies the other day and she told me that she actually felt pride in being all covered. Jewels, she told me, you cover.

The dead you also cover, but I didn't tell her that.

There are many women with hijab, as far as I can tell, on the streets of the Fatherland. Is the Middle East moving westward, to Germany? Or am I actually in Gaza?

•••

I think and I think, and by the time I am done thinking I am in the Black Forest. For real. It's so beautiful here that I immediately issue a fatwa forbidding burkas anywhere near the trees.

Yes, my fatwa is good. Go walk in the forest, in its dark parts, in its awesome powerful blackness and you'll immediately see that burkas don't belong here. Deer, yes; burkas no. It defeats their purpose. Indeed, I don't see a single burka lady in the whole of the

Black Forest, at least the parts that I visit.

I feel like a prophet. Me and that American Prophet should form an association, the Prophets' Verein, GmbH. I'm sure we will be pretty profitable.

Not far from here, believe it or not, somebody's built the biggest cuckoo clock in the world. I arrive a little late and can see it only through the window, but see it I do. It's totally and absolutely impractical. There's nothing you can do with it. Logically speaking, my fatwa makes much more sense. But still, I must admit, this clock pleases the eye.

Away, away from the clock lives a man known as Johannes. He is a nice man, this Johannes. He invites me to stay the night with him. He has a beautiful house, all made of gorgeous wood, and he would like to share it with others. At least for a night. He also likes to cook. Can I say no? No!

Food ready, the man asks if I want to hear his family history. Can I say no? No.

His grandpa refused to join the Nazi Party. One day the Nazis came and forced him out of his house at gunpoint. For fourteen days nobody knew where he was, and then he showed up, face fallen and spirit beaten, uttering only one sentence: "I'll never tell you what happened." And he never did, till the end of his life. Long after the Nazis were gone.

This, Johannes explains to his guest, is the story of Germany. The German people were against the Nazis, but they couldn't do anything about it. "The story of my grandfather happened all over Germany. Everywhere. To everyone. To every family. It was just a few, the SS, who did the dirty work."

And as he speaks, the Black Forest gets a little darker.

Johannes's company, privately held, has revenues of six million euros a year, he tells me. He also tells me that he loves Jews.

I love chicken. Well cooked.

Josef, a farmer, is about seventy years old. I meet him on his farm. Josef is a nice man with a thick Swabian dialect. Matter-of-factly he tells me that he took one vacation in his life, in the north, but then missed his Swabian farm and came back.

Is there something unique about Swabian people in

comparison, let's say, to the Bavarians?

"Swabians are thick-headed, unlike the Bavarians, who are happy people. If I take another vacation it will be in Bavaria."

He works eight hours a day, he has thirty cows and forty calves. He also does woodcutting and demonstrates to me how the machines work. "The young women today," he says as I try out his machines, "are lazy. They want to have a job and to work in the city. Because on the farm you have to work even on the weekend. Animals don't go 'home' for the weekend! That's why we bring in Polish women to the Black Forest and marry them. But after a while the Polish ladies learn from the German ladies . . ."

What is the most important thing in life, Josef?

"Money. To have money is the most important thing in life."

August is also a farmer. He shares his house with the cows. Too much work, he sums up his life, and too little money. "This area used to be Austria until 1806, but now it's Germany." He is a Baden man, cares not for the Swabians, and thinks that the Baden tribe is the best in the land. And what about his wife, is she a Baden lady?

"What else!"

These two guys, I believe, are the unwilling capitalists of Europe.

On the roads, some distance from the farms, there are many posters announcing the various Public Viewings of the WM games. My Germans like to use English words. I don't know why, but maybe this way they feel more international.

"Public viewing." Yep.

Say what you will about the Germans' English, there's no Brit or Yankee worth his day who will say "Nein" to a Mercedes. And Mercedes is not far from here. Should I go?

•••

Welcome to Mercedes-Benz, Stuttgart. Manfred is our tour guide for today. First he teaches us, a group of tourists, the basics. For example: This company earned 78.9 billion euros in revenue last year. Then there's a ten-minute explanation about the proper name of this company. Daimler, Benz, Mercedes-Benz, AG, and what's the difference between them all, what is correct and what's not.

We board a bus that will take us to the factory. I decide not to break my head trying to decipher what bus it is. Daimler-AG, Daimler Chrysler, Chrysler-Daimler-AG, Daimler Benz, Benz AG, Mercedes-Benz Daimler, Benz Daimler AG.

For all I care, it can be a Ford.

Why are you so complicated? I ask Thomas, a member of the Visitor Communication department of Mercedes-Benz, or whatever it's called. Thomas, you see, was sent to help me out in case I have some questions.

"Because we are Germans," he says.

Poor Thomas, he didn't expect such a question. I think he wants to leave.

"I will meet you after the tour, if this is OK with you," he says.

Yes, of course it is.

Tour starts. Here they make engines for the A-Class. Today 711 engines are to be made. At this moment, 12:54 P.M., 291 are done. They have until 11:00 P.M. to complete the rest. No robots in this part of the factory, just people. Robots are not part of the tour. Too bad, I love robots.

I don't know about the rest of the plant here, but this part reminds me of pictures from the beginning of the Industrial Revolution. Very depressing, to put it simply. The floor, as you might expect, is clean but really ugly. And so is the rest of the place.

Another interesting thing: Unlike the BMW plant, here there are no workers with coffee cups. I look at some of these faces, and they're not very cheerful.

Do you like working here, are you enjoying your job? I ask two young workers.

"Not much," comes the reply. "But what can we do? We must work."

"Smoking is forbidden in workplaces and offices," Manfred says, "and alcohol as well. Alcohol cannot be bought in the factory store."

Thomas of Mercedes-Benz's Visitor Communication confirms that alcohol is not sold here for the reasons Manfred specified. But there's another reason, he adds.

What is that?

The company doesn't want to offend the religious sensitivities of some of the workers whose religion forbids alcohol.

To make this a reason for not selling alcohol is PC gone extreme.

The more time I spend in this country, the more I get the feeling that its society is too extreme. I'll have to think about it, but not now. Now I have to talk to Thomas.

How come I didn't see even one worker who is having coffee in your plant? At BMW, I saw quite a few of the workers having coffee—

"We don't pay for workers to drink coffee."

I love short, clear answers. Now at least I know the difference between MB and BMW.

How does he think the workers would reply to my question?

"I don't understand it. I work for money, not for enjoyment. Our intention is 100 percent quality."

So it doesn't bother you they are not happy?

"Me? No."

As we talk, a well-dressed man walks by, and Thomas moves nervously in his chair. His name is Volker Stauch, Thomas tells me. According to Thomas, he oversees 17,000 employees here. In Stuttgart, he is the Big Boss. No one above him. His official title is Senior Vice President for Powertrain Operations, Mercedes-Benz. He's in charge of the plant here and of some other plants across this big land.

Would he mind having a little chat with me?

Gladly. Top Men love journalists.

An exhibition here lists different milestones in the company's history. Usually, the date of the event is also listed. But I noticed that not listed is the date when this company paid compensations to forced laborers during World War II. I ask Volker if he knows the date.

He gets pretty emotional as he responds: "My mother lived in Poland and she lost her home. At that time, that was Germany. My interest is in that. That's MY history. I am interested in that. She had some difficult nights with Russian soldiers!"

Do you have the date when the company paid compensations to its forced laborers?

"I know that the company asked people to write a book about what happened here, but I don't know the details."

He is an emotional guy, Volker. He loves his mama.

There's no one like Mama. A few thousands dying here or there? Who cares! But Mama is different. Mama is Mama.

I have to ask my Half and Half in Hamburg if Italians talk like this as well.

I stick around for a night in Stuttgart and then move to Frankfurt, capital of the Unwilling Capitalists of Germany. Where else!

•••

## Chapter 14

### How the Emir of Qatar Became My Friend and How China Ended World War II

The first person I meet in Frankfurt is Hikmet. Do you know Hikmet? Hikmet is a taxi driver. He would like to attend a Public Viewing of the soccer game this afternoon, the one between Germany and Serbia. But he can't, sorry. Today is Friday, and Hikmet has to go to the mosque. On Allah's Day, Hikmet would rather be with Allah. Allah can do more for you than FIFA.

"We have a big, beautiful mosque in Frankfurt," Hikmet tells me. "With a minaret," he adds with a smile, referring to the Swiss ban on minarets.

In two more years, Hikmet promises me, he'll take his wife with him and move back to Turkey.

Does your wife wear hijab? I ask my new friend on earth.

"Yes, she does."

Your mom too?

"Yes, she too."

And a burka as well? I ask. I have no idea why this burka thing keeps popping into my exposed mind.

"No, no burka."

Your wife too?

"My wife?"

Burka?

"No."

Why not?

"It's not in the religion!"

What do you mean?

"It's not mentioned in the Quran."

And the hijab?

"The hijab?"

Is it mentioned in the Quran?

"You mean—?"

Where is the word *hijab* mentioned in the Quran? Did you see it with your own eyes?

Hikmet stares at me, the new imam of Frankfurt.

"You know the Quran?"

Yes, answers Imam Tuvia.

"It's not mentioned, true."

He laughs now. It's between Muslims. Between men. Mentioned, not mentioned, who cares? We, men, don't wear it anyway. We share a laugh. We understand each other. I bid Hikmet goodbye and go to meet a Jew. Just to be even-handed, like the EU. When in Europe, I figure, do as the Europeans do.

•••

My Jew for today is Roman Haller, director of "Claims Conference, Successor Organization" in Frankfurt.

What is Successor Organization?

"Incoming Money," he tells me. That's in plain English. What this office does is locate properties that were in Jewish hands before World World II and "reclaims" them.

He introduces himself:

"I was born in Poland, but I am not Polish because I left Poland as a baby. It's impossible for me to say I am German because of what happened to my family here. What am I? I am a citizen of Munich. I am Bavarian, I can say that. I am a Jew and I am a Bavarian."

I ask Roman how much money did Daimler pay out for its conduct during World War II and in what year did they pay it. He can check for me, he says, but, "As far as I know, only 15 percent of forced labor at Daimler were Jewish. Everybody was screaming that the Jews take money, but most of the money went to non-Jews."

At the Claims Conference here, he tells me, "We deal only with properties. And the Jewish properties have to come back to Jewish hands. Full stop."

How about claims that have nothing to do with property? Should they continue to be made, as they are now, or should they be stopped? Roman Haller will be glad to answer me this question, he says, provided I stop writing. I stop and he talks. Whatever he says now is off the record.

All in all, he tells me before I leave, "there is less anti-Semitism in Germany than in the US." I am happy to hear about it.

# I Sleep in Hitler's Room

I have been suffering constant anti-Semitism in New York for the past thirty years, hardly surviving, and it's great news to hear that the situation in Germany is better.

•••

Outside his office, loud groups of people, or *Vereins*, are at the ready. They are excited. It's time for another German win. Yeah, this is a *Verein*. Kind of. Same idea. People who want to watch the games in groups. Sitting home and watching TV, coming to you from the same channel at exactly the same time, is not good enough. We must see the games with other Germans, many Germans. All of us together.

Walking the streets of Frankfurt on game day requires training. It's a sport by itself. You have to maneuver among the crowds. They are excited, the people. Especially those next to Public Viewing areas, such as Rossmarkt.

Thousands upon thousands of two-legged creatures, many carrying German flags, are at the ready. There are some here, I suddenly notice, with Serbian flags as well. Will they spoil the party? The people, some of whom took trains from long distances just to be here, to watch the game with the others, are singing excitedly intelligent poems with flowery lines such as "Deutschland vor, Schieß ein Tor!" (Onward, Germany, shoot a goal!)

Suddenly, nobody knows how it really happened, Serbia scores a goal under the nose of the Germans. Serbian fans shout in delight. After all, they are the ones who did it, right here in Rossmarkt. Yeah. Don't dare to remind them that they're not in South Africa, that they are in Frankfurt, Germany, watching a giant TV screen. But the Germans here are in a bad mood, worse than the Palestinians in Gaza. At half-time, a man with a mike on the stage urges the people to be happier. We are just one goal behind, he reminds them. Waste of time; they are too depressed.

The second half starts and the German team doesn't score. One young lady, with the colors of the German flag on her face, rubs them off and exits.

There are ten thousand people here. Who are they, really?

147

With press card in hand, I am permitted to go to the stage and stare at the crowd from above, facing the multitude. This is magnificent. When viewed from the stage, under the huge screen, the thousands of faces project back like a strange painting, faces upon faces made into one atomic unit of worshippers. Some, I am not kidding, pray to the screen, and I feel like God. They scream in my direction, being the imprecating devotees that they are.

Those who don't scream, the silent majority, stand almost motionless, like the trees in the Black Forest. Visually, this looks like a painting by a deranged man.

Whatever it is, it is hard for me to take my eyes off them. It's magnificent in its beauty and amazing in its ugliness, all at the same time. You can't duplicate this image. No lens, no TV can capture the awesomeness of this moment. Frightening.

•••

Rumor flies into my ears, and I can't share the name of its carrier, that the emir of Qatar is in Frankfurt today. He is staying, where else, at the Steigenberger Frankfurter Hof. Now, this is a nice hotel. And this nice hotel has nice people in it. And the nice people of this nice hotel are welcoming me as a guest of their hotel. Four kingly days at no charge. I even get a tour of the place by a beautiful saleslady who shows me to the Thomas Mann Suite and some other interesting hideaways in this huge building. Yes, this is called the Thomas Mann Suite because the man stayed here. Mann, the Emir, and Me. A gorgeous triumvirate. The emir's presence, by the way, is a big secret. I am not supposed to know. When I ask an official here, I am met by:

"How do you know?" And then:

"Oh God, did I just tell you?"

No, I say, the emir and I are intimate friends!

The Holy Triangle widens when I meet a fourth man: Patrick Bittner. Now, this is a man for you. A chef. Chef of the hotel's French restaurant. Not just a chef, a runner too. This man, believe it or not, runs 25 km every day. Not in his car, not in his motorcycle, not on a yacht. But by foot.

Patrick dear, what's your motto? Anything you would like to

be remembered for?

"Food is like women. Food needs to be treated with respect."

Great. By the authority given to me by Zeus, I order you to answer me this question: If I allow you to have only one, food or women, which would you choose?

"Food."

When you prepare a dish, do you converse with the food and ask it for advice? Do you talk to the food?

Zeus knows how I came up with this question, I certainly don't. But Patrick, go figure, understands it.

"Yes I do."

There are forty-one suites in this hotel. The Presidential Suite, in case you are interested, goes for 4,600 euros a night. And Patrick's restaurant, you'll probably not be shocked to learn, is the most expensive in the area. Dinner for two will cost you, on average, around 400 euros. Last night, a staff member shares a little secret with me: A group of ten came for dinner and had spent 3,000 euros by the time they left.

What food, you might be curious to know, do walking banks eat? Well, good food. I know, because I tried it. Gift of Patrick.

Here are some of the foods and the drinks that, following bits and bites of various delicious goodies intended just to whet the appetite, enter my belly on this Friday evening:

> Alsatian goose liver with elder, yogurt and green pepper.
>     This comes with a 2005 Monbazillac wine, a Château Le Thibaut from France.

> Line-caught John Dory (Saint Pierre) with mashed potatoes, chanterelles, and green peppers.
>     This comes with a 2006 Riesling, a Nonnberg, Erste Gewächs from Germany.

> Turbot from Brittany with young artichokes, capers, and tomatoes.
>     This comes with 2004 Grüner Veltliner, from Austria.

The fish, the waiter tells me, have just arrived in Frankfurt.

Twelve hours ago, he explains to me, they were calmly swimming in France. The man makes me feel almost like a cannibal. But I eat them anyway.

Continue:

> Saddle of deer from the Eifel with kohlrabi, peas tortellini, and Mexican spice.
> This comes with a 2000 Hautes-Côtes de Nuits from France.

This, as mentioned, is just a partial list of what is served at dinner. There are sweets as well, more wine, different breads, and, of course, three different butters. Rich people like more than just one butter on their breads.

How was the food? Well . . . if there's a heaven, Patrick is the head chef up there. Not only does his food taste otherworldly, but he prepares it like a painter. Each dish, and there are quite a few here, looks like a painting. Charles Schumann called it "food design." But I like it. So I'm not a cannibal after all. I'm an eater of museum pieces, only these museum pieces taste good. No wonder the emir of Qatar eats here.

And Oscar too. Do you know Oscar? Oscar is a rich man, very rich, an employee whispers into my ears. Oscar watched the game and witnessed Germany lose. That made him sad and he went on a drinking binge. He showed up at the restaurant of the Frankfurter Hof with his expensive wear but minus his shoes. He forgot them along the way. Somewhere. Rich folks don't handle defeat well, it seems.

How did he manage to get here in one piece?

"This is my home," he says. "There is no better food in the world than here."

I go outside to have a cigarette. Smoking, after all, is forbidden inside. Just as in Dachau. A tall man walks by, next to the huge euro sign and the European Bank. He is in his fifties or sixties, seems to be a man of average means, but suddenly he stops by a garbage bin. He picks up empty bottles and puts them in a plastic bag.

He is a man who reached bottom.

The contrast between this nameless man and Oscar, between the haves and the have-nots, is just too hard to digest.

Do I live in a dream?

Where am I?

When will I wake up?

Where?

At the Steigenberger Frankfurter Hof, naturally.

There is a breakfast manager here. I didn't know, but now I do. He knows me, by the way. Everything about me. "You cut your hair," he says to me as I sip my morning berry juice. I am taken by surprise. How does he know my hair habits? Is he my close friend and I've forgotten? Is he a member of my family and I never knew? Is he my silent business partner, from Goldman Sachs or some other Jewish media holding, finally revealing himself? No, none of the above. He is a Steigenberger Frankfurter Hof manager. Steigenberger Frankfurter Hof managers, let it be known, know their clients. They get a list in the morning of who is who, pix included, so that they will be prepared to serve the esteemed guests.

No, do not worry: Steigenberger Frankfurter Hof people are not the CIA.

They're better.

If the US government consulted Steigenberger Frankfurter Hof before going to Iraq or Afghanistan, they might have saved themselves a fortune.

I sit here now for hours, entertaining stupid thoughts like that, while I'm constantly served and ever eating. My whole world now is about taste and service. More and more of each.

Each fish comes with its own wine, I learned yesterday. And each bite in the morning comes with its own drink, I learn today.

I love learning!

Abdul is my next teacher. He sits outside, my new rich pal Abdul, enjoying a cigarette.

Abdul is very interested in politics. Some people are. He's from California and he reads a lot about the Middle East. The last topic on earth I would like to discuss today. But Abdul does.

"I like Prime Minister Netanyahu," Abdul says. "He is a strong leader and you need strong men in that area."

I have been in Germany for some time now and never once have I heard anyone expressing thoughts even mildly close to this. What's going on with Abdul?

I try to feel him out. In outer appearance, he looks similar to President Obama. Well-spoken, dark skin, sharply dressed, and smartly opinionated.

Your name is Abdul?

"Yes, that's my name."

You must be the only Abdul on the planet who thinks like this. What makes you—

"Listen," Abdul interrupts. "I have two cousins in the Middle East. One Jew, one Arab. Sometimes one cousin is right, other times the other cousin is right. This time, this cousin is right, the Jewish cousin. You have to be tough to survive in that part of the world."

And I ponder: Why is it that so much of our thoughts are determined by where we live? Why aren't more Germans thinking like him? Why aren't more Americans thinking like the Germans? We all think that we are independent thinkers, but are we? I look at this Abdul and ask myself how come I never met a Günter who thinks like him.

Sometimes reality is too complex to handle. Maybe I should go to the opera. "*Daphne* von Richard Strauss" is playing at the Opera Frankfurt tonight.

I sit next to a Japanese guy who asks me if I'm going to review the performance.

This Frankfurt is packed with spies.

"Daphne."

The theme of love and death surfaces here, as on other stages in this big land. The music is majestic and the orchestration here superb, yet the attempt that these opera singers make at acting is not at all convincing and should be scratched. But all in all I'm having a great time.

I am going back to my local Better-Than-the-CIA Hotel. On my bed is a piece of chocolate and a sheet with a bedtime story. Every night we get one. We. Members of the club. My own little *Verein*.

Just a little advice for you, my *Verein* member: If you stay at this hotel, don't get too wild at night. Don't tell anybody I told you, but here it is: The beds, the gorgeous beds, have wheels under them. If you get a little unruly you'll find yourself in a different country when you get up in the morning. Unless you have your passport with you, stay calm here.

And stick around for breakfast.

As I am doing, at this very moment.

A staff member, one of those CIA agents, comes over and tells me that "Since you are Jewish—"

I am what?

"I was given the information about you—"

Oh, yes . . .

"—and, as is my practice with members of the Muslim community, I will not offer you bacon."

I hear this and try my best to hide the wursts and all other questionable goodies that I've put on my plate just minutes before. Oh, it's so hard to be a Jew!

But, yes, it's entertaining as well. At least sometimes.

I continue eating and drinking for two or three hours. Why not? This is my gym for today, exercising my mouth muscles.

•••

Once I'm done with my morning workout, I go to meet a Frankfurter financier. Bank of America Merrill Lynch. That's what the card says. About as reasonable as Daimler Mercedes AG. The card also bears this financier's name, but I can't use it just yet because Bank of America Merrill Lynch must approve this interview first. There's a process for this and it takes three different departments to approve it. In the meantime, I have to give this person a name that's not his. Let's call him George.

George was not born in this country. He started in banking many years ago and today he is one of the top people at BOA ML. Not the top of the top, but almost. If only he wanted, he could buy the building across the street. But he doesn't need it. Not today.

What is life for you?

"Do you know Thomas Mann? He asked this question . . ."

You can be more original, can't you?

"I avoid answering, don't I?"

Yes, you do. What is life for you?

"As a banker?"

Let's start with that.

"My job is important. It's takes up a major portion of my time. Including weekends. It's a complicated business. We have huge competition; it's tough but interesting."

What's the goal? Making money?

"No."

What is it, then?

"Having fun."

Working weekends is fun?

"I haven't told you the other things yet."

Let me hear.

"Yesterday we had a party—we drove a huge lorry with a shovel in front—at the airport, and I saw a lot of people I know and like. Last weekend I was visited by friends from abroad, friends I hadn't seen in decades. This evening I am playing golf. Next week I am going fishing, fly-fishing. Are you familiar with fly-fishing? It's an artificial fly that you put on top as a bait. When I have time to spend, I take half a day for fishing; that's the best! Then I see the opera. Music is important to me. Literature is important to me. And it's all framed by my job. You need money to finance this way of life."

You have enough money today to maintain this kind of life even if you quit your job this very moment. Right?

"Yes."

So, what's the goal now?

"The primary goal is to make money for the shareholders."

Let me re-rephrase the question: What's the drive?

"To beat JPMorgan."

What??

"They are the best, and we want to beat them. Be number one."

That's it?

"Till we beat them. Then we'll see."

OK. Let's leave the companies aside for the moment. Let's talk about you. You've made a lot of money, have you not?

"Yes."

And you want more?

"Yes."

How much money is enough? When will you call it quits? When will you say, I have enough?

"You are asking me a tough question."

When is "George" going to say, Enough!?

"I am not going to tell you that."

Aren't you a millionaire?

"Yes. I am a millionaire, but there are millions of millionaires. I need money for things. For my family. For relatives whom I want to help."

I'm sure you've already set aside enough money for these purposes. Haven't you?

"Yes."

So, what's the goal? Why keep on working?

"I would also like to study a new language. And I would like to go to university and take a course in music."

Hard to believe what the man is saying. Can you believe it? That's why I'm not a millionaire; I can't answer questions like George. A whole semester costs 500 euros, and this millionaire tells me he must keep on working so he can afford the tuition. I love it!

How many people work under you?

"None."

Don't fool yourself. George is not a janitor at Bank of America Merrill Lynch. No, not really.

"In my position you don't have employees under you. Your employees are virtual."

Is he the iPad director? Nope.

"In my position, you have clients. You meet the clients and then you create teams."

Who are your clients?

"Siemens. Lufthansa."

You're a big shot. You make tons of money.

"I do."

And you won't tell me how much is enough?

"No."

Not enough yet?

"Not yet."

The emir of Qatar is still at it. Not enough for him. Not yet. Not for him and not for you.

George laughs, like a child caught eating a forbidden fruit. He points to a bicycle on the street opposite us. "You see that? That's my Porsche."

I feel bad for you, my poor man. You don't have a car?

"No."

Really?

"Really."

And your wife?

George laughs. "She has a small Mercedes," he says.

The man tried. What has he got to lose? It's part of the spiel.

George has to leave now. It's Sunday afternoon, and there's a corporate meeting he must attend.

"So, you saw *Daphne* last night," says George before leaving. "He had a questionable past," George comments, referring to Strauss, the man who once dedicated a song to Josef Goebbels while at the same time he did his utmost to protect his Jewish daughter-in-law.

And I thought that today I would get a rest from the Jews and the Nazis.

But George had to kill those two birds for me with one shot.

That's what happens when you meet a financier in Frankfurt am Main on a Sunday.

He leaves and so do I. He goes to his corporate meeting. I go to Rossmarkt.


Italy against New Zealand. No German flags today, sorry. The game ends 1–1 and I go to the local McDonald's. I order a meal and a latte and sit outside to consume my four-euro expenditure.

A man sitting next to me, obviously in thirst for a couple of ears, starts talking to me. His name is Herr Kraus and he loves traveling. That's his hobby. He was born in 1936 in Berlin and he cannot recall ever seeing an SS man or a Gestapo member. "I grew up in war," he says to me, "I didn't know any other reality and for me it was normal." What he does remember, however, is the air bombardment by the Allied forces. "My father told me that Rome will pray for us. That was my religious education."

•••

It would be interesting to see what kind of education the young of Germany are getting these days. To find out, the next day I head out for two schools in Frankfurt.

The first is Freie Schule für Erwachsene (Free school for adults). This is the place of the unlucky guys and girls, the ones who were doomed into different kinds of schools, those that guarantee a future in low-paying jobs. There's a very complicated formula in this wide land, one that my little head does not fully comprehend but that determines which school you'll get into. One kind of school trains you to become a doctor, one trains you to become a technician, and the third one will teach you how to bake a pita and clean the toilet. Not exactly, but more or less that's the system.

The students here are doubly unlucky. Not only are they from the Toilet Department of Education, but they also happen to be dropouts, meaning that at some point in life they quit Toilet Cleaning 101. The good thing is, these boys and girls have decided to go back to school, and that's why they are here. No, they will not get what is called here Abitur, which is reserved for the Lucky Boys and Girls *Verein*, but they will get Second Best AND a CHANCE to study more and MAYBE at SOME POINT get an ABITUR.

Most likely no "George" will come out of them, no Volker, no Otto, and of course no Half and Half and no Rabbi Schmidt. But these people want better than what they have now, they wish for more, and they try to fight the system.

Today is test day. Oral exam. If they pass they can move on, if they fail they're out.

In a few minutes these students will present what they know, or don't know, to a committee of teachers: the Judges.

The judges are all white. The examined are a "mosaic" of people: blacks, whites, and whatever in between.

If they get a score of 6 or higher, they fail. The best is 1.

Objective: Get as close to 1 as you can.

The subject is history. The details are up to them.

First student chooses to give a presentation on the Warsaw ghetto uprising.

Is he Jewish? I ask.

"No," he says. "But this story means a lot to me."

OK. It's a free country, as Alvaro the Italian taught me.

Facing his judges, this teenager talks about the Jews and about what the "Germans did to the Jews."

The white Germans listen as this foreigner speaks about the "Germans," which is them. This is so theatrical! Better than any German theater I've ever seen.

It's Absurd theater, to an extent. I don't know if I should laugh or cry when I realize what this student is doing. He turns the tables; he turns his judges into the accused.

The Warsaw-ghetto admirer gets 2 minus.

Next student, please!

His topic: World War II.

What's gotten into his head? World War II? Couldn't he find something easier?

Well, it was his choice.

He gets some facts right. Like the extermination of Jews. (I can't believe we get to this topic again!) Then he quickly moves on to the end of the war. Russia, he says, ended it.

Only Russia, asks one of the judges?

"America, too, I think," says the student.

And that's it? asks the judge.

"China, also."

This guy should get a 9, at least.

But one of the judges, who is the Last of the Mohicans, won't allow him to fail. Her name is Ines, and she's a liberal woman of the kind you rarely see. She's the real McCoy. She's not a liberal like your average liberal politician, the kind who abuses the term *liberal*. She's a Liberal in the real sense of the word. She believes that EVERYBODY deserves a chance in life, even our discoverer of China.

The discoverer of China deserves a great mark because he "delivered his presentation with full confidence." She must be kidding. But, no, she's real. She's a rare bird of a human indeed.

She fights now for every "less point." And while you can't really agree with her arguments, you know that the Fatherland is lucky to have Ines as a Daughter.

She wins. This China discoverer gets 4 minus.

Full stop, as Roman of Claims Conference says.


The second school I go to is Wöhlerschule. The students here are the best of the best, and they look it. Well groomed, well mannered, well dressed, and well poised for the future.

I sit in a classroom, and the students present are in *Mathematik Leistungskurs*. Make no mistake: These are the smartest of the smart. Advanced math. The next Rabbi Schmidt is coming from here; the next Sheikh Jens. But not Half and Half. All of these pupils, lo and behold, are German German. "It just happened," the teacher tells me. "Usually our classes are much more mixed."

How come this one is not?

"It's because this is the math group."

Yeah, of course. How could I miss it! To be really smart, you gotta be white. I look at these extra-fortunate youngsters and I ask them:

What would you like to be when you grow up?

After two minutes of silence—they are totally unprepared for this kind of questioning, as soon becomes evident—I detect a sound:

Student 1: "I want to be free."

Be what?

"Free."

Free to do what?

"Whatever I want."

Good. What is it you want?

"To be free!"

That's it?

"Yes."

I think he should get his Abitur on the spot. Today. This hour. This very minute.

There's a mathematical reasoning to what he says, an exponential derivative, and his brilliance must be recognized. This boy is pure genius. Not that I get him, but how many people understand geniuses? That's the whole idea of being genius, isn't it?

Student 2: A pained expression and half a laugh.

Student 3: "I don't know."

Student 4: "I want to be a doctor."

Praised be Goethe! We have a winner! Doctor of what? I ask.

"Doctor."

Yeah. Got that. In what?

"Doctor in, in, eh. Doctor!"

Dentist?

"No, no dentist!"

Psychiatrist?

"Maybe."

Gynecologist?

"Maybe."

I get nowhere. So I ask another question:

Are you happy to live in this country?

"It's OK," one of them says.

If there's a war between Germany and France, how many of you will join the fight to protect Germany?

Not a single one of them. Now, this is surprising.

But I shouldn't be surprised. "This is not America," one of the boys explains to me. "We're not like the American students. We don't recite the pledge of allegiance every morning."

It's good that I came to Germany to find out what I had been doing in New York every morning. Somehow I never knew.

"My great grandfather," one of the students suddenly speaks out, "was a train driver during the war. In the service of the Nazis. I don't know if he drove people to their deaths."

"My grandfather," says another, "was in the SS."

Is that why you are not going to protect your country? I stop this sudden group psych-revelation.

"Yes. This is our history."

Do you think about that history much?

"Yes."

Why are young people like you thinking of a war that ended so long ago? Is it because your teachers shove too much Holocaust studies in your faces?

No. Not at all. On the contrary. Speaking with much passion, one student almost pleads with me, in the presence of his teacher: "Our teachers don't teach us enough. Just numbers and dates. They don't go in depth. They don't tell us what really happened. We want to know more."

This is not what I knew or read about young German students. But reading the papers is one thing, reality is another. Other students nod in agreement while he speaks. And yet another adds: "They don't tell us how it happened, why it happened."

Are they just shoving numbers and stats at you without bothering to teach you in detail what really happened?

"Yes, that's what they do."

I tell them a story about the war, an example of what happened in this country long before they were born.

At the time, young women of the BDM, the Bund Deutscher Mädel, were taught they shouldn't use deodorant or lipstick, because these were inventions of the Jews. Why did the Jews invent it? The Jews, Nazi theologians argued, were born deformed and are regularly emitting strange odors. But the German woman, who is beautiful from birth and naturally smells good, doesn't need artificial ingredients.

The students look at me, transfixed by what I tell them.

Our teachers, they say, should teach us these things!

Their teacher sits next to me. He is shocked and ashamed. He stares at his pupils. "I didn't know," he says to me.

Yes, I can't blame them for having this one dream: Be Free.

As I leave the school, the only thought that crosses my mind is this: I love these kids.

•••

I might be a little psychotic. After I leave the blessed kids I go to see heroin shooters. Don't ask me to explain this.

The heroin here, where I've just arrived, is legal. It's a government program that allows addicts to inject themselves with heroin, supplied by the government.

As I enter the premises, a man tells me that "one hundred people, plus or minus five, get heroin shots here every day, and a hundred others get methadone treatment."

The youngest person treated here is twenty-three years old, and the average age is forty. All who come here have tried other treatments and failed. They come up to three times daily, get heroin at a supervised dosage—the max is 900 milligrams daily—and they inject themselves.

Werner Heinz, the person responsible for the psychological social services here, says it's important that the people feel they are not excluded from society. Many of the patients, as Heinz calls them, started taking drugs at the age of twelve or thirteen, and "they stopped their biography," as he puts it.

I assume there's a psychological need in you that makes you work with these people. What is it?

"I feel an intellectual challenge working with them."

Give me more!

"I come from the left side of society, politically. There is an anger that I carry with me. In 1968, I was sixteen years old, and 1968 influenced me a lot. The early writings of Marx influenced me, and I acquired sympathy for the Third World. The Third World is far away, but a counterpart to that world is here, with the heroin people."

Werner also tells me that when people start using heroin, "what they experience will take a normal person twenty years of meditation in the Himalayas to experience." The problem is that with time this effect evaporates and all that remains is a terrible addiction.

Dr. Hamid Zokai, who is the psychiatrist here, enters the room.

Why are you here?

"I had a lot of personal problems, I had a personal crisis at the time."

I love it! You can't get it better than a psychiatrist sharing with you his deep neurotic, maybe even psychotic secrets. My face lights up like that of a child with ice cream.

Werner, seeing my happy face, warns Dr. Hamid that everything he says will be read by many Germans.

Dr. Hamid thinks about this and decides not to talk about himself. Too bad. Werner, with his Third World dreams, put the fear of God in Dr. Hamid's heart, depriving me of a first-rate story today!

But there's no time to think about this. It's feeding time. One by one the addicts enter the building.

My phone rings. What timing!

It's "George" of Bank of America Merrill Lynch. He needs to send a letter to London, he tells me, to get an approval from the Compliance Section for him to talk to me under his name. The response will come in twenty-four hours, he says, and most likely I will still not be able to use his name and, if he goes through with this process, he would like me not to mention Bank of America Merrill Lynch either. What's my preference?

Don't contact London, I tell him.

"OK. You don't mention my name, but you can mention Bank of America Merrill Lynch. I'll see you tomorrow."

Got you, Mr. George.

For the record: Neither "George" nor Bank of America Merrill Lynch Compliance Section in London are shooting heroin.

Back to the addicts; they are here.

There are "stations" the addicts must go through before getting their portion. First they come in. At the first station they leave their bags, if they showed up with one. Then they take an alcohol test. If they are drunk, ship out. This is a respectable place. If they are sober, they move on. Next Room, *bitte*. Here they get their portion. But this is not the end. With heroin in hand, they proceed to pick up cleaning materials. You must clean yourself and your little corner once you are done!

Addicts are not leisurely shoppers. Addicts have no time. Addicts rush. Very focused, like a tiger that hasn't had anything to eat for a month, the addict rushes to a table and immediately gets to work. Roll up a sleeve, unbutton a shirt, or pull down some pants. All depending on how they fancy to shoot their liquid dream into themselves. Some like it next to their private parts. Just so. As close as possible. Fully concentrating, more so than a research astronomer focused on the moon of a distant planet, they check for the spot, the vein. And then they inject.

Here is an older man, he likes it in his thighs. There is a young woman, she likes it in the middle of her pubic hair. Everybody and their customs, everybody and their preferences. And then it's done. Roll back whatever they've rolled up or down, clean the mess, and move to the last station, a closed section. Here they smoke, relax, have a talk, or meditate with the spirits. They must stay here for some time before they are allowed to leave.

Every step of the process is precise, like a Daimler engine. Exact and on time. None of these people have any control over what they are doing. The heroin controls them. It's their master, and they are its slaves. But you wouldn't know it if you met them on the street. They look normal. Not like bankers, mind you, but normal still.

In this Capital of the Unwilling, this corner of the city houses the utmost Unwillingness, unwillingness greater than which you will not meet. This is the end of the road. The next stop from here is the moon.

Thomas, an older addict, is relaxing at the moment. "This place," he says, "saved my life." He started heroin, he tells me, at age sixteen. "My friends were artists, musicians. That was in Munich. The good music was written under the influence of heroin. I wasn't an artist, but my friends were. I started then and haven't stopped since. I was in jail. Many times. I was thieving— not from people, only from corporations—and was in prison. I was selling dope on the street and got caught. In Munich, when I was in prison there, they didn't give me heroin. Not even methadone. They gave me codeine. Was not easy. Codeine, to calm me down. If I don't have heroin, I puke and I have to urinate every twenty minutes. I was in jail in many places. Altogether, eleven years. But now it's good. I come here in the morning, get my dose, and then I go to work. I work in the zoo. I have to do public work. Three thousand hours, the court said. I work with apes. I feed them and I clean them. Then I come here, get my dose. After I get my dose I go to eat lunch. I get a big meal for one euro. It's a government program. Very good. I go back to the apes after I eat, and after that I come here by 4:20. People who work can come as late as 4:20. I get my dose and I go to the park. Meet friends, play with them, and at night I go back to my flat and go to sleep. Three and a half years like this. The government pays my rent, and they pay for my food. And for the heroin. I don't have to sell dope. Now I have to get my second portion, my second half, excuse me. I took only the first half."

That's it. A whole life, a full biography, from A to Z, of a man named Thomas.

When you first see this, it flies by you. And you go on. Back to the streets of Frankfurt. Prostitutes and hijab wearers, financiers and beggars, all mixing with each other.

It's a beautiful day. Nature is nice. No ash clouds and no rain. I stroll the streets and window-shop. Here's a small wallet in a fashionable store for only 500 euros. I am not sure, but this might be on sale. Some people use wallets to store their money, others use money to fill out their wallets. It all depends on how much you've got. This is Frankfurt, Germany, the seat of the European Central Bank. It is here where, for the right sum, all your sweet dreams can turn into sugary reality.

And then it hits me, the Nightmare. Suddenly. The men and the women and their shots. Their faces suddenly stare at me. The holes in their bodies jump into my eyes. I don't know how it happened, but it did. The people who "stopped their biographies" come to me. Like mice in a cage. The humans turn into ghosts. And these ghosts are with me now. Hours after I left them, they return. To haunt me. They insinuate themselves into the most private corners of my heart, they violate every sacred part of me, and they darken every light within me. They demand attention, and they want me to die with them. They offer me no way out. I can't push them away with the power of my muscles, because they have entered my mind. I can't shut off my eyes, because they have infiltrated my soul. They possess me. They are the walking dead. And they walk over my head. If they have anything to teach me, if they have anything to say, it is an awful message: Human life is really worthless. A little liquid in the system and see how ugly we all are. We are made of crazed flesh and that's all there is to us.

I am trying to run away from them, or have them leave me alone. But it's not an easy task. My heart goes out to them, no matter how empty and shallow all of them might be. But I know I can't help them; these machines are beyond repair.

You can't turn a mouse into an eagle, even in Frankfurt.

Let me leave Frankfurt! I take the train out. Out to Nauheim.

•••

Have you been to Nauheim?

When people disappoint you, try to befriend buildings. Nice buildings. Villas. Old-style villas. Nauheim is blessed with a great selection of them. Houses so beautiful you want to eat them, to lick their facades. If you are ever in a crisis that you deem larger than you, try Nauheim before you start injecting yourself with certain liquids.

Bad Nauheim, as it's officially called, has invented a subtitle for itself: *Die Gesundheitsstadt* (the health city). Blow your own horns, kid. Why not? And raise your cover charge accordingly, wherever and whenever you can. Consequently, every Healthy thing here is costly. The *Gradierbau*, or *Saline*, as the locals call it, is an interesting invention: Dripping waters over tree branches that are fixed on a huge wall. Don't ask me, but people here think it makes you breathe better. I try it. I sit down, smoke a cigarette, and really enjoy the sound of wasted water. It's an experience. I don't belittle it. I know that the next time I'm in the Sahara Desert I'll miss it terribly.

Bad Nauheim is a money factory, where you get charged for everything and anything. But, at least as of this writing, they don't charge you for strolling the streets. It's good for me. The beauty of this place pushes away the heroin-shooting mice in my head.

When night falls I go to Butzbach. Heard of Butzbach? It's a place, a town. A delightful dot on the map. I am staying at Farah's. Farah is a Persian woman I first met in Tunisia. She didn't like Grand Ayatollah Ruhollah Khomeini and she moved to Germany. She hasn't been to Iran for many, many years, but she's proud as hell to be Iranian. She is happy to be in this country, but she doesn't give the German people very high marks.

They are very exact," she says of the Germans, "and when they make mistakes they make them very exact as well." She has many sayings, Farah. Her aphorism of the day is "The Germans think they killed the Jews, but who they really killed is themselves." "They are people who don't like to be themselves."

Farah, by the way, has a soft spot for the Jews. With the financial crisis going on in the world, she asks me, "What will happen with the Jews?"

Should something special happen to the Jews? I ask her.

"Now the Jews will be blamed," she says.

The Jews? Why the Jews?

She looks at me as if were totally retarded. "They are the financiers!" she says.

Jews again. Almost every day.

I never felt so Jewish in my life as I feel here, in this Germany.

I came to Germany to find the Germans, but what happens is that they find me.

Who was the man who said that the Germans don't have a sense of humor?

Whoever he was, he's wrong!

My financier "George," for the record, is not Jewish. And he's ready to meet again. After all, he still owes me an answer, an explanation for what drives him. We meet, where else, at the café of Steigenberger Frankfurter Hof.

Yes, I'm back in Frankfurt.

•••

So, why are you still working so hard to make money? What drives you?

"Chess," he says. "The game. It's a game. Not poker, but chess. It is a complicated game, you need skill. Those are exciting things. I don't do it for the money, I do it for the game. If I happen to make a million or two, that's great. But it's not about that, it's about finding out what makes the other side tick."

Why aren't you playing chess at the Kleinmarkthalle (a local market place), right here in Frankfurt? I would love to see you playing next to the wursts and the Frikadelles (German meatball) and the chickens. I can arrange a chess table for you, if you want. Should I?

"Very funny. I owe Deutsche Bank quite some money for my various properties. I need to make money, you understand?"

OK, let's put everything on the table: How many buildings do you need?

"George" looks at me as if I were Mr. Lenin. But I am not. I swear. I don't know one word of Russian.

"George" is very clear-minded. We talk about many things; his mind is sharp, and his arguments are always to the point. Except on this one issue.

Why is he so complex on this one point? I feel, after long talks with him, that he's actually driven by greed but can't bring himself to admit it.

I have time. I don't work for Bank of America. So why not use my time to help a helpless Unwilling European Capitalist? I try to guide him into the Promised Land.

Say after me:

I—

"—I—"

—am—

"—am—"

—greedy.

"Won't say it."

Why not?

"I would feel low."

He doesn't deny his greed, he just can't admit it, because he "would feel low." I point this out to him and ask him if that was a "terrible Freudian slip." "George" stares at me, as if I were the Real Devil.

Yes, I know. I use the terms Capitalist and Unwilling Capitalist often. But it's not because of me; it's because I keep hearing it, or some variations of it. I'm always the Capitalist, because I come from New York, and the German is always some kind of a socialist, because—well, just because. Using this logic, "George" is some kind of a socialist while I'm the Pure Capitalist. Something in this picture looks funny.

I Sleep in Hitler's Room

Yes, I know: I own Goldman Sachs, AT&T, Macy's, Verizon, and American Airlines, and I control the foreign policy of the US government. But I have debts as well, the war in Iraq costs me a fortune!

I'm getting nowhere with "George" talking finance. I must change the subject. There's this terrible silence between us, the greedy American and the righteous European. What topic should I choose? Well, why not my favorite one: the Germans.

What do you think of the Germans? You've lived here many, many years—

"Germans are consensus-driven, by and large not very charming, not very humorous, are ponderous and heavy, tremendously organized, excellent engineers, not natural financiers, tend to extremism, and many of them have demonstrated innate cruelty."

Wow!!! Anything good?

"They created fantastic music and literature."

What did you mean, "consensus-driven"?

"Everything must be decided by consensus. Bosses with employees, companies with unions. In every segment of society. They decide together."

Should I tell "George" of my *Verein* Theory? No, not yet. Let me check and verify it some more before I announce it to the world.

"George" leaves, to make more money, and I am stuck with a question in my head: What is this strong drive, the drive for money, that makes us all so obsessed?

The most plausible place on earth to find an answer to this question would be in the money temple, the local stock exchange, wouldn't you agree?

I go there. I arrive. I am at the Frankfurt Stock Exchange.

•••

I owe a debt of gratitude to the good people of Deutsche Börse, as it's called here, who are kind to me and let me be here on my own, not with the tourists babbling and mumbling and clicking their digitals all over. I get what they call a "private tour" of this property. I need it. I need time to meditate on the Almighty Euro. I want to unite with the Almighty Euro, I want to be born again, to hear His Voice calling me, and to totally devote myself to Him. For this I need quiet surroundings.

I am also thankful to them for releasing the security man from breathing his secured air behind me. It's me and the Almighty only. I pray to Him: Blessed be Thou, Almighty Euro, and praised be Thy Name.

One floor below me, of which I have a perfect view, is where the Almighty's army resides: the brokers. Many of them will leave this place in about two years, when machines will perform most of the trades. But now they are here, each trading different stocks. One trades in BMW stock, another has Siemens, and so on.

Let me take a look at the Almighty's soldiers. That one on the left is surfing the web, the one on the right is using his iPhone, another drinks coffee, an athletic guy watches—what else!— soccer, two ladies are chatting in a lively manner.

Besides being an army, it's also a big show. The huge electronic boards all around, displaying the various stock symbols, are purely for theatrical purposes. None of the brokers ever looks at them. The brokers, each of whom has six screens and two keyboards at their disposal, wouldn't even notice if the boards went dark or changed to Hebrew-language programming or to ancient Greek. But theatricals are good for money. Quite a few media organizations set up shop here. DW-TV, CNBC to my left, Reuters and DAF in front of me, among others. Seeing it from here, for real, you laugh at how "cheap" this all is. But on TV it probably looks great.

What one cannot ignore in this place is the flag. Sorry, flags. German flags all over. In all sizes and in all places. On walls, on chairs, on desks. Germany is in love with itself. And the brokers let it be known.

I am intrigued by the brokers, and I want to talk with them.

I am a naïve man.

"If you want to talk to the brokers," I am told, "first you need to get approval from the banks that employ them."

Why the banks are so scared of the media is something I'm not clear about. Maybe they want me not to work too hard.

So, I just watch what's cooking down under. A German TV crew enters and walks the floor. They get two people from the floor, a man and a woman, and they position them next to each other. The TV crew, consisting of two women, make their wish known. They want to see the brokers giving a thumbs-up. So, two thumbs go up. Then they get the man to give two thumbs up, and the woman another two thumbs up. They check it on the screen. Not good. They get the brokers to give the thumbs-up together, each one thumbs up. They check it, and decide No. OK: Let the man give two thumbs up while the woman stands by his side posing with a big smile under her blond hair. Yes. This is good.

The TV ladies go for it and broadcast a "spontaneous" thumbs-up at the exchange.

This is News.

I feel bad for the German nation. They watch TV and think it's reality, but in reality it's just a show, "Unwilling TV."

A man fom the press office comes to join me. "How many flags do you usually have here?" I ask him at the sight of so many.

"Only now [WM season] do we have them," he answers me. "Usually we don't have any flags, not even one. Our history, you know. We are not America."

Oh, my Germans: Why are you so extreme?! Can't you take a middle ground for once?

I am given a little toy, a green bull. That's nice. I walk out.

•••

I drive to Farah's to bid her good-bye and thank her for being such a great host. She shows me an old Quran she has, a family heirloom. She says that Islam as practiced today is not mentioned in this book, that the Quran is a spiritual book, that she remembers the elders in Iran who studied the Quran and had shining faces. But those days are over. And now she's in Germany.

"I feel like a Jew," she tells me. "The Germans say that they respect me and my culture but they don't get any of it, and don't make any real effort. They just talk. They understand nothing about my culture, about the spirit of my culture. I understand theirs, but they never bothered to really understand mine. To them

I am a foreigner, no matter what they say. I know. Farah knows. Farah knows people."

I arrive at the main station in Frankfurt, ready to board a train going somewhere.

This is Germany. Flags abound, and people are buying. Three colors to the flag, all of them earthy, hot, serious, dooming, stubborn, and almost very clear.

Can anybody explain to me this country, and in plain English?

Kai Diekmann, the editor in chief of *Bild*, the biggest paper in Europe, as I'm told, is willing to give it a shot.

To Berlin I ride, Answers is my destination.

•••

## Chapter 15

### Twelve Million People Read His Paper Every Day: Interview with the Man with the Biggest Penis

After passing through X-ray screening, à la modern-day airports, I am led to his office. Two other gentlemen join the meeting. Are they lawyers? CIA? Mossad? No. They are just nice folks who speak good English and go by the names of Tobias and Ulrich. Nice to meet them both.

Time to talk. Kai enters. Gel-haired, white shirt without a wrinkle, black-framed glasses, clean-shaven, he approaches me and shakes my hand. He sits opposite me, behind him an artsy *Bild* painting, and he is all ready for the talk. In his hands he holds a big plate full of fruit salad, which is probably his lunch. He bites into the chunks of fruit with great craving, which makes me think that the man hasn't eaten for quite some time. Yet his attention is not focused on the food but rather on the upcoming interview. He seems to be ready for some tough questions, big-time. That's why, I assume, he has here with us The Two Gentlemen of Berlin.

Not wanting to disappoint him, I ask him the most personal, intimate question I can come up with: Is Germany one nation or a collection of tribes? The Two Gentlemen of Berlin look as if a rock had just hit their unprotected heads. What is this?! Their eyes roll in disbelief. But Kai, keeping focused, replies.

"Definitely a nation," he says. "Especially after unification, and after the government moved to Berlin. Now there's a center. Everybody looks to Berlin."

What makes a German German?

"Germans are great at rebuilding. You know what I mean? But we have a problem maintaining it."

There's going to be quite a lot of rebuilding to be done in Afghanistan, if peace is ever achieved there. Does he support having German forces in Afghanistan?

"I think it's good that our forces are in Afghanistan. We are the strongest economic power in Europe."

This is an explosive political issue in Germany. Not all see eye-to-eye on this, to say the least. I'd like to know Kai's take on Germany's various political parties. So I ask him:

What's the difference between the conservatives and the liberals?

"It's about how much freedom we have."

What?

"Conservatives want different types of school, more choices, while the left wants the same school for all. People are not all equal, and I don't want to make them all equal."

It's not exactly what I wanted to know, but it's interesting to hear nonetheless.

Whatever the differences between the various political parties, Kai still believes in consensus. "Consensus-building is very important. And this may be the answer to your first question about the defining characteristic of this country. It is consensus. A consensus-building society. We spend a whole lot of money to maintain consensus."

Not that consensus is easy. "This is the only country in the world where the majority wants to raise taxes. Why? Because taxpayers are the minority. And I am totally against raising taxes. More than 50 percent of the people get more from the government than they pay for it."

Consensus is one thing, multiculturalism is another. "Multiculturalism here has gone wrong. The idea was to let them [workers from Turkey] live in the same way they've lived before, but many of those who came to Germany were poor people. Many of the Turkish people here still live in the Stone Age. We did not put enough pressure on the immigrants to learn and adopt to the culture here."

This brings me to my favorite fashion item: hijab.

Are more Turkish women wearing hijab in Germany today?

"No. There are more of them wearing bikinis."

I want to ask him where I can find them, but I decide to stay polite and stick to politics.

What's the story with your paper regarding Israel? Is it true that you have here a Legacy to Protect Israel—

"Worse . . . Every journalist working for us has to sign on to four 'principles':

"To reject all forms of political totalitarianism.

"To uphold the principles of a free social market economy.

"To support the Transatlantic alliance.

"And very important: To promote the reconciliation of Jews and Germans and support the vital rights of the people of Israel.

"In my opinion, the state of Israel is where the survivors of the Holocaust found refuge, after the Germans murdered six million of them. And because of this special relationship I am deeply convinced that whenever Israel's right to exist is in danger we cannot be neutral and our place is to be on the side of Israel. This is our responsibility: We have to take care of Israel.

"This does not mean that we do not criticize Israel. We do.

"What I ask our journalists to do is to always take a closer look, not just follow the mainstream. This is what I tell my people."

What do you think of Obama?

"I think he is going to be a big disappointment. He's a one-term president. He is very charismatic, politically very naïve, and very left. But first of all, I don't like his attitude toward Israel. He gave dangerous speeches, not understanding at all the Arab world."

One of Kai's office workers tells me that Kai hardly grants interviews anymore, that in fact he gave only one other this year. I'm intrigued why he granted this interview to me of all people, but I'm more intrigued about his leadership of this paper and how he sees his job here. This man, after all, is one of the most influential people in Germany today.

I ask him the same question I asked Sheikh Jens of *Die Zeit*: Is the *Bild* the best paper in Germany?

"*Bild* is the most successful paper in Germany, the most successful in the whole of Europe. Twelve million read it every day. In its category, it's the best. We manage to explain politics, and other things, to people who probably would not understand it otherwise. We have got a totally different readership from that of *Die Zeit*."

Who are your readers?

"Mostly the typical German citizen. Our reader structure is very similar to our [country's] demographics. It's a little younger and it's a little bit more male. As for influence, we reach more academic, educated readers than does *FAZ* [popular name for the German daily *Frankfurter Allgemeine Zeitung*]. If somebody told me I'm allowed to read only two newspapers, that's it! I'd decide for *FAZ* and *Bild*."

And if you are allowed to read only one paper?

"Of course, *Bild* . . . You know why? *FAZ* is a newspaper governed by logical criteria, it simply reports what is going on. *Bild* has an emotional approach, we are not only reporting what's happening, we are also reporting what people think is going on, what they feel about it and how they speak about it, and very often this is more important than what actually happened. To give you an example: In New York, when you check the weather you don't get just the temperature, "minus two degrees," but you also get the wind-chill factor. With the winds, it feels like minus twenty. So if you go out, you don't take the coat for the minus two but for the minus twenty. This is what *Bild* is doing, and this is what makes *Bild* so important. There's nothing like *Bild* in the whole world."

What's your contribution to *Bild*?

"I always had one strategy, and I think this is the most important thing: I always said, *Bild* has to be so 'boulevard' so that there's no other newspaper that could attack us from down under. We always have to be so boulevard—so simple, so funny, so surprising—that no other newspaper can be better than we are from down there, can get to the masses better than we can. But, to get new readers, to change the image of the newspaper, to be attractive as a platform for politicians, it is important to open the newspaper up at the top. To attract more readers who'd usually not read *Bild*, thinking it's just for the man in the street. And this is what we have done for nine and a half years now, trying to open up *Bild*. And we managed to do it."

What does this "opening up" mean?

"Very simple: To fill the newspaper with subjects, with content that would be different from what's in *FAZ*."

He tells me of an exhibition that *Bild* has put on at a museum: the sixty most important pieces of art in the last sixty years. An editor from *FAZ* even called to tell him he's ashamed it was not his paper doing it. "This would not have happened in *Bild* fifteen years ago," he says. "Fifteen years ago culture in *Bild* was, you know, on a stage if a light fell down and somebody was killed. That was then *Bild* reporting about culture. Today we are serious players. I lifted the standards. The only interview President George W. Bush gave to any German newspaper, a one-on-one interview, was to *Bild*. Every important book, if we want it, we get first serial rights to at *Bild*. This was unimaginable years ago. And we don't even pay for it. This was my idea. If we want to see the pope, we go to Rome for a one-on-one meeting. Another thing that I brought to the paper is politics. Page two of the paper today is dedicated to politics. The whole page."

Talking about his paper, his baby, Kai gets close, and quite friendly. We have eight hundred journalists working in *Bild*, he says. "If you want to be the best newspaper in Germany, you need eight hundred journalists." Personally, he says, he knows three hundred of them. He is the one with the authority to make final decisions. And he does. Every day. And as many times a day as he thinks it's important to be in touch and on top. In short: Everything that's published in *Bild*, whatever edition, must get his approval.

But the most important thing for him, strangely enough, is Israel. When he talks about Israel, he gets passionate. "A journalist who is against Israel has no place on our team," he declares. "If he's an anti-Semitic asshole he'll be fired."

All during the interview, and we are talking for more than an hour already, Kai shows much more passion when he talks about Israel than when he talks about Germany. He had just come back from London, where he attended a party with Elton John, and he is a little tired. But when the name *Israel* is mentioned, he jumps like a lion to defend it.

I try to push the envelope and I make a comment against some Israeli settlers, particularly the extreme among them. I compare their philosophy to that of the Nazis. Kai lets me have my say, but he definitely doesn't accept one word of it. If I ever entertained the idea of writing for *Bild Zeitung*, forget it. I stand no chance. This man is committed to the Israeli cause. This man is definitely not a Jew. I don't think I ever met a Jew that committed.

Being that he's not Jewish, and likely not circumcised, it's time to talk about the really important stuff: His penis. I ask Kai if he has a small penis.

This gets him really animated. "That's not true," he says. "You can see on the wall, over there!" He gets up, asks me to come to the window of his office, and then points to a location outside. "You see that red flag there? That's the building of the *TAZ* [the paper *Die Tageszeitung* paper]. You see that yellow sign on the wall? To the left of the yellow sign, that's the top of my penis. Four stories high. My penis. That's true. You don't believe it? It's true."

Yes, he's right. Projected all over the building, from the bottom to the top, is an image of a huge penis, supposedly Kai's penis. And Kai Diekmann, this guy next to me, is seen at the bottom. With sizable balls, by the way, as he proudly presents his junk to whoever wants to see. That's culture, I guess. German-style. Some artist, hired by *TAZ*, created it. I try to imagine this image in New York: the penis of a newspaper editor on the Empire State Building. Will never happen. Even if God himself orders it, no God-fearing New Yorker will ever dare to do it. But this is Berlin. This is Germany. Sophisticated. Cultured.

It turns out that *TAZ*, for whatever reason, published a fictitious news item about Kai Diekmann, their chief ideological enemy. Kai, they said, was having an operation to enlarge his tiny penis. Very complex operation, mind you, where parts of dead corpses were used to create his new, enhanced organ.

Kai, taking a step that could only backfire, sued *TAZ* for 30,000 euros. He lost in court. And the folks at *TAZ* hired an artist to create this image.

What does this have to do with news? As much as the penis of Barack Obama would have.

Kai leaves me to my thoughts and leaves the room, but only to come back with a black folder. Here are quite a few documents. Some *TAZ* stuff, plus a fake *TAZ* that *Bild* published at the time. Yes, they did that.

"They did it to provoke me," he says. "They hoped that I'd tell them to take it off, but I said, 'It's great.' If you go out of this building, and go there, you'll see me. It's me. My face and everything. But I will always say, 'It's a great piece of art but it's not me, it's their lawyer.' And then they got crazy. They said, 'It's not our lawyer.' So I said, 'It's a left-wing columnist from the *Berliner Zeitung*.' And then they had a big discussion, because they are feminists. The chief editor then was a new girl, and she publicly stated in the newspaper that she didn't want to park her bicycle for the next two years under the penis of Kai Diekmann. Then we secretly published a newspaper—it looks like *TAZ*, the same layout—with the title *We Are Penis*, where we argued that the mural had to stay. And everybody thought it was the real *TAZ*. We had great fun!"

But Kai is not a man to step down and accept defeat.

"When the *TAZ* turned twenty-five, four years ago, they asked their most beloved enemies to publish their jubilee edition. They asked me to be chief editor for a day. I did it. And even today, that one issue is the highest-circulated ever in the history of *TAZ*. When they turned thirty, they made the mistake of sending me a letter, which they sent to many others, offering me the opportunity to join their corporation."

Kai accepted. And he loves it! He goes to their annual meeting, asks stupid questions, and "I have great fun."

I have fun, too. He and I get along.

He gets up, brings in his iPad and his iPhone, sits next to me and shows me tomorrow's edition. His iPad, by the way, is the shiniest and cleanest machine I have ever seen. You won't get it from Apple in a minter condition.

We start with the front page. His Apple brings up tomorrow's front page as it now stands. He doesn't like the way it looks and feels. He doesn't even like the fonts used. Why not?

"This is like old-fashioned," he says. There's nothing new to it. We need something different. This will not go to print; it must be changed. "There are only three people allowed to do the newspaper, my two deputies and me. I am here from nine o'clock and I preside at all the conferences. I pick the pictures."

I get up, thank the Jew-lover gentile Kai Diekmann for his time, and tell him it was a pleasure meeting him. He takes one look at me and says, "But you are not a Jew, ah?" He doesn't mean it in a bad way, he's simply still shocked by the comments I made earlier. Before I leave, I take one look at this Jew Lover and "box" him: I register him in my brain under "Jewish Bride." Kind of a "Jew Lover." Yes, "Jewish Groom" would better but it is already taken, supposedly, by God.

Kai surprised me, I must admit. I expected to meet a bully, based on what some told me, but what I saw was a believer. A man driven to do what he believes is right. We might not see eye-to-eye on this or that issue—where Kai sees a great Jew, I see a potential little Nazi; where he sees bikinis, I see hijab—but he's driven by ideals and he says what he thinks. I respect this.

Did I achieve what I set out to achieve, did I decipher the German character? No. Kai might influence twelve million men and women in his country, but he's only one man. A man with a big penis on a Berlin wall, and a much bigger love for the Jews in his heart. This is not the Normal German, at least not the one I've seen so far.

Perhaps I should cross the political divide and get me somebody from the left—from, let's say, Die Linke (the Left [Party]). They impress me as educated people, maybe they know that which mere mortals don't.

Where should I start?

The man who answers to the name Gregor Gysi would be a good start, I think. But how do I get to him?

# I Sleep in Hitler's Room

Through his sister.

•••

## Chapter 16

### Artists, Leftists, North Korea and a Poem

I would like to introduce you to . . . Gabriele Gysi. Please applaud.

Gabriele is also the ex-girlfriend and lover of Frank Castorf, the artistic director of the prestigious Volksbühne theater in Berlin. She made him famous, did his p.r., they lived together for five years, and once he became famous he had affairs with other women. That's when she decided to leave him, thirty years ago. "I knew the type," she says to me. "My father was like this."

Many years later, in 2006, he asked her to become his personal rep and made her the *Chefdramaturg* of the Volksbühne in 2007. He threw her out in 2009. "He is selfish, he is a bitch, he thinks only of himself. . . . He had many fights in the theater, but there are people there he can't fire, because, according to German law, they can't be fired—for example, those who have worked for more than fifteen years. They didn't obey him, and there were always fights. He asked me to come and help him. I did. I fought for him. I defended him against his enemies. They asked him to fire me. He thought that if he fired me they would be good to him. So he fired me. That's Frank."

Gabriele is the sister of Gregor Gysi, the *Fraktionsvorsitzender* (parliamentary leader) of Die Linke in the Bundestag and arguably the most recognizable of eastern Germany's politicians.

She is a strong supporter of Die Linke and she loves Obama. If Obama ran for office in Germany she would vote for him. Certainly. Before Obama, America was bad and "treated the whole world as if everybody were an Indian."

She asked Gregor to meet me, she tells me, but he stipulated two conditions: Though he is willing to meet and talk politics, he doesn't want to talk about anything personal; also, though I never raised this issue, "he insisted that his Jewish background not be discussed." Period.

Strange, since a quick Google search will immediately scream this fact in anybody's face. But still, that is his wish, and I cannot accept such a condition.

No meeting with this man shall take place.

How did you get to be Jewish, by the way?

"The mother of my father was Jewish, and the grandfather of my mother was Jewish. That's why my mother had a *J* on her student ID card and couldn't get a doctorate; the same happened to my father."

Are you Jewish?

"We grew up godless. But we also grew up in the context of this experience."

Whom do you relate to more, atheist Jew or atheist Christian?

"The atheist Jew, naturally."

She also informs me that "there is no anti-Semitism in Germany. There's more anti-Semitism in the United States."

How do you know this about the United States?

"Because more Jews live there."

What else do you know about America?

"Google is a military instrument of the United States government."

What!

"Yes, it is! What, you don't think so?"

What will happen if Die Linke wins?

"This is an American question."

Why?

"Because Die Linke will never win."

Why?

"Because all the media are against them. And they have no army. It will not happen. Never. People will never believe in them."

Do you think your brother thinks like you?

"I am sure Gregor is not worried about what he will do when he becomes chancellor . . ."

What's your dream in life?

"Life without TV."

Her TV, of the big-screen variety, is on in the other room. It's soccer time.

You have issues with TV—what are they?

Before the war in Iraq, she tells me, she caught American TV faking news. "American reporters were shown on American TV walking around Saddam Hussein's private home. They went to his kitchen, opened the fridge, and claimed that the items inside were parts of weapons of mass destruction [WMD]." American reporters, so she claims, "were doing propaganda for the American government."

She and André Schiffrin, I think, should form a *Verein*.

So, soccer is on. Are you pulling for Germany to win?

"I would like North Korea to win."

Gabriele, I'm writing this all down. This is going to be in the book. I want to make it clear: Did you say that you'd like North Korea to win?

"Yes."

Well, that's her wish. Politics and soccer are connected by an umbilical cord. And she has her preferences.

Gabriele is a gracious hostess. We combine interview and dinner here. The lamb she prepared for this evening is outstanding, one of the best I ever tasted. And even if she doesn't always make sense to me, I still can see where she comes from. She is a believer, and her faith is Atheism. President Ahmadinejad of Iran is waiting for Prophet Mahdi, who will never show up, and she waits for a Die Linke chancellor, who will never materialize. Everybody is Waiting for Godot, that great and brilliant invention by ancient Jews and Christians. But she is not blind. No matter how she worshipped Frank Castorf in the past, and still defends him as a talented artist, her eyes have never closed to what she sees as his endless games. "No other director can succeed Frank at the Volksbühne," she tells me. "When other directors work there, Frank always goes to the actors and says to them, 'Do you like what he did?' 'Do you REALLY like it?' The actors get the hint and they say 'No,' and the new director is out."

Gabriele comes from the elite of German society, and she is an integral part of it. But this does not make her a lover of Germany. Her home is Die Linke, and her heart is in North Korea. She's for peace, but the nuclear buildup in North Korea is obviously not in her worries. What *is* there, she tells me, is the German education system. "They rewrite history in the schools. They teach about the six million Jews but not about the twenty-three million Russians."

I think Gabriele should meet other Berliners. Mr. Lippmann for example.

I meet this eighty-two-year-old at the bar of the Park Inn Hotel in Alexanderplatz.

"My parents are in Auschwitz," he says when I ask him to tell me about his family.

They were deported in 1943, in the "last transport of Jews from Berlin. We didn't know they were killing Jews until after the war." He stayed in hiding for two more years, which is how he survived. When the war was over, he didn't leave Germany because "after the war everything was cheap here."

That's it? That's why you stayed, because of money?

"No. After the war, it was easy to go out with the girls in Germany."

There were many of them, and very few men.

Unlike Gabriele, he says that the "Germans are anti-Semitic. I know, I live here."

Why are they anti-Semitic?

"It's in them. People have tendencies, like fear. Why? It's in them. Germans have anti-Semitism in them. It's inside them. But I won't leave this country, I was born here."

Mr. Lippmann does not have children. "I didn't want to bring children into this world," he says to me.

Before coming to Germany, I had no clue how complicated and complex this country is.

•••

I move on. I go to meet Holger Franke, who founded the famous Theater Rote Grütze in 1972 in Berlin. He would like Germany not to win the WM because a win would help the present government, which Holger regards as a catastrophe.

Would he like, let's say, North Korea to win the cup?

"It would be nice if North Korea could win, but they are already out."

Another North Korea lover here. What party does he belong to?

"I voted for Die Linke," says Holger.

Then, upon reflection, he admits a big sin:

"When I watch the game, in the moment, in my heart, I want Germany to win."

What did you feel when people screamed and sang "Deutschland!" on the streets after Germany's victory?

"I felt ashamed. I have no erotic feelings for the German flag."

Holger should know a thing or two about eroticism. The main idea behind his theater was to open up eroticism, "to make eroticism part of public discussion." His theater became a success practically over night, and precisely because of this reason

I am all for open eroticism. I ask Ricky, Holger's wife and thirty years his junior, to open up and tell me what's going on in the couple's bedroom.

"My husband has a sexy ass and I kiss it every morning," says Ricky. "Three days after we met we had sex. He was married at the time, to a wonderful singer, but I sat next to him, we held hands, and I saw the stars on his face. We were sitting on the terrace, it was a full moon, and I said to him, 'This is love.' His wife was not home at the time. Holger's daughter had a mobile home outside and we went there. We closed the door and then we—"

Holger remarks: "It was not an affair, it was love. For my wife it was horror, for me it was terrible because I had to decide between my wife and my lover. I loved my wife too, but with Ricky it was like a dream, a dream that lived in a bubble inside me and suddenly burst into reality. We were like two children."

OK Holger, what happened after you and Ricky closed the door at the mobile home? Tell me all!

"Would you like some red wine?" comes Holger's reply.

He might believe in, and preach, open eroticism. But preaching is one thing, action is another. Holger spent many years teaching and preaching the message, but somehow he forgot to include himself.

Holger, sixty-eight years old, is not an idiot. He sees the paradox between his decades-old teachings and his last ten minutes with Yours Truly. So Holger offers to go for a little walk, where I can see his wonderful neighborhood. Down deep Holger hopes that I'll stop asking him about his sex life.

Not far from Holger's house is Caravan Town.

On a small piece of land that used to be a no-man's-land between East and West Berlin, there's a little caravan neighborhood. Established by young people with a taste for alternative lifestyles, these squatters decided that a no-man's-land is their land. It's a community, so to speak, of people who live in little structures that look quite primitive, very similar to those of Jewish settlers in the early days of the settlers' movement in the West Bank. And like their brethren in the Middle East, the people here have a political agenda: Bio life. They are not connected to normal electricity, as each of them has a solar system supplying them with energy. No running water. And they grow some kind of trees. In addition, they do some sort of community culture. Today, for example, there's a music show. When the show is over, what a surprise, the participants applaud.

Who are these creatures?

Franziska—or, for short, Franzi—is a tall blond with a constant smile. Her father, she tells me, is a philosopher and psychologist; her mother is in the pharmaceutical business. This woman doesn't look poor. Yet, she has chosen to live rent-free.

Do you take a shower once in a while?

"Yes."

Where?

"A pool not far from here."

Anytime you need a shower you go the pool?

"People around here know me already. When they see me walking with a towel, they invite me in."

How did you get here? I mean, could I also become a member and move in?

"I worked with this community and helped out for a year and a half before I moved in."

Is there a social structure here, a kind of boss?

"The one who is here the longest is the one who has the last word if we can't decide together."

There you go. Another *Verein*.

She shows me to her home, a wooden structure on wheels. A warm place, nicely built. Did she build it herself? Yes. She's an architect. She's also a "Die Linke supporter."

"I grew up to hate this country," she tells me.

I meet one Die Linke after another.

Is this the same Germany as the one in the south?

Well, for one thing, they drink here more or less like the Bavarians. You can tell this by the quantity of empty beer bottles next to the caravans.

There are other similarities: The students I met in Munich wanted free higher education; these settlers here want free housing.

So far, what I know is this: Demand free housing and free education, drink cases of beer, be a member of some *Verein*, be PC, denounce Israel, eat Bio, be on time, love your neighbor's iPad, scream "Deutschland!" or pull for North Korea, have no knowledge of what your family did during the war or call yourself Jewish, be very clean or very dirty, participate in one demonstration or another, discuss every detail of every issue until the other side gets a severe headache—and you are German.

Did I get it right? I don't know. I have no time to think about it. Only minutes away is a soccer game between Germany and England and I've got to see it.

As the German team meets the English team on the field of the Fanmeile (a huge square) in Berlin, twenty million Germans are in attendance. I can't vouch for the accuracy of this number, but personally I have never seen so many people in my life standing in one place. Rossmarkt, by comparison, was a bus stop.

Just take a look at what happens here! As the German team scores 3–1, beer starts flowing skyward. The people are so excited that they irrigate the skies of Berlin with their beer. They jump, they sing, and they scream "Deutschland!" from the top of their lungs. Funny, in the midst of the twenty or fifty million Germans here I notice three Arabs standing just next to me. Like Muhammad and the mountain: If I don't go to them, they come to me.

But they want to leave. "Halas," they say to each other.

Halas? I ask.

"Halas," they say. "We are going."

Why?

"Germany is winning," they say, utterly defeated.

They leave. And Deutschland scores another goal.

That's it. The crowd is in heaven.

When the game is over, and all sing "Deutschland!" including yours truly, I make my way out. I try to follow the crowd. Not an easy task, since they go in different directions. I cross Yizhak-Rabin-Street—yes, there's a street like this in Berlin, I am not kidding—through that famous DEM DEUTSCHEN VOLKE (for the German people) building. No, I am not lying, there's a building like this here, it's the Reichstag. And I make my way to the Central Station, Berlin.

I board a train and get off at Rosa-Luxemburg Platz. This weekend, you see, the Volksbühne Theater has a special event called "Idee des Kommunismus" (The idea of communism). And I, who have just been introduced to some Die Linke people, want to acquire a deeper understanding of them. Theater, when well done, has the capacity to explain to us what logic does not.

I am ready. Today's Communist Conference theater performance is *Lehrstück* by Bertolt Brecht, directed by Frank Castorf. Gabriele told me that Castorf is the second-highest-paid director in the city; he must be good.

Play opens.

# I Sleep in Hitler's Room

About twenty actors are in this production. All sing. Then all scream. When the effect of just screaming wears out and wears thin, actors break chairs and tear a pillow to pieces. When they're done, a stuffed man is brought onto stage and two actors cut him with a knife and scream at him as well. If you're a sadist, you'll take great pleasure watching this theater. And nobody will know you're a sadist, because this is culture. Great, right? Then, suddenly, coming totally from left field, an actress declares that she's Jewish and starts talking in Hebrew, reciting a poem by H. N. Bialk.

How did we get into "Jews" again?

There's no real beginning, middle, or end to this play. None of the actors have developed any kind of personality. All are members in good standing with the Screamers *Verein*. At one point I fall asleep but wake up when an actor comes over and actually wakes me up. Eyes open and ears alert, I see another actor who goes on reading, loudly, from books by Lenin.

Yes, of course. This play, after all, is part of the Communism Conference.

Does it really have to do anything with communism? No. With art? Not with that either. What is it, besides sadism? Go figure. There are some flashes of genius here, but they're too few and too far between. Overall, it's at best a children's voiceover class. Its only achievement is the presentation of humans as brutal, idiotic, machinelike, and ugly. Was this the intention?

In the lobby of the theater, as you make your way in or out, you can pick up a free gift: a box of matches. On it is written, in big green letters, one word: CASTORF.

The man must think he's a god.

I leave the theater more empty-hearted than when I entered. I walk, making my way down the streets of the former East Berlin. As I pace on the sidewalks I ponder questions of utmost importance to the future of Germany and me when my eyes catch two fourteen- or fifteen-year-old girls snapping pictures of one of the sidewalks.

You like sidewalks?

They point down at two small golden brass squares.

What's that? I ask them. They point at the writing on the squares and say:

"These are the names of the Jews who used to live here before the war."

Why are their names here?

"They don't live here anymore."

Why not?

"Because we killed them."

I am stunned by this answer, at the simplicity of the way it's phrased.

Did they ever meet a Jew personally?

"I know of one Jew," says the girl on my right. "A friend of my mom is a Freemason and her boyfriend is a Jew."

You sure?

"Yes. He goes to the church of the Jews."

All the above is just too hard for me to digest and so I go to the Deutsches Currywurst Museum, to bite into something German.

Now, this is a museum. Real culture. Oh, what a museum! Here you can prepare a virtual Currywurst on your own. You can acquire knowledge here, no kidding: Cardamom, I learn, helps potency in men. Included in the entry price: half a portion of real Currywurst.

At the nearby Checkpoint Charlie, a fake soldier will issue for you a visa on a piece of paper and, for a few euros, even stamp it for you.

I hop on a train, out of Berlin.

•••

Time to get in touch with the world outside Germany.

Here's the Top News, brought to you by the BBC:

> Turkey has barred an Israeli military flight from Turkish airspace, in apparent retaliation for Israel's raid on an aid convoy bound for Gaza. The banned flight was carrying Israeli officers to Poland to tour Auschwitz.

Does any of this have to do anything with Germany? Not really. Or does it?

On to Dortmund. At a time when half of Germany is busy with Public Viewing, there's an interesting artist in Dortmund who is busy with Public Thinking.

Yes, correct. Public Thinking. Brought to you by Rolf Dennemann, the artist. Rolf is also a director, producer, and whatever in between. I've known Rolf for a few years and have worked with him. From time to time he contacts me in New York, letting me know of a strange, though always refreshingly original, idea he has just come up with. Same this year, with his public thinking. And he even has a place for me to stay in Dortmund, Jugendgästehaus Adolph Kolping, a youth hostel. Should I take him up on his offer? I think so. After being spoiled in four- and five-star hotels, I might find it quite exciting to experience a youth hostel.

My eyes are greeted by group of German youngsters, about forty beer bottles between them, as I approach Adolph's abode. Seeing the bottles makes me wonder if I made the right decision. Well, too late. *Wilkommen in unserer Welt* (Welcome to our world), says the sign at Adolph's lobby. My new Welt, just to fill you in, is a closed room with no air conditioning and no open windows. It's hot and stuffy inside, on this, one of the hottest days of the year, but Adolph is nowhere in sight and the clerk working here never heard of Ritz-Carlton's Twelve Commandments.

This is not Autostadt.

A band, mostly sweaty men, shows up. It's a band from Berlin, and they are part of Rolf's event. They perform one of Rolf's songs. Rolf, it becomes apparent, decided one bright morning to become a songwriter as well. In English, no less. I ask them to recite for me the words to his poem. Here goes:

Time is not money, time is life.
It's not very funny,
In my hat there's a knife.

I once sat in a café,
It was a hot one by the way,

I Sleep in Hitler's Room

I was burning out my brain,
Thinking about my little games.

I once sat on a sandy shore,
Watched the seagulls in the sky,
Kissed a girl called Elinore
I was hot and she was shy.

*Chorus*

I was hanging out at noon,
Knowing that the end is soon,
I was feeling rather sad,
I made many people mad.

Now society is insane.
It's time that we should remain.
All the vomit floods the planet.
The system is dead.
You will forget it.

Do what you want,
Do what you like,
Hand around and stay alive.

At this point the singers are not sure. Maybe it's "Hang around and stay alive."

But then the end:

Time is not money, time's life.

The band members want to drink and smoke now. Problem is, they're told that they can't drink outside and they can't smoke inside. How does one achieve both goals, drinking and smoking, at the same time? Good question. They sit at a table and drink and smoke anyway. Somebody somewhere told them it's OK, because

194

it's really late. Yoyo, the bass player, says he likes "to criticize society."

Why?

"Because I can."

•••

## Chapter 17

### The Biggest Mosque, the Most Comic Mayor, the Funniest Piano Player, the Sexiest Tattoo, the Most Important Shower

It slowly becomes clear to me that the Public Thinking will actually take place in two or three days. I have time to spend . . .

I drink the night away and in the day of morrow go to the mosque. If I get to Duisburg, my dear friend Christof suggested to me a while ago, I should visit the biggest mosque in Germany. I love big. Today is Friday, and Friday is the Muslims' Sabbath. It should be mine as well.

Why? Why not?!

Allah accepts his creatures' prayer requests five times a day, at very certain moments. The exact times are different every day. Toady they are: 5:29, 13:19, 17:20, etc. I shoot for 13:19. Yes, I verified it. It's correct. Jews, I know, disagree. The hours that they think God accepts prayers at are altogether different. But 13:19 sounds reasonable to me. Don't ask me to explain this. I go to the mosque. What a gorgeous piece of real estate! What a beautiful building! Allah must be rich. The muezzin starts. It's time to pray. The mosque is packed. Must be at least a thousand men here. How do these Turkish people get so many people to come? It's not even a weekend yet. Jews can't get a fraction of this number in their wettest dreams. Well, 13:19. That's the time!

But, truth be told, it's not that easy to be Muslim. Lots of push-ups during prayer. Jews, if they were asked to do this, would certainly strike. Push-ups! And when they sit, these Muslims, after they have left their shoes at the entrance, they sit on the floor. Don't ask questions. That's the way Allah likes it. Otherwise, don't bother Him. Or move to another religion. Last time I went to pray in a mosque was in Amman, Jordan. For some reason, it was more fun. I don't know why.

But this is Germany. And everybody is looking at me when they walk in. Why? I try my best to get lost in the crowd. I kneel, I bow, I get up, I sit down. Everything. But I am obviously still conspicuous. What, they don't have Turks looking like me? A man comes by. He dangles a pair of socks at my face and says "Ein euro" (one Euro). I ask him in Arabic what's his problem. He doesn't understand a word I say, but once he realizes I'm Arab, pure, he flies away. No point to argue with Arabs; he knows he'll lose.

"There's no God but Allah and Muhammad is His messenger." I love the way this is recited! I repeat it. Why not?

As in many churches and at some cultural events, there's a passing of the hat. Only here it's not a hat but plastic containers. People put money in; but only notes, no coins. Quite a sum is being collected, and pretty fast.

The service is soon over. And after all the bows I go to visit the imam. His name is Yusuf Incegelis.

How does it feel to be Turkish in Germany? I ask him.

"Very happy."

Happier than in Turkey?

"It is not possible to feel better than in Turkey!"

Then he says he is going to leave. Can't talk no more. His excuse? He speaks neither German nor English.

Do you speak Arabic? We could talk in Arabic.

He smiles, and carries that smile to the other side of the door. He's out.

Mohammed Al, president of the community, is sticking around. He's ready to talk. He says that he came to Germany when he was six years old. "Turkey for me is a place for vacation."

How does it feel to be Turkish in Germany?

"We feel good as Muslims in Germany. There's discrimination here, but it's not so strong that we'd say we don't like it here. Every country has some discrimination. But Germany is now an immigrant country, which makes it good."

What is Turkey for you?

"My origin."

How do you feel about Jews, Israelis, Germans? Can you sum it up for me in one sentence?

"Most Turks living in Duisburg love Germans, love Jews, love Israelis and are happy to live in Germany."

You must be kidding. Do you really mean it?

I repeat to him his response. He looks at me in disbelief, as if these were the words of some deranged Turk, but quickly catches himself and says:

"Yes, this is what I think."

Somebody told me that Turkish men can marry German ladies who are not Muslim but Turkish ladies cannot marry German men unless they convert. Is this true?

"Yes. Muslim men can marry non-Muslim women. Muslim women cannot marry non-Muslim men."

Why so?

"It's in the Quran."

Where in the Quran? Can you show me the verse?

"That I don't know. I heard of it, that it is in the Quran, but exactly where in the Quran, I don't know. This you have to ask our theologian, he knows."

Who is the theologian?

Wonder of wonders: Hüseyin enters. HE is the theologian.

Hello, Hüseyin. Do you know where in the Quran it says that a Muslim man can marry a German lady who is not Muslim but a Muslim lady cannot marry a German who is not Muslim?

"Yes, I do."

Where?

Oops . . .

"Today, I don't remember. I forgot. You have email?"

Yes, Theologian.

"I will send you an email."

Excellent.

Meanwhile, until the email service is ready to send me Hüseyin's message detailing a Muslim Turk's permission to marry a blond, blue-eyed German, Hüseyin will be glad to show me the mosque and explain to me its treasures: "The mosque cost 7.5 million euros, half of which was paid by the EU."

The huge and gorgeous chandelier, with the 99 names of Allah engraved on it, is "a gift from the Turkish government."

All the wooden pieces in front, "assembled without using one nail, is a gift from Ankara. The government."

"We have nine hundred members, each member must give ten euros monthly. The poor can pay five."

Hüseyin presents me with a gift before departing. A brass coin depicting the mosque, and a traveler's guide to the area.

A man approaches me. He says he's a journalist and asks:

"Are you Muslim?"

Yes, of course.

"Oh, I prayed next to you. I felt you when you prayed. You have a heart of gold."

I am happy he is impressed with my prayers. Maybe I should come more often. You never know: If it continues like this, I might become the next imam of Duisburg. I'm not kidding.

The more I think about it, actually, the more I like it.

But I would need to know more about Duisburg, all the different angles of it, before I make my next move. Who can help me?

I need some officials to chat with, some big guys. But how do I get one? Experience has taught me that getting an interview with the big shots is a big headache. I prefer finding them in restaurants, pubs, special events.

So, what's cooking today?

# I Sleep in Hitler's Room

There is a festival called Tramzeit. It's in the north of Duisburg, in a park, with all kinds of relics of this place during the Industrial Era. The festival is sponsored by, among others, Sparkasse Duisburg. I like the word *Sparkasse*, it's better than *Bank*. *Bank* is, so, so Capitalistic.

I go there.

Beautiful place! Tons of people, mostly young.

Any big shot?

Yes. Adolf Sauerland, the *Oberbürgermeister* (super mayor) of Duisburg, is a member of the conservative CDU, Christian Democratic Union, the party headed by the current German chancellor Angela Merkel.

Adolf and I are both very cultured people and we both like to attend cultural events, especially the private parties, for the select few, that follow such events, which is where we meet and where I interview His Honor.

You're of the CDU. How did you get to be a mayor in Duisburg, not famous for its right-leaning politics, to say the least?

He shoots straight. "Being elected," he says, "is not a question of politics. It's only a question of money."

He goes on to elaborate that his election was direct. "The people voted directly for me."

What's your dream?

"To change the structure of this industrial city. We take the old industrial places and transform them into cultural institutions. And it creates another kind of work, another kind of employment."

So, is it your dream to make Duisburg a City of Culture?

"Yes."

I look around at this place of a future Culture Capital, and the faces staring back at me are all white Germans. So, a question is in order:

All the people I see here are white folks. Where are the Turks?

"Last week we had an event, Istanbul meets the Ruhrgebiet [the Ruhr area], and many Turks showed up."

Nice. That was last week. Why don't I see them this week, like now?

"They are here, all over."

Turks all over? Where?

"You can't tell, they look the same. You stay long enough in a country, and your face changes. I have relatives in America, in New Jersey, who were born in Germany, but now they look different. Their faces changed."

This man is funny. He is a politician with a sense of humor. I like it!

Let me ask you a question: Are there more women wearing hijab this year than in previous years?

"The percentage of women wearing hijab is declining, but the German population is declining even more, and that's why you see more hijab. It looks like there are more women with hijab today than in the past few years, but that's because there are fewer Germans around."

His Honor missed his calling. He should have been the Theologian.

Adolf tells me that he goes to the mosque "twice or three times a week."

Do you also fast on Ramadan?

"I am Catholic." He doesn't go there to pray, he explains, he goes there to keep in touch.   OK. It's time to figure out this guy in more detail.

I'll repeat a sentence, you will tell me who said it to me. Deal?

He nods, with a wink and a smile.

"Most Turks living in Duisburg love Germans, love Jews, love Israelis and are happy to live in Germany." First: Agree or not?

People sitting next to us start laughing.

Adolf says, "No. I don't agree."

Now: Who do you think gave me this statement?

"The imam."

No. One more chance.

"Muhammed Al."

How did you know?

"I know him."

Is he a bullshitter?

"Yes."

What would you have said to Muhammed if he tried to sell you the same line?

"You are a bomb layer, this is not the truth."

Some people in the community, especially independent artists, complain that as of next year Adolf will be cutting their budget, threatening small culture organizations with sudden demise. He says he has no more money. He must pay for the opera, the Duisburg Theater, the Philharmonic, and there is not much left.

The sign of his fight with the small arts organizations comes to the fore when a couple, he with hair down to the middle of his back and she with her hair standing up like a bush, passes next to us. "You see," says Adolf, "this is Culture . . ."

But I am still with my Turks.

Does the Turkish presence change the culture in this land? If so, how?

"Twenty years ago nobody knew of Döner, today it's second to the Currywurst."

What else?

"Food is the first step to accepting another culture."

What else?

"When going to an appointment with Turkish people, you don't have to be on time."

Else?

"It used to be that you were ashamed if you came late. Today, people come ten, fifteen minutes later. People now are more relaxed. Basically, we would have more heart attacks today if not for the Turkish community."

And what changes happened with the Turks? What have they learned from you? Are they getting more heart attacks now?

"They learned that when they come late they have to apologize. Before, they just came half an hour late. Today, when they come half an hour late, they say: 'I am sorry I am late, but there was an accident . . .' The Chinese arrive too early, the Germans are on time, the Hondurans come at some point of same day."

You should have been a comedian—

"Politics is comedy."

What's next for Adolf, after Duisburg?

"That's it. The top."

Come on, now you talk like Muhammed Al. Give me a better answer, more honest.

"OK. My dream is to be the pope. Only problem is that I wouldn't be able to have sex."

Adolf likes his city, he loves it. He does whatever he can to put it on the map. Culture is his way of doing it. He also tries hard to keep the peace here. He goes to the mosque to keep in touch and on friendly terms with the Turkish community. He thinks they're important for his city. The way he sees it, the Turkish people have a big role to play in Duisburg. They have big families, unlike the German Germans. The young belong to them. And the young are the future.

Night descends on the park, and as soon as this happens an unbelievable light show begins, displaying its magic. Old rutted steel machines are covered with multiple light colors and shadows, many shapes, and various frequencies. Miraculously, the rutted steel turns into shiny diamonds. It's magic!

Tons of young people are dancing. Loud. Sweating. They are full of energy.

Adolf Sauerland looks at the crowd and smiles. Tons of people make him happy.

Adolf asks how long I plan to be in the vicinity. I say that I'm actually in Dortmund for an event and after that I leave. He wants me not to leave and offers to put me up in a hotel in Duisburg for a few days, following my Public Thinking. I accept.

Now I have considerable time to explore the area.
To Marxloh I go.

•••

And find Mustafa.

Marxloh is a Turkish area, or at least known as such, and is financially at rock bottom. "If you want to rent an apartment and you say you are from Marxloh, nobody will rent you anything," says Mustafa. He should know. He tried and he failed, even though he has enough money. "I told the landlady that I would pay her one year in advance," Mustafa recalls, "but she said, 'No. I don't know what you will sell from your room.'"

Mustafa has a blue-eyed blond girlfriend, he tells me. But that's OK.

Why is it OK?

"Because she respects my culture."
How does she do that?
"The shower is always ready for me after we have sex."
You take a shower after sex?
"Yes, sure."
Sure?
"Yes."
Why?
"It says in the Quran."
Sure?
"Yes!"
You know where in the Quran?
"Yes."
Sure?
"Yes!"
Where?
"In that sura, what's the name of the sura—"
If I gave you the Quran you could show it to me?
"Yes."
Do you have the Quran here?
"Yes."
Can we take a look together?
"We can, yes, but not now. I am so tired today!"

Mustafa loves Marxloh. He and some friends opened a campaign called "Made in Marxloh." They distribute postcards and stickers with this slogan.

What was made in Marxloh?

"It's about having pride, it's not about money. We are proud to come from here, from Marxloh."

By the way, in case I didn't know, Mustafa tells me:

"My girlfriend, she is partly Jewish."

Really?

"She told me."

Rabbi Helmut Schmidt, you have many children here!

And if you two have a child, will you take him to the mosque?

"Yes!"

And to the synagogue as well, since the mom is a Jew?

"If I go with him to the synagogue, that's OK."

I Sleep in Hitler's Room

Why should you go with him, you also want to be a Jew?

"No. I will go with him so that I can teach him what's right and what's not."

Will be interesting to see if such a child will also take a shower after sex, when he's old enough to understand.

Mustafa turns to his friend, sitting nearby, Halil. "Do you remember the women we saw, especially the one in hijab. Wasn't she sexy? Very sexy, right?"

Wait. Women wearing hijab are sexy?

"Yes."

Sexier than the ones without it?

"All depends on how you wear the hijab! Hijab can be very, very sexy! It's like a jewel."

Yes. This is Duisburg. Its images, its prejudices, its passions, its words of no meaning, and some of heavy meanings, a place where people have totally opposite ways of looking at the same thing. And one thing I know: I like this Mustafa. The man has a lot of life in him and much, much warmth.

Mustafa shares with me that he doesn't view himself as Turkish. "Turkey is only about money. It's not me. Neither is Germany. My identity is Marxloh. Duisburg."

"Come again," he says as I get ready to leave, "and I will show you real people."

But reality will have to wait. Dortmund is calling.

•••

There's a tattoo event in Dortmund, the Fifteenth International Tattoo and Piercing Convention. Who could pass on such an opportunity? Not me. Doesn't take me long from the moment I find out about it till I find myself joining in.

The place is packed. Which is not big news by itself. Many events, I lately notice, are packed. Almost everywhere I go. Except for the synagogues.

So many pierced and tattooed people in one place is a strange sight to encounter. Each of them probably thinks he or she looks unique, but to an observer they are all part of the same *Verein*, the Nuts *Verein*.

Here's Tim, tattooed over half his body , waiting for his turn to start tattooing his other half.

How much is this pleasure?

"Today I will spend two hundred euros on my left arm. This is first part of a tattoo work that will in the end will cost me fifteen hundred euros."

Why are you doing this?

"I want to modify my body to make it conform to my personal taste and being."

Can you explain to me what's on your tattooed arm, the right one? I don't really get it.

"Odin, God of Thunder, with two ravens, Hugin and Munin. Plus, a Viking funeral scene."

Wow. This man is a walking encyclopedia. What do you do for a living?

"I am employed by a social-insurance company."

Is your left arm 'naked'? I mean, is that what you feel?

"No."

Then what's missing? Why don't you leave your skin alone?

"It's very boring to be un-tattooed."

What's boring about it? Aren't you a handsome man? Is that what you think?

"Tattoos make it more—"

He is smiling, either to himself or to me. Let's try to understand him.

Is it more sexy?

"Yes. The girls really like it. They like the bad-guy image."

You know this for a fact?

"Yes."

Your tattoos attract girls?

"Yes."

Do you have a girlfriend at present?

"No."

Maybe you need more tattoos, to attract the ladies. Is that it?

Tim nods.

What about the ladies, would you prefer your girlfriend, when you get one, to be tattooed as well?

"Yes."

Let's imagine it together: What tattoo would you like on a woman's breasts?

"Some tribal stuff."

What's tribal?

"Black ornaments."

What would you like on a girl's ass?

"A little heart or a kiss. Big lips in a kiss."

Very nice image. And what would you like on her private parts?

"Flowers with tribals."

What do you have on your ass?

"Nothing."

So your ass is not very sexy?

"No."

What else can you tell me?

"I would like to have all my body tattooed."

That's your life's mission?

"Yes."

Tim is not alone in the world. Here's Rolf, a man into piercing. Rolf has metal stuff all over his face. His upper lip is full of piercings, forming a metal moustache. But not only there. His lower lip is distorted from the constant weight on it. By a cautious estimate, he has fifty to sixty piercings on his face. Looking at him, if you dare, is a guarantee to have nightmares three nights in a row. At least. Who is he, a refugee from a mental institution? Let me see if this man can even use his mouth to speak.

What do you do for a living?

"Computers."

Computer analyst?

"Yes."

Why so many piercings?

"Tattoos are not enough, they don't give you 'feelings' like piercings."

You feel them all the time?

"Not ALL the time, but—"

You feel them now?

"I feel them now."

The weight, the metal?

"I feel them."

Why are you doing this?

"The girls like it."

You sure?

"Yes, the girls like it!"

Do you have a girlfriend?

"Not yet."

But you're sure the girls like it?

"Yes."

I stop a gorgeous girl passing not far from us. Could you come here a moment, please?

She does.

Do you think this is sexy?

"Yes."

OK. Would you like to go out on a date with him?

"Yes."

How about this evening? I can arrange it for you.

"Not this evening, but—"

Tomorrow at some point?

"No, no."

Why not?

She takes me aside and begs me to stop.

But Rolf still has hopes. He and Tim.

And so do many other people in Dortmund. They have their hopes. Today it's Germany versus Argentina. A group of fans walk the street outside singing "Argentina is homosexual." I have no clue how and where they got this information. It would be nice if Tim and Rolf were gay; they would make an outstanding couple.

At half-time, Germany stands at 1–0 over Argentina. Then the rain pours down mercilessly on the fans at the Friedensplatz's Public Viewing. You would think they would run for cover, but no. They get even more excited. They are charged. Flags up as high as can be, they scream-sing DEUTSCHLAND! Over and over. Their loyalty, so to speak, pays off. Germany wins 4–0. The crowd cheers when they see Chancellor Merkel on the screen and boo at the appearance of the Argentinean coach, Maradona.

Play over, the fans pack the streets, their cars and the trains. In the train I'm on, a group of black-clad young men pick on a fellow passenger and are about to start a fight. I am not sure what this is about, but one side is neo-Nazi and the other is not. The black-clad recognize this guy from a demo in Bochum, where he was part of a counterdemo, and now they want to exact revenge. A woman jumps and stands between the warring sides, in the style of: Hit me before you hit my man. How did this Nazi thing come up again in my presence? Can't we have a rest from this?

This is Germany.

The shouts and threats finally calm down when the train comes to a stop. Both sides get off. What follows, I don't know. Don't want to know.

Germany won the game, but the real fight looks to be still on.

•••

Off the train, I go to meet Rolf Dennemann, artistic director of Hanging Around, in a local café. I listen to him.

"I love the Ruhr area more than the rest of Germany," he says. "The best. At the same time, I hate it, this is the worst place to live. I love the humor of the people here, but it's very provincial. The projects I'm doing, I prefer them to be shabby and emotional, rather than clean and politically correct—and I can do this better in the Ruhr area than anywhere else in Germany. Here, the down-to-earth person is at home. This area was never a place for the bourgeois, where you pay three and a half euros just for coffee."

I don't know if you noticed, but this is what my small Coke costs, right here.

He looks at me.

What's the amount of money you raise a year, lowest and highest?

"Sixty to a hundred eighty thousand euros."

What are you trying to do with your work?

"That's my life. I have to do this. It's a silly answer, yes. I prefer to work in the open area, I want to breathe, not be in a black box."

What do you really want to achieve? Just to breathe?

"I did a work in a cemetery. Theater and dance. People come to the cemetery, they have to walk between the graves, and in each place they meet different dancers, different theater pieces, two graves were talking to each other. This is very good. People who usually don't go to theater do come to see this. And they never forget the experience.

"This possibility, to give people art and have them experience it, makes me feel good. The people who attend my productions are not your average theatergoers, the ones who come to the theater and then talk about the last time they saw the play and compare between what they saw in Paris and what they see now."

Are you doing your work for yourself? Or for the people?

"I can't do it without them, and they wouldn't have it without me. I do it for both of us."

How many people show up for your productions?

"For this festival we thought we would have five hundred people, but only twenty came."

So, let me understand: You go to the mayor of Dortmund and say to him, Give me a hundred eighty thousand euros because I have a plan to put on a performance for twenty people. Is that it?

"There's no law in Germany that specifies how many people are to attend. Money is awarded for creativity. That's the history of this land."

Isn't this fucked up?

"No. I think it's absolutely important. Thinking only of money, of commercialism, kills art. All over."

What is important?

"I would like to sit and watch people eating, walking, drinking. And I need money for this."

Charles Schumann: Meet your partner!

Let's see if I got you: You want the city of Dortmund to pay you money so you can look at mouths and legs of people?

"Yes."

Really?

"Yes, because this leads to some creative work."

That's Rolf. He understands zero in p.r. and can hardly handle an interview, but his ideas, I vouch to you, are always refreshing and brilliant. His country has still to discover him, and it's sad that German critics haven't found him yet, that they've been too lazy to come over and see this man's work for three decades going. It's their loss more than his.

212

# I Sleep in Hitler's Room

Rolf's Public Thinking is about to start. And these are the rules of this game: You come in and a young girl asks you what you want to think of and about. You can choose from ten topics, or make up one by yourself. Chairs are spread all over in front of a former factory, and you choose your chair and Think Publicly. Which means, in this case, when others like you also think about their choice topics. In other words, this is something like a *Verein*, a *Verein* of people who come to think next to each other. In Germany, if you didn't know by now, we like to do things in groups.

Perfect. I participate and make up my own topic: soccer. This, of course, exempts me from thinking. I look at the sky and at the clouds moving slowly. (I learned this trick from Arab merchants in East Jerusalem. On tense days, when commerce is zero, they sit in front of stores, smoke their shishas, and watch the sun move. Try it. It's nice!)

How many show up for this Public Thinking? It doesn't really matter. I lie down, for about an hour, and think of "soccer." I have the time of my life.

In front of me is an exhibition hall. Years ago the building used to be a factory, but now it's used for art exhibitions. In New York, old factories are being converted to flats for the richest stratum of society. Here they turn into art centers. I like it.

The people of steel fathered stubborn children, no doubt, who demand their right to create. It's nice. They should put a big German flag on top. This country deserves it.

At Dortmunder U, a museum and culture center, not many show up either. And this building costs millions. I go there after my Public Thinking.

Today's exhibition is about political provocation. It's called Agents Provocateurs. Here you can see all kinds of political demonstrations and actions through deed, word, or image. Pictures and videos are presented to demonstrate the issue at hand. To my right side is a film about three beautiful women. They are in a pool, camera capturing them in the water—which adds a beautiful layer to the images. They undress each other, slowly and sensually, and then dance-swim in the nude. It is an erotic film, and I think Holger Franke will love it. On the opposite wall is a video of a man walking with his clothes set on fire and a photo of Milica Tomić strung up on a lamp post, as a reference to Nazi troops hanging antifascists in Belgrade.

For the artists who have created the pieces in the exhibit, every one of them must be loaded with meaning: historical, political, cultural. What I see here is an exhibition on the theme of Sex and Death. Again.

•••

The Ruhr area has begotten quite a few interesting children. One of them is Helge Schneider, whom I go to visit in Mülheim. First thing the man says to me is:

"I wanted to come to New York but they have 110 volts, and my organ is for 220 . . ."

This man is a famous comedian, piano player, entertainer in this country, but I don't know him. So I ask him: Who are you?

"I have lived here since I was born, fifty-five years ago. I never went away."

But who are you?

"I am a male citizen of the Ruhr area, and I want to remain a male citizen of the Ruhr."

Why?

"My place of residence is now on the passport, and it's too complicated to change it. But I'd like to see other cities, like New York."

OK. Let's try the question once more. Who are you?

"A male citizen. A piano player, naturally. What else could I be?"

More specific. Who are you?

"I am a piano player who is interested in people. And sometimes I try to make people laugh. Since I was a boy I've been working at it."

How do you do that?

"It's my special way of movement, perhaps my face."

You have a funny face?

"No."

Why are the people laughing?

"I don't know."

Were they laughing when you were a child?

"Yes. And when I come on stage, they laugh."

Helge contemplates: "This is my last interview. Ever. No more talk shows. No more interviews. And perhaps I'll change my name."

Helge Tenenbom?

"Perhaps."

Some say that Germans lack a sense of humor. What do you think?

"We live at a time when it's fashionable for ladies not to smile; they think it will give them wrinkles. When people lead hard lives, they laugh more."

Let's try the question once more: Do Germans lack a sense of humor? Yes or no?

"I don't think that Germans lack a sense of humor. When I go to Switzerland I think they're not funny, but they think they are."

The Swiss think they're funny? Be serious!

"I can't say anything more about the Swiss!"

What makes humor?

"Often humor comes from sadness. Like when somebody died. If you go to the funeral of an old person and somebody laughs, you'll see that the others join."

So, what is it that makes us laugh?

"I don't think about these things. Humor is much more complicated than aggression. It's a basic part of being human. For me life consists of three things: Birth, humor, death."

Are you thankful to Germany for being so successful in it?

"No. If I feel thankful, it's to my destiny. Not to a nation, not to a country. I didn't study anything, I don't even have Abitur. I just play music. I'm under no pressure to think about how Germany was so high, so low, and now high again."

Helge tells me he doesn't care who wins the WM, the World Cup. He's for everybody. Helge must be very PC. Or, as he puts it, "I am a 'nationalist.' To me, all of us are the same."

I have no idea why, maybe I've had had my fill of PC people lately, so I give it to him. I tell him that, yes, like all those artists anywhere and everywhere, he is a peace-loving man, a make-love-not-war sort of a guy. And then I go on to tell him that I too have heard this slogan in the artistic and academic world for as long as I can remember. Yes, all of us in theater, music, and dance are good people. Not one of us is bad. And now, how surprising, he repeats the same tired slogans. Wow. But does he know what? I don't buy it. Can't he be more refreshing, please? Let's face it: Aren't we all big bullshitters? The artists' community likes to preach against war, hate, racism, discrimination—as if we were the only good people in an ocean of depravity. Isn't he, am not I, and isn't everyone in the Arts—aren't we all just little supremacists thinking we're better than everybody else?

"We all are big bullshitters. That's true. Cross out what I told you just now."

What's your dream, Helge?

"I have no dream. I live. I want my thoughts to be free, but I have no need to have a dream. Martin Luther King had a dream, but when [German chancellor] Angela Merkel says she has a dream it sounds like comedy, like a comedy on German TV. On TV, I like only *Columbo*."

What do you think of now?

"About my baby. About the wash in the basement. About my next show in America, if it's too early or too late to call the United

States. I think about the news, about the newsmakers who make up the headlines. About Israel and Palestine."

Another German and his Mideast . . . But I don't say this to Helge. I just ask him, What do you think about Israel and Palestine?

"For example: I heard about the ship that came from Turkey. And I imagine how it feels to be there. Israel, the ship, Palestine. I think that everywhere you are is shit. I have an interest in politics; sometimes I think about Ahmadinejad, about Iran, the Middle East. And then I think: Should I go there and talk to the people? Tell each of them to apologize?"

Great idea! Why don't you do that?

"Maybe one day I will."

Like Rudolf Hess?

"Who?"

You know. Hitler's deputy who flew to Scotland on a solo peace mission. Don't you remember?

"Oh, him. Yes, yes. Am I like him?"

I am ready to go with you to Gaza next week. Deal?

"I would like to go by myself."

OK, before you go, let's try to imagine you've already arrived in Gaza.

I point to Helge's manager, Till, who sits with us, and say:

Your manager is the Palestinian and I am the Israeli. Make peace between us!

"You are the Israeli?"

Yes. Convince me to make peace with the Palestinians.

Helge takes his job seriously and starts his imaginary peacemaker role. "Open the borders. I talked to the Palestinians and they are very friendly. All Israelis and Palestinians who want to work can be involved in cleaning up all the mess in the area, and everyone will get twenty dollars an hour. Thirty-five hours a week. This is the beginning."

Will you offer the same to the Palestinians?

"Yes."

The manager is not very active here. Let me change hats with him. I am going to be the Palestinian. Any problem with this, Helge?

Helge agrees, and I play the Palestinian.

I don't want the Jews here. You, Germans, killed them; you take them. I didn't send them to Auschwitz, you did. I was born here, my papa, my grandpa, back through history. Take your Jews and pay them whatever you want. Take them back to Germany and keep your twenty dollars!

Helge gets scared. This is not what he had imagined in his peacemaking dreams. He says: "I am done. I did my job. End of my peace efforts for now."

Obviously the Middle East is on his mind. I ask him why.

"You see the news and it's the Middle East all the time. Also Hitler. Every day you can see Hitler on TV, on one channel or another."

Speaking of Hitler. Did you ever ask your parents or grandparents about the war years?

"I saw a picture of my uncle in a black uniform, and I think it was the uniform of the SS. I also saw a document, belonging to my aunt, that was stamped by the authorities, certifying that she's Aryan. But I never asked my parents about the war. My father had a hunchback and was very short, a dwarf, and my mother was also deformed, she had one leg shorter than the other. I don't think they were involved in the war, and so I never asked. As a kid I was ashamed of my parents, and when we went for a walk together I always walked a hundred meters ahead, so that people wouldn't see us together. Only after I got older, when I had turned fourteen year, was I proud of them."

If your parents were not deformed, would you be different?

"Probably. My father was short, and I had red hair and I was skinny. And my classmates used to make fun of me. They called me Egghead."

Deformed parents, red hair and a skinny body, plus a perfectly kosher Aryan family . . . That's a lot of baggage to carry, isn't it?

"Yes. But this is the only life I know, I didn't have another. For my father, the dwarf, all people were equal, the ones on top and the ones at the bottom. And this I learned from him."

I try to imagine it: a dwarf who looks around and from his position, unless he tilts his head, sees only legs walking. He can't tell the difference between this pair of legs and the other pair of legs.

I guess this is what Helge means when he talks about all people being equal.

Helge can't help it. Again he must show his guest how PC he is. All people are equal. Yes, I agree that, legally speaking, all people are equal. Meaning, every person should have the same chances, opportunities, and rights. But are all of us equal? No. Some of us are dwarfs. Not all of us have the same talents. Not all of us are beautiful. And not all of us are smart.

I look at Helge, a funny man with a very sad beginning. Is this what made him funny, the harsh realities of his life's beginning? I don't know. There are similarities between Helge and his country. But Helge is not a country, he's a man, and a comedian. You can laugh while listening to him, but if you choose to cry instead that would be equally appropriate.

Bavaria voted against smoking in public. This is one of the harshest antismoking laws in Germany. Smoking Prohibited, says the sign in Dachau. History goes in cycles and circles. In "celebrating" this prohibition, Till gives me a nice little gift, a Cuban cigar. I hold it and think of how much absurdity this one little item contains within it. The commodity is a no-go in the United States. Some kind of embargo. The United States against Cuba. Strange little law.

Cigar in my pocket, I move on to Duisburg.

•••

What should I do in Duisburg?

There's a Tourist Information desk in the shopping area, maybe I should check with them. The girl at the counter welcomes me with a smile. The people of Duisburg are very welcoming people, she tells me. Is she a Duisburg girl? Yes, she is.

What's interesting in Duisburg?

A boat tour is nice, she informs me, but the last one has already left.

Is there a good place to eat? I ask her. I like Turkish food. Where's the best Turkish restaurant in town? Anything good in, let's say, Marxloh?

"Marxloh," she says, "is in Turkish hands." There's nothing to see there unless "you are interested in the mosque."

Mosques are good. But does Duisburg also have churches, synagogues?

She shows me a picture of the synagogue, very beautiful, it seems. It's like an open book with different leaves.

Can I attend some services? That would be nice. Would you know when they have services?

"There are services, but for members only."

What kind of services are they?

"Friday night services every evening at 18:45."

Sounds intriguing. I go to the temple.

The place is closed, all its doors locked. Nobody in. And as at the Jewish center in Munich, you wonder to yourself what this is all about.

Synagogue-with-no-Jews done, I go to see the Muslims. Marxloh, to be specific. I hook up with Mustafa and Halil at the Medien-Bunker Marxloh or, for short, Bunker. They show me a film made by the Bunker people. Here's a demonstration in Marxloh against the G8. People are seen holding a variety of signs, reflecting what they're demonstrating against. I read: "Free Palestine." Free it from the Jews, I guess. At least this is the interpretation I got when I was in Qatar last year; they also wanted to Free Palestine. But we are not in Doha. How the Palestinian issue snuck into Marxloh is a puzzle to me. And in the first place, what does it have to do with the G8? Is Palestine part of the G8? Is Israel?

I don't know and I am here to learn.

Mustafa explains to me that Israel unites the people of Marxloh, who are often divided. There are Turks here, but not only them. There are also Kurds living in the neighborhood. And these two people don't even talk to each other. "A man can share his bread with you one moment," says Mustafa, "and the next moment not even look in your direction—if he discovers that you are Turkish and not a Kurd," or vice versa. But the hate of Israel unites the Turks and the Kurds of Marxloh. This is the point where their minds and emotions meet and they unite to fight this mutual enemy. Both were "enraged" at the way Israel acted with the flotilla to Gaza, he explains to me, and both took to the streets. United. In hate.

Jews again.

People here are obsessed with Jews. But I want no part of it. I leave the Ruhr area, which this year is the Culture Capital of Europe, and take the train to Düsseldorf.

•••

Once in Düsseldorf I go to see Heine Haus. I love Heinrich Heine, the German Jew and great nineteenth-century poet, but Heine Haus, I soon enough realize, is a bookstore. The original house was demolished, they tell me, and then rebuilt, and now it's private. There's a café here, but it's open only when there's a special event. Will you open it tonight for a Public Viewing? I ask the lady who sits in front. I think it would be nice to see soccer at Heine Haus. The lady thinks I crossed the line and doesn't even bother to respond. I leave. In the window outside, which supposedly showcases the best they have in the store, I check the display. Here's what I see: A book about Palestine, a book about the Holocaust, and another book written by an Israeli leftist who is a strong critic of the Israeli government.

Country obsessed!

Germany will soon face Spain in South Africa. I think I should go to a Public Viewing. Better than Israel versus Palestine.

Esprit Arena is the place I choose for my Public Viewing. Tickets are between 6 and 9 euros. Why people pay money to watch TV while standing, as most here do, is not a question for me to answer. Maybe a professor of sports could explain, not me. I'm not really qualified.

The game starts. It's obvious from the get-go that the Spanish players are better. They control the field, and the ball is mostly around *their* feet. They are also better as a team, coordinating very well with each other. The audience, quite a few thousand, seems to register this fact and is laying low. I find myself, strangely enough, hoping against hope that the German team will win. God, am I becoming German? Sadly, against my newly developed hopes, the game ends and Spain has won, Germany has lost. The audience is depressed. They brought their flags, but for nothing; some are clad with clothes made of flags, with their various noisemakers and rivers of beer—all on the assumption that Germany would win.

It is not to be.

People are crying. Some cover their faces with flags. Others lie down like defeated soldiers. They take it personally, as if they were the actual players. But more than just that: to them Germany lost, and Germany is them. The source of their pride is no longer an entity to be proud of. Their honor, their sense of worth, the core of their being has been beaten. Crushed. Here is a young man so despondent he's kicking a wall. The big TV screen on which the game had been shown now shows a kid crying uncontrollably. This beautiful blond being, draped in the colors of the flag, just can't stop crying. The thousands here watch. They wish to comfort the kid, but they can't comfort even themselves. A bunch of teenagers in front of me lie on the grass of the stadium, hugging and caressing each other. The arena looks and feels as if it were a funeral home. As I point my camera at them, they ask me not to take their picture. Shouts of "Deutschland!" are not heard except from a lone lunatic who obviously didn't get the news.

Walking back, down the streets of Düsseldorf, I notice a funeral home, a real one. In its window, for those into coffin window-shopping, there are soccer balls and German flags. The dead, it seems, didn't get the news either.

Will be interesting to know what Helge and his wife, Maria, think of all this. He's German, she's Spanish. How do they view the game and its result?

•••

Maria, wife of Helge, though they are not officially married, is much younger than Helge, who's about twice her age. But when you listen to her talk, you realize she's mature far beyond her years. She thinks outside of the box, she has her own ideas. For

222

example, she tells me that Hitler hated Germany and that's why he did what he did.

What?

"Hitler was an artist, with an artist's mindset. Artists are not nationalist."

Really?

"Hitler did not use his power to help people, he was thinking only about himself.
Artists, who at their root are selfish creatures, cannot be nationalist."

I never thought about this, but she has a point. An interesting woman, Maria.

"I remember that picture of Obama with the slogan 'Yes we can,' and when I looked at how people worshipped him, I thought: It's similar to what happened here, when the people worshipped Hitler. It's the same thing. People look for a leader to worship. Back then it was Hitler, today Obama."

Does Helge agree with her?

"I don't think that Hitler hated Germany, or that he loved it. He did what he did because he believed in what he said and did. It was about ideas."

You played Hitler in a German film recently, how did you prepare to play him?

"I listened to an audiotape, a tape recorded in secret by the Swedish ambassador. There Hitler is heard talking in a way that seemed strange and naïve. He talked quietly, quickly, and much. Something like, We have twenty thousand tanks . . . He didn't raise his voice, he was just counting his tanks, planes . . . And that's how I played him in the film."

I tell him about the lipstick and deodorant, the story I told the students in Frankfurt. Helge says he knows it.

How do you know?

"I recognized it the moment you said it."

How?

He gives me a long answer, but the most interesting part of it is this: "My mom was in the Bund Deutscher Mädchen [BDM]." Interesting. When I asked him about his parents earlier, he didn't mention a word about this.

Will Germany become Nazist again?

"No."

Why not?

"Too many Turks."

Suddenly, don't ask me why, I have a moment of truth and say to him:

I ask you questions about politics and some other heavy issues. But between you and me, how can you really know? In our generation we make gods out of celebrities. But, really, aren't we nuts? I mean, should I also expect you to solve complex mathematical equations only because you made it into show business? What I am doing is senseless, isn't it? You really don't know any better than anybody else. Do you?

"Celebrities are businesspeople. In former times we asked these questions of Kant or other great philosophers, like Alphons Silbermann. Now we ask these same questions of Paris Hilton or Bastian Schweinsteiger [a German football player] . . . That's why I told you: I am not giving any more interviews. You're the last one. I am not the one to be asked these questions. Because I am one of the few who knows the answers . . ."

OK. Let's talk personal. Did your mother talk to you about her years at the BDM?

"No. They don't talk about those years. I saw a picture, when I was a young kid, of the Bund and in the middle of it was a man I recognized: my music teacher. I showed him the picture and asked him if that was him. He hit me on the face and threw me out. I used to get 1 in music, but after that incident I got 6."

You carry heavy baggage, you and the German people. Don't you?

"Yes."

Maria breastfeeds their baby. Then she shows me to the family's sheep. Yes, they have sheep. I love sheep! And when sheep are around I don't talk about WM, even if my original purpose was to discuss it . . .

•••

Helge's manager is also here. We have a chat.

Till was born in Dresden and spent his formative years in East
Germany, the GDR. He tells me that he spent twenty months in
jail. Why? Because he wanted to go to West Germany. Till says he
lives in the present and looks ahead to the future; he doesn't want
to revisit his past. But I push a little.

The Stasi [the former East Germany's ministry of state
security], I assume, had a big file on you.

"Yes."

Did you see it?

"I went to the government office that had it and reviewed it for
two hours."

That's it?

"It's a thick file. I couldn't read it all. I asked them to send me
a copy."

Did they?

"Yes, they did."

What's in it?

"I didn't read it."

It's in your house and you never opened it?

"Yes."

Aren't you intrigued?

"That's the past."

Are there accounts by citizens who testified against you?

"Yes."

For example?

"My neighbor told the Stasi that I had a brothel."

Say that again—

"I used to have many friends who came over, young men and
women, and he thought that I had a brothel."

Did you confront this man?

"No."

Why not?

"That's the past."

Are their other testimonies in your file?

"Maybe."

Aren't you intrigued?

"That's the past."

Were there other people in your family who had trouble with the regime?

"My brother. Gregor Gysi was his lawyer."

You know this Gysi?

"I talk to him for professional reasons from time to time. Just a few days ago he wanted Helge to appear in a presentation that he made at the Volksbühne Theater."

I tell Till of Gregor's objection to having his Jewishness mentioned.

"He's Jewish?"

Why, you didn't know?

"I never knew he was Jewish."

His story sounds interesting to me, so I go to meet Tom Dahl, Till's brother. He was a musician in the GDR, but he wanted to leave the East. One day he went to West German Ständige Vertretung (Permanent Mission) to ask for a visa and was subsequently arrested by the Stasi. He spent twenty months in jail.

"I asked that Gregor Gysi represent me, because he had a good name. Gregor told me that he believed that I was not guilty but that I had no chance. He appeared in court four times, but that was a show."

On Gregor's part as well?

"Yes, of course. Gysi was a member of the Stasi."

About five years after the wall came down, Tom got his Stasi file, but it contained only the information from his time of imprisonment. As for the rest of the documents about him, Tom was told that if he asked for them they would try to find them. Did he ask for them? No. In fifteen years, Tom tells me, he didn't find the time to send the letter of request. A busy man.

Did your family "sing"?

"I don't know."

Maybe your father betrayed you?

"Maybe."

Don't you want to know for sure?

"I know."

You know?

"Yes. I am sure he did."

You sure?

"After I was arrested he didn't talk to me."

Didn't?

"He was a Communist."

And—

"I became the enemy."

Enemy?

"Yes. When I was in prison my mother would come to visit me, but my father (his stepfather) would stay outside in the car. He didn't want to see me. I still remember this."

The wall fell. Since then, have you met the people who put you in jail? For example, the judge?

"No."

Did you try to trace him?

"No. For what?"

To say Fuck you!?

"No. Why would I do that?"

I play a little with Tom:

Look, look! He is right there! The judge. Say something to him, man!

"FUCK YOU!"

So, that's what you really feel?

"Yes."

But you wouldn't ask for the file . . .

"Maybe. At some point. I don't know when."

Tom and Till, the two East Germans, force me to rethink everything I know and have learned about Germany and Germans. Now there's a question mark that I have to put next to the line "I know Germany." Perhaps I have to throw the line in the trash altogether.

East Germans have more than one piece of baggage to carry on their shoulders. While the rest of the Germans carry the baggage of their country, or their families, of killing "foreigners" such as Jews, gays, gypsies, or Russians, the East Germans have one more piece to carry: killing their own brothers and sisters, betraying their own friends, or sending their own relatives to prison. This is one load too heavy to carry.

How do they cope with it?

Perhaps one way of doing it is: I won't read the file.

It's amazing.

An hour or two later, Tom drops me off at the Bunker in Marxloh.

These Turkish activists, a fine group of people, invite me to stay in a hotel nearby. I accept. This gives me time to get to know the Bunker people better as well as the general Turkish community in Marxloh.

Here in the bunker, at the top floor, I find a group of young people whose goal is to reclaim poor, no-hope districts. The spirit animating this group is provided by Mustafa, Halil, and another person who is not here. That other person is German German; Mustafa and Halil are Turkish German. I sit down to speak with Mustafa, once more.

How important is it for you to be Turkish?

"Not at all. Last time when I was in Turkey with Halil, we met a famous Turkish director. He was talking about Germany. He was trying to explain how come Germany is such a powerful country after being almost totally destroyed in the war. He said Germany's rise was so rapid because they stole all the money of the Jews. And I said that was not enough to make Germany successful, that there were other reasons as well for its success. I didn't contradict him, I just added to what he said. When the director heard it, I could see that his face changed immediately. He stopped talking, and I was told that I was thickheaded."

What are you trying to say?

"In Turkey you must respect the man of higher education, and you can't disagree with him. That is Turkish culture, not mine."

His culture is "Marxloh." "I am a 'Turkish German,'" he says.

What does that mean?

"I will tell you a little story. When I was a boy, I found a hundred deutsche marks on the street. I had a very close friend, and I spent the money on food, sweets, ice cream, everything, for both of us. Together we spent all the money in one week. That was a lot of money for me, but I shared it with my best friend, a German German. The following week I needed fifty cents to buy something, but I didn't have the money on me. I asked him if he could give me fifty pennies. He gave them to me. Then, a day later, he came to me and said, 'Can you give me back the money?' I was surprised, because I had spent so much money on him just the week before. You understand? He was German German. Different culture. I don't want this culture; that's why I want to preserve my own culture."

Don't you think that a Turkish German kid would behave the same way?

"No. Never. Look at Turkish neighborhoods. Everyone is with everyone. You don't have to make appointments with your neighbor. You just knock on the door and walk in. You understand me?"

Got it. But that's Turkish culture, that's Middle Eastern culture, that's the East. Why not just be Turkish? Why Turkish German?

"I love German order! Trains being on time, police security, things running properly . . ."

Whom are you attracted to more, German women or Turkish women?

"German! I can't stand the caprices of Turkish girls."

Why don't you like Turkish girls?

"When you go out with a Turkish girl, the first thing she expects of you is that you pay. Then you sit down and talk. About what? The whole talk is about jealousy, marriage, what's forbidden and how to manipulate prohibitions. I can't stand it!"

Should I tell Mustafa that Orthodox Jews are just the same? Maybe next time we meet.

•••

## Chapter 18

## Peace and Love: Why Jews Like to Shoot the Dead

Mustafa has a mother he loves, his biological Turkish mom. But he also has a second mom, a German woman he calls Mama. A white, German German woman named Gitti Schwantes. She is a peace activist from Marxloh, and she's the spirit and power behind Rosen für Marxloh, or Roses for Marxloh, a peace-and-love initiative that's basically a rose garden.

Gitti, whose house is adjacent to the Merkez Mosque, the "biggest mosque in Germany," is a very busy woman these days. The *Süddeutsche Zeitung* is coming to interview her, and so is a radio station. She feels wanted, and she believes she deserves the attention. After working at it for years, she finally got the various permits and the financing to build a rose garden on the mosque's property. Why she would need permits from the government to build on the mosque's property isn't clear to me, but I guess that's the law here. What's really important, I quickly learn, is the purpose of it all. The garden, she tells me, will offer people of different religions the opportunity to stop by the mosque and feel good about Muslims. In other words, this is a p.r. tool for promoting an image of the mosque and of Islam as being full of friendliness and love.

Gitti came to Marxloh with her husband in 1972. The two of them, both intellectuals, believed in justice and wanted to help and empower to the workers. Her husband, an economist, took a job in the factory. Not because the man was a working-class guy, of course, but because he wanted to "infiltrate" the working class and gain their confidence by having a job just like them. After ten years, when he thought he had gained their trust, he tried to push them into a social revolution against the establishment. But they said no to that.

Soon after, Gitti and her husband divorced.

This must be a sore point, but I touch on it nevertheless.

Trying to spread love all over, you ended up not being able to love even each other. Is that correct?

"Oh, this is terrible, the way you put it."

But isn't it true?

"Yes, this is true."

And now, what now?

"We are building a rose garden, next to the mosque."

Why that?

"So that people can meet each other."

And love each other?

"Yes."

Same dream as before?

"Yes."

Who are the people you want to have love each other in the rose garden?

"Muslims, Jews, Christians."

And you think that your rose garden will achieve this?

"Yes."

Why and how?

"Roses have a good smell."

And that's why people will go there?

"Yes."

You will achieve world peace, love between the three religions, because of a rose?

"I hope."

You and your husband spent decades trying to achieve love between Germans, and failed. Now you think you will—

"Why didn't you come two years ago—?"

Nobody has ever challenged her before, and now she feels like a total idiot. But two minutes later, she regrets her regret.

"No. People will come and talk to each other--"

You really think that Jews will come to a garden, on the mosque's grounds, to meet Muslims? Can't they meet them in a

Turkish restaurant? There are great Turkish restaurants around. I've tried them. Do Jews and Christians go to those restaurants?

"No."

So why—

"I don't know. But the garden will be nice—"

Would you go to a rose garden built next to an NPD [the "neo-Nazi" Party] office?

"NO!"

Why will those who hate the Muslims come to your garden?

"I don't know."

Maybe it's time to stop?

"Too late to stop."

Why?

"What will I say, that a man came to me, asked me questions and I didn't know how to answer? That's a shame."

Are you religious?

"No."

Your parents?

"Yes."

Do you believe in God?

"What do you mean?"

The God of the Bible, for example?

"No. Not anymore."

Do you believe in freedom for women?

"Of course!"

You are a nonbelieving feminist, can we say that?

"Yes."

And you support the Muslims here and their mosque?

"Yes, yes."

Do they believe in the same God who is the God of the Bible?

"The same."

Their women have to wear hijab, kind of like Orthodox Jews?

"What are you trying to—"

You're not an Orthodox Jew, are you?

"Me? No."

Why are you supporting a religious institution that believes women—

"Muslims believe in peace."

How do you know?

"They told me."

And you believe them?

"That's the meaning of the word *Islam*."

How do you know, do you speak Arabic?

"No, I don't. But they told me."

*Islam* in Arabic means *submission*.

"To whom?"

To Allah.

"OK."

Did you attend a worship service in the mosque?

"I went in one time, and then I left."

Are women and men praying together?

"No."

Who gets the nice part of the mosque and who gets the other part? Where are the men and where are the women located in the mosque?

"The women have to cook, don't they?"

So, you believe that women should stay in the kitchen and let the men have fun?

"Are you a therapist?"

You didn't answer my question.

"I didn't."

Why not?

"I don't know."

You are supporting an institution that believes in a God that you don't believe in, an institution that holds the view that women should stay in the kitchen and that they should cover their bodies, practices that you're against, all this while you are, as you just—?

"I want to believe in peace, I want to believe that—"

—all those good things that you know have no basis in reality?

"Yes, maybe."

Because?

"People make mistakes, it's human."

To support a system that believes in what you don't?

Gitti gives no answer. She just stares at me.

I met quite a few people like you: White, intellectual, freedom-and-peace fighters, who for some reason support Islamic institutions that preach the exact opposite of what they believe. I am trying to understand why.

"I can't stop now!"

Shukaryeh, a single Turkish woman looking for love and company, shows up. What does she think are the reasons behind Gitti's involvement with the mosque?

"Maybe it makes her feel good, because what she does makes people love her."

So, purely egotistical reasons?

Gitti, she tells me, is also working for the mosque. She is a member of the council. But she's no Muslim. "I should have been the member of the council . . .!"

As the evening moves forward, Nurcan enters. A thirty-year-old Turkish German, she is dressed "modern," with arms and shoulders showing, and of course she doesn't wear hijab. Nurcan works as an Integration Officer for the city of Duisburg. She is feisty, full of life, beautiful, funny, and very sharp.

Tell me, Nurcan, are more women in your community wearing hijab this year than in years past? I mean, is the trend growing?

"More hijab, much more."

Do you have any idea why?

"The first generation of Turks in Germany were religious people. The second generation, like my generation, is much less so, but the third generation is even more religious than the first."

Why are you living in this country and not in Turkey?

"My brother passed away in Turkey, in a car accident, and I went there. I wanted to stay in Turkey, because I didn't want to leave him alone. But then I decided that living in Germany was better."

Why?

"It's safer in Germany."

What do you mean?

"In Turkey, when you go to the bank they don't even look at you when you talk to them. When I was in Turkey and I experienced it, I wanted to shoot them."

One bad experience in a bank and you judge Turkey?

"It's everywhere. They don't care about human life there, unless you have money."

What are you talking about?

"In the hospital, you have to bring your family member to watch over the sick or the sick will die there."

What do you think about the leaders of Turkey?

"Erdogan is the second-worst person after Hitler. We have recordings of what he's said in the past, and now he says totally the opposite. He's a man who tries to provoke people and make one faction hate the other."

Is there a difference between you, a Turkish German, and other women of your age who are German German?

"A Turkish German woman of my age appreciates her life here more and has wider horizons than the German German woman does. I know Turkey and I saw poverty there. I appreciate my life in Germany more, because here it's different. A Turkish German has more ways to look at the world, because she has another culture as well."

Do you think that the German Germans look down to you?

"Yes."

Do you look down to them?

"No. I used to look up to them, but not anymore. Now I work with them and I know them better . . ."

So what do you think of Marxloh?

"People say that even the police won't come here, but I like Marxloh."

Adolf Sauerland is right. The Turks are a blessing to his city.

I am so impressed with Nurcan that the next day I go to meet three generations of Turkish families, all living in one building.

•••

Hamiyet, a young mom, leads off the encounter. She's of the middle generation, a hospital nurse by profession, and she's proud to be who she is: Turkish Muslim. Right off, I have no clue why, she's on the attack. It is strange, since I'm here to join them for lunch, and hospitality is normally the name of the game.

"Why did you Jews reject the sabbath when Allah offered it to you? I want to know!"

What is this woman up to? What den of what animals have I entered?

"I just want to know why you Jews did that! Why? Why?"

Yes, I am familiar with this thinking. After all, it's the Muslim's belief that Allah first gave His Book to the Jews but they falsified it. But why this question now? Whatever happened to hospitality? Forget hospitality, what happened to human behavior?

What is this attack?

I try to calm the storm and answer her. I start by saying that the three Abrahamic religions base their faith on similar stories but that there are differences.

Hamiyet cuts me off.

"No," she says, "it's all the same."

Take the binding of Abraham's son, for example. There are major differences between the way it's told in the Quran and the way it's told in the Bible.

"No, it's the same."

Well, let's look at the name of that son. In the Bible it's Isaac, in the Quran it's Ismail.

"Isaac and Ismail are the same!"

No, they're not.

"How do you know, are you a specialist in this? You don't even know the Quran and you just talk!"

Well, I've got news for you: I am a professor of Quran.

I have no idea how this title crosses my mind, but why not? In Coburg, I met that professor of sports, and if that woman could be professor of sports I can be a professor of Quran.

Don't ask me to explain this to you, but Hamiyet believes that I really am a professor of Quran. She says: "As a man who knows— you are a professor—why can't you see the truth?! The Truth of the Quran?! There are differences between religions, that's true, but Allah made one final version, the Quran. That's it. No more!"

You believe it, and that's fine, but not everybody does. Can you accept this?

"The Message of Allah ends with Prophet Muhammad, Sallallahu 'Alaihi wa Sallam. Why can't you accept this?"

Let me ask you: How do you know that what you say is right?

"It says so in the book!"

Hamiyet wouldn't like to know this, but she talks word for word as Orthodox women in Israel do. And both wear coverings over their hair. They actually look the same, talk the same, and walk the same. The similarities are frightening. I can see a Hasidic woman in front of me, not a Muslim. Or, equally so, Muslim women who are actually Hasidic . . . like my own sister, an Ultra-Orthodox woman who talks exactly like Hamiyet and thinks almost exactly like her. Just exchange Muhammad with Moses and you have the same thing. "How do you know the Bible is true?" "It says so in the Bible."

Bingo.

But there's no time now to contemplate these similarities.

Samide, Hamiyet's sister, doesn't get it either why this professor is not yet Muslim.

Samide adds that she knows what the Bible says. I cannot play games with her.

What do you know that the Bible says?

"That all Prophets were sinless."

Who said that?

"It says so in the Bible."

Did you read the Bible?

"No."

Then how do you know?

"My sister read the Bible and she told me."

It's a hot day in Marxloh, about 40 degrees Celsius. And these ladies wear hijab.

Why are you wearing hijab?

"So as not to tempt men."

Do you think your hair will tempt them?

"The Quran says that women should wear hijab so that they won't be raped."

This is a strong argument.

We finally sit at the big table in the kitchen, ready to start the meal.

And Hamiyet says that the Quran says that the Jews want to make trouble and war.

You think so?

"Yes. That's why there's conflict in the Middle East."

Is she talking about Israelis or Jews?

For her it's all the same. "Jews killed Jesus!" she shouts at me.

But Jesus was a Jew too, wasn't he?

"Jesus was not a Jew. None of the prophets were Jewish."

Time to change the subject.

What are your thoughts about the Gaza flotilla?

"What are yours?"

I wasn't there and I don't know.

"If you don't know, if you are dumb, you shouldn't write a book. The people there were innocent but the Jews killed them. They killed one guy, a nineteen-year old, they shot him. Then they shot him again. And again. And again."

I heard this line often during my travels in the Arab world. Jews shoot and kill, then shoot the dead body again, and again, and again. Why? Because Jews love to see blood.

I don't buy their accusations, but I admire their honesty. They go straight for the meat: the Jews. They don't play the game of "I'm highly critical of Israel but I love the Jews." No, they don't do that. They say what they think. They have a faith, they have ideals they believe in, and they don't shy away from saying out loud what they think.

Hamiyet, you said that the Quran says that women have to wear hijab—

"That's true."

You read it in the Quran?

"Yes, I did. You want me to show you?"

That would be great. Please.

"Should I go bring the Quran?"

If you don't mind.

"Yes, I will bring it."

I have it on my iPad, if you prefer.

She loves this! The professor of Quaran carries the Quran with him wherever he goes. We check the electronic Quran but don't find any hijab there.

"I have to bring my Book."

Hamiyet brings the Quran and puts it on the table.

"Right here!" she says; the book still closed.

Thanks. Can you show it to me inside?

"You know the Quran on your own, don't you?"

Yes, of course. But I don't remember this particular verse.

"You want me to show you?"

Yes.

"It's in Sura Al-Nisa."

That's a long sura. Can you tell me what verse?

"Yes, I can. You know, when I started reading the Quran in Turkish, I didn't understand anything. I knew it in German. It was the first time I read it in Turkish.

Interesting.

"Then I read it again—and still didn't understand it."

Interesting.

"But on the third try, something happened."

You read about hijab . . .

"Hijab?"

Where is the verse about hijab?

"Inside the book."

Where inside?

"I am very tired today, I still have to go to work."

One of the sisters intervenes, "You can Google!" she says. And she does. She finds it through Google. I tell them that we have to check it in the source, in the Quran itself. We open the Quran, to the sura and verse that they got from Google, but don't find the hijab commandment in the original. A two-hour discussion follows, with the sisters passionately shouting statements about their faith. I take a moment with beautiful Samide.

Samide, tell me: Would you like to be a Virgin Bride in paradise?

"Who wouldn't!"

Hamiyet, who hears this, immediately interrupts. She raises her voice at me.

"Why are talking about this, are you trying to mock us?!"

Hamiyet speaks loudly unto her sister, in Turkish so I won't understand. But she uses some Islamic terms I am familiar with. Samide, on orders of her older sister, changes her previous statement. She wants to go to heaven to meet Allah, no Virgin Bride. And then, without any warning, she goes ballistic on me.

"I don't like what you do. I am upset with you!"

I calm her down. It takes some time. At the end, we hug and embrace.

Good night, love!

•••

Morning comes and it's breakfast time at Mustafa's mom's. The food is excellent and I announce my intention to come every morning. When we finish our Turkish coffee, mom turns her cup upside down on a plate. The neighbor, a coffee reader, will tell what will happen . . .

Mustafa's sister, a very intelligent teenager, tells me her dream is to move to Turkey to live there. "I am a stranger in this land, the Germans look down on me." She really doesn't like Marxloh, though she understands why her brother is trying so hard to improve the image of their birth city.

How about your friends in school, do they also want to move to Turkey?

"All of them."

Then Mustafa suggests that I see Zülfiye.

Zülfiye Kaykin, Turkish-born, came to Germany in 1977. She got her education here and, as she grew up, started feeling she was discriminated against. Zülfiye, state secretary of NRW (North Rhine–Westphalia) Ministry of Integration, used to be the general manager of Duisburg's Merkez Mosque.

Zülfiye spent nine of her better years totally dedicated to the mosque. She was the mosque's face when dealing with the German government, which gave 3.6 million euros for the construction of the mosque. But after fights with the mosque's board, which she blames for spreading false rumors about her during internal struggles for power, she resigned.

What rumors did they spread about you?

"That I misused a hundred twenty thousand euros of the mosque's money."

Are you telling me that they used you as their 'face' with the German authorities only as long as they needed you but, once they didn't, since the German government had already paid what it committed to, they just wanted you out?

"Yes. I looked good as their front: modern, blond, educated. I was used."

She doesn't wear hijab, except when she goes to the mosque. "When you come to pray you have to cover your head."

Why is it that men don't have to cover their heads?

"Why do you say that? Men must cover their heads as well."

Sure?

"Yes!"

Do the men of this mosque cover their heads?

"Yes!"

I saw them and they didn't.

"What you saw are men who don't follow the rules."

One thousand of them?

"What are you saying?"

I prayed with them.

"You did?"

Well, Zülfiye is a politician. She tried to trick me, and it didn't work. But once she realizes that I was in the mosque and saw what I saw, she gives me a sweet smile . . .

I tell her of the interesting encounter with Hamiyet et al. and ask her how she explains these anti-Semitic outbursts.

"If it's true, then it's because we've not been integrated by the German community."

Integration between Turks and Germans is a matter between Turks and Germans. How did the Jews get in the middle? What do the Jews have to do with this?

Zülfiye goes around and around but does not answer. Finally she admits that "these feelings exist in the community" but insists that they don't originate with the mosque.

Well, you just admitted that anti-Semitic feelings exist in the community. My question to you is: Is the mosque trying to fight this way of thinking? Should it?

"I will talk to the imam and next Friday it will happen."

When will you talk to him?

"Later."

Wouldn't you like to talk to him right now?

I offer to use my phone. If she gives me the imam's number, I can dial.

No, she has her own phone. Zülfiye calls him. They have a long conversation. Long, long. When she finally hangs up, she says: "The imam is shocked and will speak about it next Friday. This is pure anti-Semitism and he will totally denounce it."

242

Zülfiye, let me quote to you what Mohammed Al said to me, and I'd like to have your comment. "Most Turks living in Duisburg love Germans, love Jews, love Israelis and are happy to live in Germany."

Zülfiye laughs. She says: "And that's why thousands of Turks demonstrated against Israel in Duisburg last month . . ."

I don't know what she's talking about. Thousands of demonstrators about—

"Against Israel. We have this about once a year. Ten to fifteen thousand go to the street to demonstrate against Israel."

Sitting in the salon of her home, Zülfiye explains to me how the Duisburg Merkez Mosque works—or, more precisely, how nine hundred mosques in Germany work. In Turkey there exists a council of eighty theologians, governed by a president. Following consultations, the president dictates to imams of nine hundred mosques throughout Germany, which are part of DITIB (*Diyanet Işleri Türk-Islam Birliği*—the Turkish-Islamic Union for Religious Affairs), the text of their Friday speeches. Only after this speech is delivered can individual imams add something about local issues.

It's extremely hot in Zülfiye's place. Her husband tries different combinations with fans that he keeps bringing in, but they don't help much and we all sweat. I think it's time to leave. I tell her: Zülfiye, I'm coming to the mosque on Friday to hear the imam's condemnation of anti-Semitism.

Zülfiye, or so I judge from the way her eyes move, didn't expect this from me. She makes an immediate half-reversal, a "clarification" of sorts: "The imam will say, 'We have to be careful what we say.'" Not for naught is this woman a politician.

I should have let it rest, really. She's a nice lady, after all. But for some reason, like a one-year-old who can't stop kvetching, I press on: Is that it? Is that all he's going to say? Didn't you say, just before, that he—

Zülfiye is a woman of Law and Order. She tells the Kvetcher: "This is all he CAN say. That is the policy."

The "This is pure anti-Semitism and he will totally denounce it" has gone through a major surgical operation in just a few minutes. But I understand. Law is law. And in Germany, I have heard many times, the law is very, extremely important.

Zülfiye and I exchange looks, and then we both laugh. I tell her that she passed the test: You are an excellent liar, and I'm sure an excellent politician. We shake hands. We understand each other.

See you at the mosque, Zülfiye. I'll be there on Friday to check on the imam.

•••

But before I do, since we have a few days till Friday, I meet Rainer, a professional photographer. He's a German German and he's the third person in the trinity that includes Mustafa and Halil, the team that makes up the Medien-Bunker.

"I just came back from Palestine," he greets me. "You don't go to Palestine?"

He loves to say "Palestine," I can clearly see.

As-Salamu 'Aleikum, Mr. Rainer. Do you also visit Israel from time to time?

"I was just in Tel Aviv."

I see that it's hard for him to say "Israel."

You went to Israel?

"I wanted to go to Gaza but they didn't let me." *They.*

Rainer, I have the impression, would like Israel to disappear. It would make him feel better, much better.

I assume you are on the Palestinian side. Is that so?

"No. I am open-minded. I know that there are two sides. I'm just looking for justice."

And you think that both sides must improve—

"Exactly."

You're a photographer, right?

"Yes."

Did you take pictures to show the injustice?

"Yes, I did!"

So, did you capture the injustice that the Israelis commit against innocent Palestinians?

"What are you trying to say?"

What did you capture with your camera?

"The Separation Wall. I walked along it for 50 kilometers."

Obviously, you're on the Palestinian side, aren't you?

"Why would you say—"

You walked for 50 kilometers, taking pictures--

"Justice, man!"

Did you look for justice closer to home? Let's say Kurdistan, Chechnya—

"What are you trying to say?"

Why are you so fixated on Israel?

"Is there something that you have in mind—?"

Just wondering why a German like you is so interested in Jews like them?

"Can we talk about this tomorrow?"

Yes, of course. What time?

"Eleven o'clock."

Perfect.

Day follows day, and "tomorrow" is now. I show up at the Bunker for our scheduled interview. Eleven comes. No Rainer. Twelve. No Rainer. One. No Rainer. Two. No Rainer.

•••

I leave the Bunker and go to the mosque. Got to pray for the Germans. Halil joins me. As we approach, just by the rose garden, the imam and the president, Mr. Al, pass by us. Each looks like a million dollars: dressed up and sharp. They must have a good life. I approach the imam. I want to know if Zülfiye talked to him about the "Jews."

The setting here is quite interesting, even theatrical. The mosque is in the background, the rose garden that's being built is right here, and everybody is talking in a different language. The imam speaks Turkish. Halil is helping out. And President Al is also getting involved in the translations, but he insists on speaking German and not English. I try to speak in Arabic to the imam but get the impression that he doesn't understand Arabic, since he keeps speaking Turkish. So I switch to English.

Will the Imam give a sermon about "the Jews" on Friday? Not really. It turns out that the imam isn't even in Germany on Friday, he's going to Turkey. So, was I fed lies? Well, this is the imam's version of the truth: Yes, Zülfiye talked to him, but he didn't tell her what she said he did. "I said that I would look into it to find if this is the truth, if somebody said those things. But I didn't promise that I'd speak on Friday. I said that I would inquire about it, who said it, and I spoke with my superior about it, and he said that nobody in this community had anything against anybody and therefore there's no reason to give a sermon about it on Friday."

How many members you have in this community?

"One thousand."

Did you speak to all of them?

"No."

I'm trying to figure out how he knows that nobody said anything if he didn't talk to them.

He explains.

"I didn't hear it. And we can't work on suspicions . . ."

Well, I can solve this little problem for the imam and the president. Gitti is here. She was with me at the house of the Turkish family and she heard it all. She would be a reliable witness, wouldn't she? I point at Gitti and ask him: Do you know her?

It doesn't take him long to cut me off sharply: "I have to go!"

Gitti, the ever vigilant mosque apologist, witnesses this in pain. Yet it takes her less than one full minute to come up with yet another theory. "Maybe," she says, "the imam is drunk. He didn't mean a word he said. He just had too much beer."

After so many years with Muslims, she still hasn't figured out that alcohol is forbidden to them. Will she say anything, true or not, just to save this imam?

At this point, even Halil is laughing. I ask myself: Is this capacity to stare at facts and stubbornly ignore them like a child, is it a German quality? Is this how I have to interpret the older Germans who say they didn't know anything during the war? Is this how I have to interpret the younger Germans who are so anti-Israel even before any facts are on the table?

Some distance from the mosque and the rose garden I meet a Turkish woman who, for obvious reasons, I won't identify by name. She speaks to me.

"A few weeks ago the mosque arranged for memorial services and celebrations in honor of the late Alparslan Türkeş, leader of the Turkish extreme right MHP [Milliyetçi Hareket Partisi] and the notorious Grey Wolves. Do you know of them? They're a racist, supremacist, anti-Semitic society. The Wolves are anticapitalist and anticommunist at the same time, because they claim that both schools of thought were founded by Jews. Some Turkish people wanted to demonstrate against this, but Germans like Gitti were against it. They have no problem with the Grey Wolves. Do you know who's a member of the Wolves? Zülfiye's husband."

I have no way of checking if he is, as I have no access to Grey Wolves records. Should I ask Gitti or the other German supporters of the mosque? Honestly, I think there's no point in bringing this issue up with them. They'll claim that the memorial services held here were for another Alparslan Türkeş, who was actually a drunk Turkish Jew, that MHP stands for Muslim Hebrew Peace party, and that the MHP and the Grey Wolves are sworn enemies.

I'm about to leave this place and its mix of cultures.

Sitting on the train, thoughts come flying at me from the opposite direction of the traffic flow. What have I seen in Marxloh? I found pride in the Turkish community, huge pride, but also much hate. I admire their spine, their passion, their commitment, and the warmth of their culture. But their senseless hate, their never-ending Jew mocking, and the ease with which their community embraces fanaticism disgust me. I'm sorry.

And then there are the Germans. What they protect is not the Quran or Islam, as they know nothing about either, but the kind of Islam that prevails in their society. Here are Germans who want to erase the shame of being the Jew killers of yesterday by uniting with the Jew haters of today. These Germans have no backbone, no pride, no knowledge, and very little humanity. Peace and Love, they say, a thousand times a day, and it's a thousand times empty. They flash two fingers, front and back, for Peace and for Love, but their hearts sing *Sieg Heil*.

But it's not only Gitti and her friends, it's the German media as well. Parading as truth tellers and honest messengers of news, here they fail at both. They fail to expose this community and this mosque for what they are: Jew haters. Not only do they fail to expose them, they also rush to hide them. Reading what they write about them is staggering. Not even the Jewish Bride of Berlin, Mr. Diekmann, with her/his eight hundred journalists, is here to uncover this shame of Germany.

Today I'm in a bad mood. My apologies. No, the problem is not the Turkish women who wear hijab here, it's the 82 million Germans who wear the burka. Eighty-two million Germans who have nothing better to do than be obsessed with 106,000 Jews living among them. It does boggle the mind.

Yes, I know that mine is a voice crying out from the wilderness. Have you ever tried to argue with a German intellectual? However strong your arguments are, he will never admit to being wrong. On the contrary: He will catch you making a semantic mistake and write a book about you to prove how ignorant you are. He will cite a thousand and one sources, none relating to the essence of what you've said, to prove beyond a doubt your ignorance and your prejudice. "The reason why Tuvia writes 'he' instead of 'she' proves beyond any shadow of any doubt that he suffers from a severe case of sexism."

The Turkish community here is a wonderful community, but they have a little disease, a little sickness: They are allergic to Jews.

While with them, I told them what I thought of them. I was not afraid that "those Turks" would hurt me. On the contrary: I was straightforward with them. I respected them more than did any of those German journalists who have worked so hard to "protect" the "Turks." We were comfortable enough with each other to respectfully disagree. It was Rainer, the German in the Bunker group, who wouldn't face me.

And there was Gitti, the German lady, who's for peace and love provided the Jew's out.

It is on this day, as I leave the gates of peace and love, that hate enters me. I hate the Germans. Hate them, their big masks, their endless discussions, their constant preaching, their implicit or explicit Jew hating, their lack of spine, their exact ways, their exact lies, their stubbornness, their hidden racism, their constant need to be loved and congratulated, and their self-proclaimed Righteousness.

Worst of all: For the first time in my life I feel like a "Jew"— and it's a horrible feeling.

Don't cry, my dear. This too shall pass.

•••

## Chapter 19

**Six Million Tourists Learn about "The Terror State of Israel," Courtesy of Dedicated German Journalists; 11,000 Virgins and 11,000 Dead Jews; One Gay Man and His Catholic Priest Boyfriend; *Everything You Ever Wanted to Know About Sex* by The Saudi Mecca Theater Company**


The train keeps moving on, and new horizons are born. Duisburg out, Köln in.

From the Turks and the Germans, on to the Gays and the Straights.

As you get off the train at the main station, the first thing you encounter is this huge Kölner Dom (Cologne Cathedral) or, for short "Dom." I love it. Its majestic beauty confers a sense of calm.

Goodbye "Jews," welcome magnificent church and your treasures!

Wishful thinking. Between the Dom and me, there Arnold stands. Arnold and company are engaged in political activism. They want to make a difference. They have been here, at the Dom's square, for many years. They have a Permanent Exhibition here, called "Kölner Klagemauer" (Cologne's Wailing Wall). This, of course, is a reference to the holiest shrine of the Jews in Jerusalem, the Wailing Wall. What a name. Cologne's Wailing Wall. Stick it to the Jews, why not? This wall exhibits posters, pictures, flyers, political statements, and news. These are Peace and Love Germans. The only problem is, wouldn't you know, the Jewish state of Israel stands in their way. Israel, they make it clear, is engaged in "Massacre," "Land Grabs," "Ethnic Cleansing," "State Terror," and other gems.

This Wailing Wall showcases photos of dead little Palestinian children in pools of blood, Israeli soldiers storming with guns over civilians, dead bodies in the style of Auschwitz, and other works of art. No dead Jew is shown here. No Jew ever died, in case you ever wondered. No suicide bombing ever happened, in cased you wanted to know. The lines drawn here are very clear: The Jews are the killers, the Arabs are the dead.

It's a nice day in Köln and I have a chat with Arnold, the man who holds one of the signs.

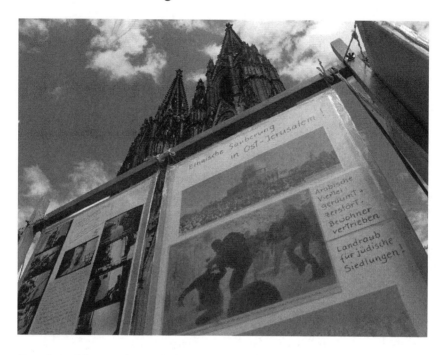

So, Arnold, you love the Palestinians and you hate the Israelis. Is that so?

"No. Both sides are wrong."

Really?

"Yes. And I am tired of them."

Let's see what the sign next to you reads: "Boycott Israel." That's your demand. Should we boycott only the Israelis or also the Palestinians?

"Both."

Then why are your posters demanding only the boycott of Israel?

"We mean both of them."

So maybe your posters should say "Boycott Palestine" and we would know that Israel is also included?

"Don't ask me these questions! I'm not the boss."

Who's the boss?

"He's in the men's room."

The boss is in the men's room?

"He needs to 'make'! What, you don't want him to make?"

•••

Let him 'make.' While the boss is making, I go to see Eva Gronbach, a young fashion designer. Eva loves to discuss her fashion ideas, she really does. Her clothes, I soon find out, contain a whole lecture. She talks and talks and talks, and I try my best to catch up. We meet at a café next to her home in one of Köln's youngish neighborhoods, where people eat Bio. The young of Germany are into natural food, bio-something, organic, real—and all other good stuff. I hope no one is going to serve me sand here.

"I love being German, really love it. This is a free country, a real democracy. Here you can be anything you want. Eight years ago I designed a collection based on the German flag. Those days were not like today. You couldn't do it back then. When I came to a restaurant or to a pub, clad with the German flag, people stopped talking. Nobody wanted to be near me. They thought I was an extremist or that I was nuts. But I love Germany. I used to hate it, with the heavy history, you know. But then I came to love it. I do. I love the German flag. It's black on top, it's heavy, but it's gold at the bottom. What's in the middle? It's red. That's desire. I have a strong Jewish desire also. You saw the golden squares on the sidewalks? I get goose bumps just looking at them. Jewish music, I love it. Sometimes I go to the synagogue here in Köln. I just go. Maybe one day I'll create a collection based on Hasidic clothes. I wanted to make a collection for men wearing the burka, but I didn't do it. I have a small baby, you know, and if some crazy fanatic comes, you never know. My collection today is made of original coal miners' uniforms, and sometimes they're very dirty and sweaty, with numbers on them and other images. But people love it. People who don't work hard, I mean menial work, like to wear these clothes. It gives them a good feeling. My coats cost about 700 euros, and the t-shirts eighty-nine."

•••

I arrive in Köln on, as has been the rule on this journey of mine in Germany, a fluke. I've had enough with all that Islamic, Jewish, German Nazi history and wanted a break. Köln smiled at me from the map, but I have no idea where I'm going to stay.

I go to the local tourist-information office and ask for a recommendation. Some hotels in Germany offer special rates for the press. Two hours later they call to tell me they found a place for me: Excelsior Hotel Ernst. And it's free. I had little clue what this hotel would be like. But now I am here. To say "five stars" would not do it justice. I have a suite. Right across is the Dom. History is staring at me. It took six hundred years, a tourist guide told me today, to build this church. It took me two hours to fully enjoy it. I can sit on the balcony and touch it. Almost. The refrigerator is stuffed with goodies, which are included in the price, as a young hotel assistant tells me. I have a Jacuzzi and two bathrooms. Marble floors in one section, modern paintings in another, beautiful rugs and carpets, and rare delicious fruits are presented daily. Love seats all over, leather chairs, and even a printer—just in case I'm in the mood to print what I write. This is a palace. Every limb and organ in my body is spoiled, and each particle in my body shouts in pleasure and delight. The food here is, let's just say, exotic. In short, this is a spiritual experience. Say what you will about justice, socialism, communism, capitalism, fairness, religion, faith, freedom, humanity, righteousness, peace, love, and all other beautiful words. They all melt like the snow of yesterday at Excelsior. This place is the only reality. This is Heaven. Life in this Suite is the only thing that counts, the only truth. I fall in love with Germany again. I mean, why not? Truly, who cares about anything? I don't. Nothing matters anymore. Not a thing.

I feel spiritual here. I feel I am a good man. I am nice. I feel excellent about myself. About the world. All people are good. As long as I have this Suite. Everybody is wonderful. I feel International today. My newspaper for today is the *International Herald Tribune*. Why? Because it has the word *International* in it. I love everybody. Love is my religion, PC my soul, Excelsior is me. I sit on one of the love seats and start reading. I like to read the most important news first, the right column of the front page. I always do that. "Scraping by in Gaza, but wanting a life." This is the lead article for today. I fume. Again? The Americans also have nothing better to do? Why is everybody bothering me with Israel all the time? Get busy with Mormons, Mr. American! Since the day the Christians started following one Italian-looking Jew two thousand years ago, they just can't stop it. When their newspaper editors have nothing to write, they write about Jews. I have an idea for you, editors, a good story to write about: Gay Games. I am not sure exactly what it is, but many folks in Köln are very busy preparing for it. It's something like the Olympic Games for gays and lesbians and transvestites and others. Something like that. Sounds very interesting to me. It would make a nice headline: "Gay Games in the Mosque." Everybody will read it. Guaranteed. Many copies will be sold and the publishers will make enough money to stay a weekend at the Excelsior. Yes.

Oh, I would like to have room service now. But what should I order? What do I need that I don't have already? Let's check the list.

On my bed are three pillows, one better than the other. On top of them is a little note for me.

To make my night's sleep as comfortable as possible, the notes says, the hotel is pleased to offer me an additional selection of pillows.

Choices are, among others: Antiallergenic pillows, horsehair pillows, cherry-pit pillows. . .

What is this? What kind of people come here? More spoiled than God.

I've got to check this out. I become intrigued.

Wilhelm Luxem, a very capable man, is the managing director of Excelsior Hotel Ernst. I am going to spend some quality time with him.

The average person usually sleeping on my bed, what is he like?

"With a big ego, but not in a negative sense."

Any particular person you remember who slept on "my bed" before?

"Henry Kissinger."

What's the rate of repeat clients?

"Quite high. Thirty-eight percent. There are people who have their own beds here. There's this person from Vienna, for example, who likes his own bed. It's the only bed he wants to sleep on. I don't know why. He shipped his bed to us, so he can sleep on it whenever he comes here, and we store it when he's away. He comes about four times a year."

You keep his bed for him?

"Yes, we keep it. Some people keep their clothes stored with us. They don't want to have anything to carry back and forth."

Do you charge them for the storage?

"No! Why would I? This is the best marketing I can have: I know they will come back. Their bed is here. Their clothes are here. We believe in service, service is very important."

•••

Wilhelm has style. He treats me, King Tuvia, as I deserve. A shiny new Mercedes waits outside for me to take me to my next exploration: Meet the organizers of the Gay Games. But, as luck would have it, I somehow find myself stumbling into a gay bar. There I meet Eric, a man with a pretty strange haircut and something like a beard.

"Life for gays is good here," he tells me, "and I feel accepted. But we will never be totally accepted, because we will always be the minority. Nature wants people to multiply and we don't. It's just a fact of life. What's your name? Oh, do you speak Hebrew? Our barman, the manager, also speaks Hebrew. Would you like to get to know him?"

Is he Jewish?

"No, but he speaks Hebrew."

How come?

"Ask him. His name is Oliver."

It's hard not to notice Oliver. He is kissing everybody, lip-kissing, and is kissed by everyone.

"All these kisses," he tells me, "and I never get sick. Somebody up there must love me."

So, it's good to be gay?

"Yes."

I have been wondering: Now that you have everything you wanted, I mean gay-wise, what's next? You spent a lifetime fighting for equal rights, for recognition, and you got them. Or at least most of them. How do you go on with your life, a man who is used to fighting but has no reason to fight anymore? What else is there to do?

"Business."

What?

"What we do here. Business . . ."

You mean, like this gay bar?

"Exactly."

Are you Jewish?

"Lo," Oliver answers me in Hebrew. No.

You studied Hebrew on your own?

"Ken," says Oliver—Yes—and continues the conversation in Hebrew.

"Years back my father came home one day and gave me a gift: The Hebrew Bible. I didn't know how to read it, didn't even know where it starts and where it ends. I put it away and forgot about it. When I got involved with a Catholic priest and we became boyfriends, I thought of the book and gave it to him."

Your boyfriend is a Catholic priest?

"We're no longer together."

Well, interesting. But how does he know Hebrew?

"When my father died I was thinking about the gift that he gave me, the Hebrew Bible. I wanted the Bible back, and I got it. I couldn't read it still. I decided that I had to. I flew to Israel, where I studied Hebrew in an ulpan [language school]."

Oliver inserts an Israeli CD in the bar's CD player, and the gay bar is now loudly singing in Hebrew.

"I threw two Israeli parties here. Last time, before we had the party, I went to the Jewish community to see if I could borrow a menorah for our party. The synagogue is Orthodox. I got in and the rabbi was in a meeting. I was shaking. Imagine if I went to the archbishop and asked him to lend me a religious item for a gay party. He would show me the door! But here I sit in an Orthodox synagogue, and I am not a Jew, asking them to lend me a religious item for a gay bar. I was shaking. And then the rabbi looks at me and he says: 'When the party is over, remember to bring it back.' I couldn't believe it! We had the menorah right here, in the center!"

Most everybody I met in my German journey up to now was anti-Israel. What's wrong with you, Oliver?

"People in Germany, the majority of them, don't understand what it means to worry if you'll see your son by the end of the day or not, because he might be dead by then. This is the reality for Israelis. I lived there a few months and I saw it. But Europeans don't get it. Not just Germans. I try to tell them that what happens there is not about politics, it's about life and a certain mentality. They think everything is about politics, like it is here. But no, over there it's not about ideas and opinions, it's about life.

"Do you want a kosher beer? I've got them. Want to try one?"

Oliver refuses to be paid for whatever I consume in his bar. "You're a guest," he says.

The Jewish Bride of Berlin would feel home in this bar.

•••

On the day of morrow, refreshed and very well fed, I go to see Paul Bauwens Adenauer. Paul is the grandson of Germany's Kennedy, or at least Köln's Kennedy, Konrad Adenauer, the first chancellor of the Federal Republic of Germany and the founder of CDU, or Christlich Demokratische Union Deutschlands, the Christian Democratic Union of Germany.

Paul is the president of the Chamber of Commerce, Köln, and owns his own company.

Is Germany one nation?

"Soccer-speaking, it is."

Besides soccer. Is this one country?

"It's on the way."

Is there a characteristic, a common trait that unites all Germans?

"Yes."

What is it?

"The Germans are romantic. They think there's a solution for everything and anything. If you watch German talk shows, you will see that they think there's an answer to every question.

There's a belief that the government can solve everything. In the United States they believe in themselves, a feeling of "I can do." That is not the case here. Here is this belief that somebody, usually government, can and should do everything. This translates into an attitude that, if something I did doesn't work, it's never my fault but some other entity's fault."

Can this explain World War II?

"In a way. There's a belief and trust in authority. It's this feeling that Hitler used and misused."

Are you telling me that the clichés are truth? Meaning, would you say that Germans like to obey?

"Germans like to follow leadership."

More so than other nations?

"Yes."

Paul too?

"What?"

You. You too?

"I hate it. I don't like to follow, I would—"

So you are not German?

"I am a *Kölsche*. In Köln, people forced the archbishop out of the city gates hundreds of years ago. That's our history."

Could it be that the reason you don't like to obey is that you come from the ruling class? Not everybody in this city is so fortunate, or misfortunate, to have a chancellor as a grandpa.

"Maybe. But I think it's also what Kölners are. It's not in their nature for them to follow. They prefer to follow themselves."

So, they're not Germans?

"No, they are the worst of the Germans . . ."

What else makes them Germans, then?

"They are good mechanics. And they like to work."

Why do they like to work?

"I don't know. They like to work more than they like to make money. Americans like the money, Germans like the work. Germans like to make things perfect. There's honor in fine work. Germans hate it when something doesn't work properly."

Paul strikes me as a smart man. I wonder if I should bring up the "Jew" issue and decide in favor. Perhaps Paul would be able to cure me of my "Jewish Hurt" in this country. I put the issue on the table:

I can report to you that with one exception, in a gay bar, the Germans I met "at random" were all anti-Jewish. Why is it that so many Germans are negative about Jews, Israel?

"I think that this attitude is stronger in other European countries than in Germany."

Let's talk about Germany. Is it true that Germans are very critical of Jews and of Israel?

"Now that you put it this way, I think it's true. I didn't think of it before, but yes."

All political alliances?

"The left wing is more critical of Israel than the conservatives are."

Paul also has an explanation for this attitude:

"Israel must sometimes be tough, I believe, because Israel is such a small country, a little country surrounded by enemies. But the average German doesn't see this, they think that problems should be solved in a soft way. That's the German's response to the history of the Third Reich. They send soldiers to Afghanistan but they think that nobody should be allowed to get hurt."

How do you explain the anti-Semitism I encountered in, let's say, Duisburg?

"There are basically no Jews in this country, just a very few. The relationship the people here have to the Jews is theoretical, not real."

Germans, those who purport to be strongly against anything that even smells of anti-Semitism, were present when I was bombarded with anti-Semitic accusations, but they didn't contradict any of it. Why didn't they object?

"Germans follow. They are not people who will stand their ground. They have no political backbone."

Soon DITIB will have a mosque here. What is your opinion? In Duisburg they send strong Jew-hate messages to their people, even celebrating known anti-Semites. Yes, they do it in Turkish and not in German. But they do it. This is what they really stand for. And soon they're coming here, to your city, and it's going to be in your courtyard. What do you do with this?

"Good question."

Are you embracing the idea of having a mosque here?

"Two thoughts in my head. There is freedom of faith, so why not have a mosque?

But when I hear what you say, this seed, this venom of Jew hating, I think it would be horrible if this grew in Köln. There's a false understanding of tolerance on the part of the Germans."

What will you do?

"I will bring it to public awareness."

After a long discussion, during which he admits to not having a clear answer or a viable path for action, he says:

"In Köln we don't go deep into these things, just the surface. We like parties . . ." Paul thinks that Köln is the fun city of Germany. "All the lazy people are assembled here. I think that's what it is."

Last question: What does it mean to come from the family that you come from?

"I am a slave to my status."

•••

Minutes after meeting Paul, I sit down with Stefan, a laid-off journalist. This is a man on the other side of cultured Köln: the poor intellectual.

Stefan says, quoting either himself or others: "When the Dom is ready and complete, the world will end."

This obviously happens to be a fact of life here. The work and reconstruction done on the premises of this Dom is constant. But it's worth it. A "complete Gothic architecture has two towers. There exists only one structure like it: in Köln."

Stefan, free from the boundaries that some media companies might require of their employees, lets his tongue loose: "Business and politicians are together. One hand washes the other. This is the biggest mafia in Germany. But Köln isn't special in that regard; this happens in other cities as well."

Arnd Henze, on the other hand, has a job. He is a *redakteur*, or editor, at the powerful WDR TV. I meet him next. I take one look at him and I "box" him. He is, I say to myself, a self-proclaimed ethical and moral man, totally PC, a self-righteous man who cares for the weak, the poor, the minority and is totally committed to total human rights. The perfect newsman. The Honest Newsman. If he could, he would choose this woman: An old Jewish black Muslim Buddhist lesbian, who suffers from severe malnutrition and is in the advanced stages of AIDS. I mean, if that were possible.

Let's talk and see who he really is.

Why are you doing what you're doing?

"To offer transparency to people and inform them, in order to maintain democracy. Democracy is about participation, and for that you must be well informed. I am aware that as a person I am biased, but my colleagues have their biases as well."

Greeaat!

Do you have an agenda?

"Of course I do. Human rights, climate protection."

What's the ratio of your pushing stories that conform to your political views, in comparison to those that oppose your views?

"I had Bush sound bites that I totally disagreed with."

Come on! That's obvious. If I had to report in 1939 what's going on I would report on what Hitler said. That's nothing to do with pushing ideas, that's pure news.

"I didn't make the comparison to Hitler, you did."

I am fully well aware of that, and I will never say that you made any comparison between Bush and Hitler. Now: Forget sound bites. Stories. Those that corroborate your views and those that do not. What's the ratio? How many of the stories that you personally report on happen to be stories that confirm your own views?

"Ninety percent of the feature-length stories that I do corroborate my views."

He goes on to tell me that WDR's "ratings go down when we report on the Middle East, because people think that we're pro-Israel." I don't know much about WDR but it's good to know that this huge media company loves the Jews. Somebody's got to love them, don't you agree?

•••

I walk along the streets of Köln, a city that had almost vanished during World War II. My eyes travel over its reconstructed walls and buildings, and I think: How painstakingly the German people must have worked! They've restored every little stone, redrawn every old line, and refilled every drop in their faucets. This must have taken unshaken determination, enormous effort, and rivers of sweat. But they did it. Dot by dot, drop by drop, tear by tear. It is admirable, it is touching, and it's fascinating.

But what does it say about the people?

Who knows?

Continue walking and you will see how cultured this city is. And how ridiculous.

Here is a church, St. Ursula, honoring a virgin who died for the Right Cause with 11,000 of her companions, all virgins as well. Yes, really.

You might wish to say that this is just a legend, but you will risk the wrath of God if you do. No kidding. If you stick around in this church long enough, you will discover in it a section known as the Golden Chamber. Here you'll find an exhibition of "prayer lines" that are made of human bones. Yep. Human bones, quite a large number of them, painted gold and hung all over in this chamber. All around. It's a disturbing image. Human bones on the walls that look frighteningly similar to the chicken bones on my plate from the day before. As if these walls in this church are here to teach you: That's all you are, a chicken for somebody to eat.

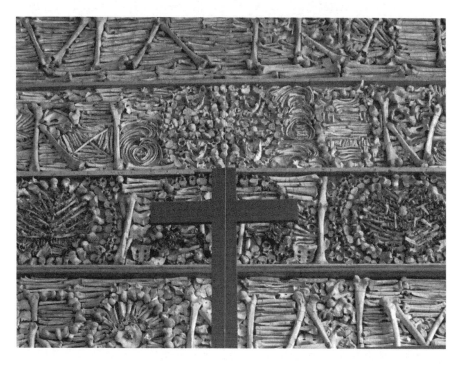

Why are the bones here? Don't ask me. Malek, a Polish German in charge of this treasure trove, stands at the entrance door and charges two euros for the pleasure of seeing these human remains. I have a little chat with him.

Isn't it frightening to see these human bones every day of your life?

"Not at all," he says. "I'm an archeologist, and I 'm used to it."

Doesn't this sort of exhibition disturb him, constantly reminding him of death?

"Every believer should always think of death!" he preaches to me.

Why?

"If you are a man of no faith, I can't tell you anything because you'll never understand." Period.

When I see these bones, believe you me, I believe anything they tell me about Virgin Ursula. Eleven thousand virgins? Yes, I believe. I'd better, before I see my own bones painted in gold and a German Pole making a bundle of euros from my dead parts.

Eleven thousand virgins. Christian virgins, not the Islamic ones. Samide of Marxloh ain't coming here. This is no Paradise; this is an awful place, with an awful legend.

Keep on walking through this city and you get to the big synagogue. One of the most beautiful synagogues I have ever seen. Its design uses simplicity in the service of beauty, arches and circles that open to a never-ending end, perhaps into the depth of the soul and of the sacred. I am told by an official here that this synagogue was built by Konrad Adenauer, Paul's grandpa. Whoever built this, it must have cost millions—at least in today's money.

When I walk in on a Friday night, I am so taken by the visuals of this place that I neglect for a moment to see that this five-hundred-seat temple is practically empty. It is only when the cantor motions to me that I must cover my head that I start noticing the people, meaning lack of people, in the place. Here is the rabbi, here's the cantor, and three Russians who work here. That's it. And me, yes. No more. The afternoon service soon ends and the evening service is about to start. Four tourists come in. The place is filling up, man! I say to myself. Evening service starts and we are, including myself, eleven people. Four tourists, rabbi and cantor, three employees, me, and one "survivor," as that man is described to me.

At least we have one German, I say to the person next to me.

"He's no German," he says; "he's Russian."

If you don't count the tourists and the employees, one person has shown up for the service tonight.

Millions of euros, huge complexes, for one old Russian Jew. If it were up to me I'd put him in the Excelsior Hotel Ernst for life; this would be much, much cheaper.

German Jewry in its past glory was mostly liberal, members of the Reform movement. The German Jews of today, the tenants of hugely expensive but empty Jewish temples and institutions, are mostly Orthodox. Usually imports. The rabbi here is Swiss, the cantor is Israeli.

The spiritual leaders of today's Jewish communities in Germany are people who didn't make it in their own hometowns. They're not good enough for their home countries, but everybody is good enough for the emptiness of Jewish life in Germany.

I can hear the wife of the chief rabbi of Munich whispering in my ears: Didn't I tell you?

The Jewish community in Germany, in Köln as in the other cities I visited, is one huge graveyard. There may be some signs of life here and there, but these are just ghosts. Dead Men Walking.

In this big building is a memorial to the eleven thousand Köln Jews who perished in World War II.

Eleven thousand virgins. Eleven thousand Jews. Köln loves eleven thousands. Nice number.

Service ends and all eleven people leave the sanctuary. The assistant rabbi and myself walk outside, strolling past gay bars while we are deep in thought, conversation, and other holy activities. The assistant rabbi tells me of a recent problem the Köln Jewish community and temple are faced with. A Köln city official called the synagogue asking for a little favor: A number of Israeli Jews, members of the gay community, are coming soon to Köln for a visit. They told the official they would like to attend a service at the temple, and he wants to know if he could fit this into their schedule.

"You understand now," says the assistant rabbi to me, "why sometimes it's better to be the assistant rabbi and not the rabbi? This is a tough question, but I don't have to answer it, it's not my responsibility."

What did the rabbi respond to the official?

"The rabbi asked for time to respond."

What is he waiting for?

"He will bring this issue to the board and the board will decide."

Yes. We need huge buildings at the cost of millions, plus imported clergy, to decide if a gay Jew can come to pray.

I think, and you can quote me, that the Jewish community in Köln and the Muslim community in Duisburg, both having such impressive buildings, should unite. Maybe they should form a mutual *Verein*, the Discriminators and Biased Ones Verein GmbH.

Here is a way to finally achieve peace between Jews and Muslims, at least between the religious segments of their populations.

I ask the assistant rabbi what he would do if he were the rabbi.

Personally he thinks it's not a good idea to let those Jews attend a service.

Why not?

"It would scare the worshippers," he says, "and they might not come to the temple ever again."

Worshippers. How did we get the plural here? There is one worshipper, the Survivor. Will it scare that old man?

"Yes," says the assistant rabbi.

Poor Jew. Isn't it enough that he experienced the Nazis? The sight of a gay Jew might do him in for good.

Köln.

•••

Continue walking and you come to a museum, a present-day museum, a Köln museum. It's called, and perhaps you have already guessed it, the Chocolate Museum. Yes: You get to see how chocolate is made, and you get to eat a piece of it too.

Welcome to Köln.

I keep on walking. Beautiful sights and places. *Fußgängerzone* (pedestrian zone), for example. A demonstration is now taking place here. Iranian Germans demonstrate against brutality they claim is committed by the Iranian regime. They have the pictures to prove it. Bloodied heads, and other organs, gifts of the regime to those who don't obey or who are different. Looking at the pictures, you can't tell if any of the victims photographed here are alive or dead. Not that it makes much difference. Given the shape these people are in, as seen in these horrific photos, death might be preferable.

I look at the demonstrators and something in them smells wrong, or foreign. I try to figure out why and what. It takes me a few minutes and then I see it: There are no German Germans here. Only Persians. All those Germans who jump to support Palestinian demonstrations against Israel, or Jews, fail to show up here. Even though these Iranians show similarly horrific pictures.

Welcome to Köln. Have a wurst and a beer, and try to forget everything else.

Köln.

•••

Tonight the Kölner Philharmonie is hosting a production of *Porgy and Bess*, the Gershwin opera, performed by the New York Harlem Theater.

Got to have some English in my system! I go to see it.

It's a sold-out performance, unlike the services in the synagogues.

The opera starts. The stage has so many people on it they can hardly move.

They sing. Supposedly in English, though no human ear can actually attest to it.

Who is this New York Harlem Theater group? Where exactly in Harlem are they located? They don't have a New York accent. Strange.

Two hours or so later I chance upon the musical director of the group.

Where in Harlem is your theater located? I ask this white man.

Well, to borrow Gershwin's title song from this very opera, It Ain't Necessarily So. He's from Munich. The group's name, you probably already guessed, is just so: a name. An excellent business idea. Maybe I should adopt it. Next year, if you happen to see the musical *Everything You Wanted to Know About Sex* performed by the Saudi Mecca Theater Company at the Köln Schauspielhaus, don't tell anybody it's me.

It's time to rest in my wonderful suite.

# I Sleep in Hitler's Room

There's a nice big TV in my suite, I think I should use it.

Helge Schneider was right. I just turn the TV on and whom do I see? Yes, Adolf Hitler. Nice little program. They talk about Hitler's sexual habits, in case we were interested to know. The learned talking heads discuss Hitler's relationship with his niece, Geli Raubal. How did Hitler have sex? It's an important question because it will reveal something extremely important. And here's the answer: Hitler, surprisingly or not, had a unique sexual desire: to have his beloved urinate on him.

This story, the history books tell us, was told by Otto Strasser in 1943. Most serious historians disregard it as true. Why are we discussing it in 2010? Hitler is still good for ratings.

Other news of the day:

In the Ruhr area there's another party going on this weekend: *Ruhrschnellweg*. It takes place on the A40. The Autobahn is closed to traffic, twenty thousand tables are arranged on this major highway, and three million people have shown up.

Is this just another variety of *Verein*?

•••

I had such a wonderful time with Paul Adenauer last time we met that I go to visit him again. Maybe he can further educate me.

Why are all those millions of Germans pouring into the streets to see –basically nothing?

"They love to be together."

That's it? Just looking for an excuse to be together, with as many other Germans as possible?

"Yes. We say: If you scratch a German long enough, a socialist comes out."

I heard that one quite some time ago. With one little modification: Instead of "socialist" they used the word "Nazi." If you scratch a German long enough—

"Perhaps it's the same thing. There's 'something' inside."

What is it?

"A sense of 'We belong together.' Members of the tribe. You have to belong to a tribe."

Is this what Hitler did, using this 'something,' and then defining the tribe as 'Aryan'?

"Yes."

Does it mean that there's a significant chance that Nazism would return?

"Yes, but not now."

Thanks, man! What else is German?

"German faithfulness. It's important to be faithful."

Wait a second: These two qualities, loyalty versus the tribal that can turn lethal and barbaric, are opposites—

"Germans' biggest problem is that they are very romantic, totally romantic. And romanticism is very dangerous. It can be turned into its opposite."

I mention to Paul this letter that I read years back. It's from a Nazi warrior to his wife, on the eve of the Christmas holiday. It was a very romantic letter indeed. In it he told her that she should be proud of him. They had a contest in their camp, he told her. They threw little Jewish children in the air and shot them before they fell down. You will be proud of me, he told his beloved, because I won the contest.

Paul is not surprised at all. He "signs" the letter:

"I killed many Jews, *Schatzi* [Honey]. Greetings to the dog."

He adds: "The German soul still has a *Nibelungentreue* [unquestioning loyalty unto death]. And this faithfulness is without thinking."

I ask Paul if he'd had the chance to think about what we had talked about last time, the possibility of Islamic fanaticism coming to Köln and how it should be dealt with.

Yes, he did.

"We, in Germany, will wait to see what other European countries do, like France and others. They have, or will have, the same problem. We'll let them act first and then we'll do what they do."

I learn a lot about Germany and Germans from Paul. If he's right, I've solved my dilemma, the one I had before starting out on this journey. The horrible Nazi past of this country on the one hand and the beautiful, romantic German literature on the other are not really two opposites.

"Germans' biggest problem is that they are very romantic, totally romantic. And romanticism is very dangerous. It can be turned into its opposite."

Is he right? Like Sister Jutta-Maria of Munich, I want to look into it more deeply.

Maybe it's time to go back in history, to see what's what and how it all originated. Perhaps a little examination of the Dom will be helpful. That's history, after all, long history. If Rabbi Schmidt taught me anything, it's this: Check history first!

I go to the Dom to meet Barbara Schock-Werner, the *Dombaumeisterin* (master of cathedral architecture), the first woman in Köln to hold this job. Wilhelm Luxem of the Excelsior, who introduced Paul to me, introduces me to Barbara as well.

"This section," she says, pointing somewhere outside, "was damaged in World War II."

I thought that the Allies spared the Dom, didn't they?

"Most of it. But most of the area next to the Dom was bombed. The British actually wanted to bomb here as well."

Why?

"Köln Nazis held on until the end."

Thinking back to what Paul taught me about the nature of the Kölners, I say to her: I thought that Kölners were not into the—

270

She cuts me off: "Yes, of course. And there were no Nazis in Germany at all . . ."

She laughs as she says this. This woman has sarcasm, a sense of the ironic.

"A Swastika was hung in the Dom," she goes on.

It doesn't comport well with the stories I've heard thus far while in this town. But facts, I guess, are stronger than fiction.

"Six million visitors come here yearly," she says, switching topics. I have to store all these numbers in my head: six million Jews, six million visitors. My head is exploding!

Barbara is a practicing Catholic, which helps her much in this job. There are five services a day here, she tells me. Sounds to me like a mosque. But I don't mention it. Instead, I ask something much more important:

Where are the nudes? I like my church with nudes.

"The Dom is from a later period. Even Adam and Eve, originally done in the nude, were ordered to be covered, and this is how you see them here."

She shows me. But I insist: No nudes in this church at all?

"Interesting question. I have to check into it. I never really thought about it. Oh, there's one nude I know, a depiction of hell. You want to see it?" Of course. It's free! We go there. But what we see is not very erotic. I ask: Any more? "I'll look into it," she says. "Now *I'm* interested!"

She shows me some treasures that tourists usually don't get to see. For example, the architectural design of the Dom, done on parchment and beautifully detailed. This is from 1270. "A woman dried her peas on it in Darmstadt," she tells me, illustrating the journeys this historical document took before it arrived back at its home.

Barbara knows a lot, there's no denying it. It's a pleasure to talk with her. She's vivid, straightforward, funny, and highly intelligent. And after a while we're going outside to talk some more, where I can also have a cigarette. As we schmooze I notice that the Kölner Klagemauer is missing from sight.

What happened to the Köln Wailing Wall? I ask Barbara.

"They're off on Mondays."

Barbara tells me of the time the Wall's people practically lived here, right at the entrance to the Dom. "For years they had a tent here, they lived here." It took time, but the Dom's lawyers eventually succeeded in evicting them, only because the tent was on church property.

What do you think of those people, of the Wall?

"It's plainly anti-Semitic and racist. There are some rich people in Köln who sponsor Walter Herrmann [founder and maintainer of the Wall]. Also, when he's in the square here, I see people giving him a lot of money. A Jewish organization recently tried to move them out, but Köln legal authorities decided otherwise. They said that it's an issue of free expression."

Will a similar Wall against the Turks be allowed on grounds of free expression?

"No way!"

The *Befestigungssteine*, the stones that serve as a foundation for Köln's Wailing Wall, are very heavy. Without them there's no Wall. But where are they now? I don't think that Herrmann, or his friends who stand there when he "makes," take them along with them when they leave in the evening. The other day I saw one of them, who was manning the Wall that day, returning from "work," and he had no *Befestigungssteine* with him.

Would you know where they store the *Befestigungssteine*?

"Not with us!"

Do you know where?

"You want to know?"

Yes.

"At WDR."

This is hard for me to believe. I try to think of an equally powerful American news organization, such as NBC, that would 'help out' a similar activity, but I fail to come up with a name. In America, news organizations of this magnitude would rather close shop than even think of doing such a thing.

Maybe I didn't get her right. I ask:

Are you telling me that the WDR—

"They help him."

They help this group distribute anti-Semitic propaganda?

"Yes."

Why?

"Ask them. You want me to show you the *Befestigungssteine*?"

Yes.

Barbara walks with me down the street and shows me where Herr Herrmann puts the heavy *Befestigungssteine* every night before going home. Right next to an *Eingang* door (entrance door) of WDR, an *Eingang* that's pretty close to the Wall.

This is a media company. Are they so dumb?

"Ask them."

I take Barbara's advice and walk into the WDR building. Try to, would be a better way of putting it. WDR is a high-security building, with electronic gates, red lights, and guards.

The woman sitting in front of the security entrance comes out to talk to me. She says she doesn't know what I'm talking about. "What stones? What wall?"

Could I speak with higher-ups? I ask her, since she so freely admits that she knows nothing. She goes inside and calls whomever she does, I have no clue whom. Meantime, I have to wait outside. Of course.

After fifteen minutes of what seems like a frantic call or calls, she comes out and says that "The *chef* said that this is all false." Never happened, never is. No *Befestigungssteine* here. Never were, never are.

I should be satisfied with the answer and go.

Good-bye.

Well, I don't really feel like walking away.

I saw them, I tell her. I can show them to you. Would you like to come along and explain them to me? I also have pictures, in case you cannot leave your post.

"You took pictures of—"

Yes.

"Excuse me," she says, and goes back to her phone.

I am waiting. About forty minutes.

At the end of this very hospitable introduction to WDR, she gives me the telephone number of one Herr Krenke, in charge of security. I should call him directly.

Can I talk to him now?

"No, he's in a meeting. Wait fifteen minutes and then call him. Not from here."

I stick around. Another fifteen minutes won't hurt. Just in case something funny develops.

And something does.

A man in a suit comes out and explains to me everything I should know. He says:

"Herr Herrmann has not been around for quite some time. In the past, those stones, the *Befestigungssteine*, were put in the nearby café. It's the café owner who allowed the *Befestigungssteine* in. But that was in the past. Now there's nothing to talk about because that Wall, you can go to the Dom's Square and see, is not there anymore."

WDR could change its name to WDT, We Dislike Truth.

Why are you lying to me? I ask this nameless, tailored WDR man. Monday is off for them. Herr Herrmann, or whatever his name is, and his group don't stand there on Mondays. But they're there the other days. What, you think I just came to town? Well, I've got news for you: I saw them every day last week.

"Really?" says the man. "I didn't know."

He disappears into the building. He should go to Marxloh, have lunch with the imam.

I pay a visit to the café and have a talk with Heinz-Josef Betz, the man in charge.

Is it you who helps Herr Herrmann with his *Befestigungssteine*?

"Me? I sell cakes and ice cream."

WDR people told me that you're the one who let Herrmann leave his stones here—

"Come, let me show you where he puts the stones."

We go there and Heinz says:

"You see, this is my business and it ends here. You see the stones? That's not me, that's WDR. They don't like to admit it, but they are the ones doing it. That place is not mine. I can't tell anybody what they can or can't store there."

He's totally right. The stones are far away from his fence. I go to the main entrance of WDR. Impressive entrance, I must say. Just beautiful. An attractive lady sits at the reception desk. I start talking to her and the Beauty turns Beastly.

"I know who you are," she says. "Go to the Dom. The church supports those people, not us."

Really? Is this the official response? Because I have pictures and I already spoke with the Dom people and also with the guy from the café—

"Wait!"

The Beastly Beauty makes a call, just as the other lady did, but this one hands me the phone. Tanja Luetz, assistant in the p.r. department, is on the other side of the line. She wants to know my telephone number and email address. She promises a response but cannot guarantee it will be in the next hour, because "people are on lunch."

They must be on a long lunch. It's now six hours later and no one has called or written yet.

After so many lies, I wonder what's next.

Germany. Anti-Semitic still.

Oh God! This is the last thing I wanted to see or find! I hate everybody, myself included, and leave Köln.

Before we began talking about the Wall, Barbara pointed at a lady, a beggar sitting next to the Dom, head covered and shaking. "Look at her legs," Barbara said. "Do you see how young she is? She's not an old lady; in real life she's not shaking. And that old man on a wheelchair, you see? You have to see him at night. He gets off his chair and goes to the pubs to drink."

Looks are so deceiving.

# I Sleep in Hitler's Room

And news companies even more.

•••

## Chapter 20

## Fact: When Two Jews Meet, Anywhere in the World, They Immediately Connect

Well, if this is still a Nazi country, then as long as I'm in Germany I want to live here like the best Nazi ever! Whatever the Führer had, I should have as well. Don't you agree?

I am in Weimar, at the Hotel Elephant. Suite number 100 used to be Adolf Hitler's room. And now I am here. A great feeling!

Yes, they changed the room somehow, the furnishing is different, the bathroom is bigger, and they made some other such modifications. But this is it. His suite. Heil Tuvia!

Forget Rabbi Helmut. Forget Half and Half. Forget Sheikh Jens. Forget the Jewish Bride. Sieg Heil! Heil Tuvia! Let the Three Ravens see this and report it to the world. Heil!

At the time, when beloved Adolfy was staying at this hotel, people outside were shouting the most brilliant, most poetic line ever composed in the German language:

"Lieber Führer komm heraus, aus deinem Elefantenhaus." (Dear Führer: Come out, out of your Elephant House.) And the lovely Führer, in recognition of his followers' genius, would then go to what has become known as the Führer Balcony on the other side, the one pointing at the square, greet them and wave at them. Kind of Heil Hitler them. And if he could do it, why not me? Yes. Which is exactly what I do. I go to the balcony, stand there as he did, and look down.

A group of older people pass by. I wave at them, Hitler style.

They love it! They wave back. What a country!

Ehrengard, whose job it is to explain to wandering visitors all they can listen to about Weimar, is walking along with me today. She tells me of this city, where the Nazis as a party had their first rally. It's here where they started winning, it's here where they first rose. They were highly motivated to make their start in this city. It was here, after all, where the most enlightened nation on the planet had its center: Weimar Republic. And here it is where Hitler and his party were most welcome.

How could people so enlightened turn that barbaric so fast?

Ehrengard doesn't know. There are some explanations, she says, and she even recommends a book that I've read already, but she tells me that there are no definite answers. I don't let her off the hook so fast and easy and ask her what she thinks of the period. Was any relative of hers involved in the war? I'm thinking of the students from Frankfurt. Was a grandpa, maybe, a train driver in Kiev . . .?

"No. No train driver. But something else."

What, who?

"Lutz Graf Schwerin von Krosigk, finance minister of the Third Reich, was my great-uncle."

That's a fat fish. At least, fatter fish than my relatives.

What did he tell you? Did he admit to doing, or at least knowing, some bad stuff?

"He told me that he knew about the KZ but not know about the cruelty."

Did you believe him?

"No."

Was that the extent of the conversation?

"I asked him: Why didn't you do anything?"

What was his response?

"You can't jump off a moving train."

That's it?

"No. He always came to a point where he said, 'You will never understand.'"

Ehrengard, who has done this tour for many years, tells me that it's the first time she's been asked these questions.

Yep. I probably went too far. And as we move on, I talk about soccer and flags.

I go back to my Elephant. Next to the Elephant is the Rathaus. An Israeli flag hangs from the top. Wasn't there last night. I try to find out why but don't get a real answer. Go figure.

Inside the Elephant, Martin Kranz waits for me. I don't know this guy, so I sit down with him for a cup of coffee and Cola Light. We talk and he tells me his story. Raised in the GDR, and a son of pastor, he could not go to gymnasium and earn Abitur.

Reason?

"Because my father was clergy."

I sip my Coke and he adds more details about his life. I jot down on my iPad: Went to army of GDR. When antigovernment demonstrations in Leipzig were flaring up he was sent to prison and stayed there for ten weeks. Other soldiers, those deemed credible by authorities, were put in charge of stopping the demonstrations. After ten weeks in jail, during which the Wall fell down, he was sent with other soldiers to Protect the Economy of the former GDR, by working in a cigarette factory. Was stupid. Four months later the soldiers said Enough! What are we doing? Hasn't the Wall fallen? They were sent home. He went to study music, because for this he didn't need Abitur. About ten years ago, when Weimar was the European Capital of Culture, Martin did fundraising to bring Israeli and Palestinian musicians to Weimar.

I stop him here. How the heck did the Israelis and the Palestinians sneak into the door of this story? How did the Jews get into the picture? Again!

Why Israelis and Palestinians?

"Why not?"

Why yes? Got nothing better, or worse, to deal with?

"Well, we invited Daniel Barenboim and he wanted it."

Why him?

"He's big!"

No other biggies?

"Why not him?"

He's a political animal, very controversial and sometimes anti-Israel.

"He wasn't then."

Really? Do you have the exact history of Daniel, when, how, and where he was when he initiated his political involvement?

No, he doesn't. And then, after a long and almost endless discussion, the answer I finally get is: "Ask Mr. Kaufman."

Who the heck is he?

"He was in charge."

So, you don't really know why Daniel was invited?

"No."

Good to know.

Martin might not know, but the facts are these: Daniel Barenboim founded West–Eastern Divan with the famed Palestinian-rights activist Edward Said; the performance in Weimar was the orchestra's maiden performance.

Martin is also a festival producer. One of the festivals he produces on a yearly basis is the Jüdische Kulturtage (Jewish culture days) in Berlin.

Why you?

"They asked me."

You're not Jewish, right?

"I'm not."

What did you learn about Jews?

"They are all connected. Worldwide. No matter what each of them thinks, no matter what political views each of them holds, they are all connected."

The Nazis would be happy to hear you say this. They think the same thing.

"No, no! No! This is not what I said!"

What did you say?

"The Jews are SPIRITUALLY connected. All around the world."

Really?

"When a Jew meets another Jew, anywhere in the world, they immediately connect. I know this. I saw this. That's what's unique about the Jews!"

Good that Martin does the festival. Finally there's somebody out there who can tell the Jews who they are.

•••

Paul Kernatsch, general manager of the Elephant Hotel, comes to say hello.

"I was born in Ireland. My wife likes to buy shoes and I like the Apple store."

There you go. We immediately connect.

I ask him to tell me the difference between the eastern Germans and the western Germans.

"Eastern German girls are more beautiful and more open-minded."

Really?

"Yes!"

Give me an example!

"In the east of Germany, pregnancy is not an illness."

I am here only one day, but I have this impression, and maybe I am totally wrong, that the eastern Germans don't take as well to criticism as do the western Germans, and that they're more stubborn. Am I totally wrong?

"No. Both observations are true."

This hotel was built, or redesigned, on Hitler's orders. Is this the only hotel he built?

"As far as I know, yes."

Tell me, how many people specifically asked to sleep in that room, the way I did?

"Since I've been here, thirteen years at this point: two people."

I guess I am in good, exclusive company. Paul goes on to show me the hotel's guest book from the Nazi period. Here is the signature of Magda Goebbels, wife of Joseph. She writes the date: October 26, 1941. And here's Heinrich Himmler's signature, no date given.

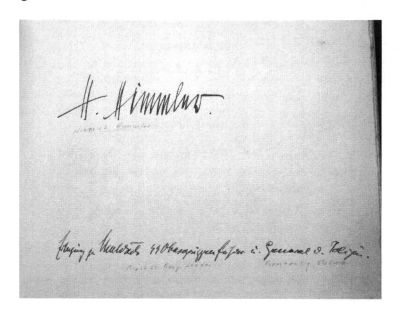

•••

## Chapter 21

## From the Entertainment Center of Buchenwald Concentration Camp to a Demonstration against Israel

Volkhard Knigge, director of Buchenwald Memorial Foundation, shows up at the Elephant. He was told that I was around, and he came for a chat.

"The KZ is the place of rebirth for those who survived and were liberated there. For survivors it's very important that the sites are kept."

Why would anyone want a place like that to be preserved? If I cut your limbs off in this room, would you like the room to be preserved?

"I can't speculate on why the survivors feel this way. This you have to ask them."

What's the nature, or the origin, of Nazism?

"It all starts with the definition of a nation. To the French, what defines a nation is its acceptance of a constitution. You are French if you accept the constitution. To the German, it's blood base. You are a German if your father and mother are."

The present government of Israel believes that a Jew is a Jew based mostly on blood. Isn't this, given your definition of the German nation according to Nazism, a Nazi philosophy? In other words: Are those Jews basically Nazis?

Volkhard goes on and on, a custom in this land when you don't know how to answer a question but don't want to admit it. But I don't let go, asking for a clearer response. Being pushed, he says: "I talk about NSDAP [the Nazi party], not others." But a few minutes later he calms down and we get to exchange some info. He even recommends a bar in Jerusalem, one he really likes: Uganda. Free-minded people are there, he tells me.

Uganda? Why Uganda?

"That's an allusion to that old idea."

He refers to the idea that Jews should have settled in Uganda instead of Palestine. Uganda, the bar, made a name for itself as a place that 'sympathizes with the Palestinian plight.' Why the director of Buchenwald Memorial gets his hands wet in the Israeli–Palestinian mess is beyond my understanding.

•••

On the next day I meet Daniel Gaede, *Leiter Abteilung Gedenkstättenpädagogik* (head of the education department, concentration camp), at Gedenkstätte Buchenwald. He is to show me around the KZ, and I meet him at the entrance. First off, he tells me he's partly Jewish. His "grand, or grand-grandfather, was a Jew." As if I didn't know. There are more Germans alive with Jewish grandpas than with Nazi grandpas. Way more! But I don't say anything. Daniel, on the other hand, does. "By Nazi law, I am one-eighth Jewish," he says. I wonder if Rabbi Schmidt knows how many Jews live in his country.

Daniel takes me on a tour of the camp. Truth is, I'd never come here on my own. But the local tourist-information office in Weimar, the office that takes care of all my needs while I'm in

Weimar, arranged this. They heard a Jew was coming, so they arranged for him a KZ visit. And so, here I am.

But I shouldn't complain. I get to see what the average visitor usually doesn't get to see. I am on an official visit, and I get an intimate look into a place of horror. And entertainment. Yes, entertainment. What kind of entertainment? A zoo. Yes, there was a zoo next to the crematorium. I would never have known that on my own, but Daniel shows it to me. He actually showed me the crematorium, but I ask him to explain to me a funny-looking structure across a narrow road from the crematorium.

"That's for the brown bears," he tells me.

Brown bears? What do brown bears do in a crematorium?

Well, it turns out that the SS had a zoo, right next to the place where humans were turned to ashes, for its soldiers to enjoy. Gassed people on the left, brown bears on the right. Together, they made for one great entertainment center.

We walk into what he calls the pathology room. This Buchenwald concentration camp is actually a theme park, in case you didn't get it by now. Disneyland in the Fatherland. No kidding. In the room I'm now in, you can see how this place operated. Here is a raised stone structure, with faucet and various cutting tools, where organs were taken out from the dead bodies before the bodies were sent to the crematorium. Sometimes a heart would be taken out for some kind of research, other times skulls were shrunk, to fist-size, and given to friends to serve as ornaments. If the dead had a nice tattoo, the skin and flesh would be cut, dried, and later be made into lampshades. What a life! Lampshades, brown bears, and little skulls as key chains. Good use of dead Jews. All prepared for you by folks with PhDs.

Don't cry when you read this, my dear, or you'll never stop.

Down under is the cellar. Here you can see hooks for hanging people.

I stand here, imagine this happening, and find myself speechless.

There's an elevator here that was used to "ship" the bodies straight into the ovens.

The company that made the ovens, Daniel tells me, felt so elated about their engineering feat that they went on to "register for patent rights."

The other day, says Daniel, he took a taxi to the camp. He and the driver got to talking. "When I was a boy," the driver told him, "I used to see corpses in there."

Yep. The kids were playing around, and they saw everything. It was never a secret. I wonder if this cabbie was ever as honest with his children.

Most likely, not.

After hours of horrific stories, these and others, Daniel sits down with me just outside the campgrounds to tell me about himself and share his thoughts.

He spent a year and a half in Israel, working for Aktion Sühnezeichen Friedensdienste, or ASF, Action Reconciliation Service for Peace. His job was to sort documents at Yad Vashem, the Israeli organization dealing with the Holocaust Memorial.

That's not all he did in Israel. In addition to his work at Yad Vashem, Daniel got involved with the Israeli–Palestinian conflict, spending eight weeks as a volunteer in an Arabic hospital in Nazareth. Nice, right?

Why did you get involved?

"I was there, living the conflict; I was in the middle of it. I wanted to find out if my belief in conflict resolution through nonviolent means was just a great philosophy or something that could also be practiced."

What did you learn?

"That it's also practicable."

How did you figure this out? How did you find that the nonviolence solution is the way?

"Look at this country!"

Germany?

"Yes."

Hello: This country? You knew this country's story before you went to Israel, long before you boarded the plane. So why did you go?

Daniel looks at me, apparently surprised that I'm so direct with him.

During his stay in Israel, he tells me, he went to Nablus to talk with the city's deputy mayor, to learn from him about the Palestinian side; he wanted to understand the Palestinians better. He's a peace lover, after all. At the end of the meeting, when he and his brother returned to their car, it exploded. What happened? A Palestinian had put a bomb in their car. Daniel's brother was killed, and Daniel himself lost his left eye.

Was this the end of your involvement in the Israeli–Palestinian issue?

"No. In Weimar last year, I marched in a demonstration for Gaza."

What has Weimar got to do with Gaza?

"The city of Weimar awarded a human-rights prize to a lawyer from Gaza."

I step out of my role as interviewer and share a moment with Daniel. I tell him that I totally agree with the notion that he has a right to criticize Israel, demonstrate against it, and do whatever he wishes. That's the essence of democracy and I have no problem with it. But what I don't understand is why a person who works in a concentration camp, a system where millions of Jews found their death, doesn't feel the need to be a little bit more sensitive to Jewish feeling and refrain from such activities.

Daniel listens to me but says not a word. His hands are shaking, and the cup of soda he holds in his right hand almost spills. He stares somewhere, not at me. I push the envelope. I ask him if his hate of the Jew is so deeply rooted that sense has simply failed him. He doesn't answer. Does he regret anything he did? No.

If the death of his brother and the loss of his own eye didn't move him, I won't either.

The story of Israel and Gaza is quite complicated, having many sides to it. But the fact, known to anybody who speaks or reads Arabic, remains this: Gaza has the world's highest concentration of people who believe in driving the Jews into the sea. Why would anybody from Buchenwald join them?

Because.

•••

286

At Divan restaurant, a Turkish eatery, there's a jam session of Yiddishkeit, a Jewish summer festival in Weimar. I go there to spend some time with Jews, living Jews with skulls bigger than fists. Olaf is one of the singers.

Are you Jewish?

"My great-grandmother was a Jew."

Olaf goes on, telling me his life story. In short, here goes: He studied theology, served as pastor of a church in the Rhineland for a short time, and then went to Berlin, where he still lives. Today he does Yiddish concerts here and there, whenever, but he gets his livelihood from "public assistance."

Why are German audiences coming to listen to Jewish music?

"For Germans, the interest in Jewish music is something like Disney."

The musicians who perform Jewish music in Germany, he also tells me, are not Jews.

I guess I was a little naïve when I thought I'd find Jews here.

Why are they doing this?

"Compensation for the past. The history of Germany."

Olaf goes on talking. He says he's against the policies of Israel. "Building Jewish neighborhoods in Jerusalem is illegal."

Again Israel?

Let me talk to another singer.

Conny, of Hamburg, is another Yiddishkeit musician. A violinist.

Jewish?

"In my last lifetime I was a Jew."

Not in this one?

"No."

But you are interested in the people who made this music?

She is.

I'm thinking: Daniel went to Nablus, maybe this Conny went to Tel Aviv.

Have you been to Israel as well? I ask her.

Conny is not amused. She gets upset. She's offended by me. She seems to think that in some way, shape, or form I connect her to Israel. She raises her voice as she says, "I don't have to go to

Israel! My music has nothing to do with it! I don't want to talk anymore!"

This outburst is strange to me. She's out. I need more singers!

Ulla, a singer who hails from Wuppertal, comes to talk.

Are you Jewish?

"No."

Why Jewish music?

"My father was very interested in Jewish history and he told me a lot about it. He was a soldier in the war and was taken prisoner in Russia."

Are you a philo-Semite?

"It depends. In respect to how Israel treats Palestinians, definitely not."

Palestinians again! What the heck is going on in this Germany?!

I am really getting lost here. But she's not.

"My ex-husband is an Arab from Jordan," she tells me. Then, with a warning, she adds: "I miss German Jews."

You WHAT?

"Since 1820, Jewish and German cultures have been intertwined. The most famous German writer of the nineteenth century, Heinrich Heine, was Jewish. What is socialism without Karl Marx? And his grandfather was a rabbi. Psychology: Sigmund Freud. A Jew."

He was Austrian, wasn't he?

"That's all German culture. You can't divide it.

"Stefan Zweig. A Jew.

"German cabaret: It wouldn't exist if not for the Jews.

"All famous German sociologists were Jewish. And they immigrated to the United States.

But I'm against the Israelis building a wall. That's like in Berlin before unification. There are a lot of Palestinian people who are very, very peaceful. I don't want the Jews to make the same mistakes we Germans did during the war."

Yes. Israel is famous for building zoos next to crematoriums, where Palestinians are routinely gassed.

Christiane, a Klezmer singer, native of Hannover, tells me her story.

"My grandma was very pro-Jewish and pro-Israel. She was religious, Baptist, and she introduced Israeli music to me."

Are you as religious as her?

"Not anymore."

Still pro-Israel?

"Yes and no. I support the right of Jews to a land but I am against the politics—"

As I write, she checks my iPad, and she stops me. She's really annoyed:

"No, not 'support' and 'against.' I don't like this! I am a skeptic. I think Israelis are paranoid. They want to solve all their problems alone—"

You seem to be very emotional about this issue. Why?

"Yes, I am. Because you will call me an anti-Semite."

Me? Why do you think that?

"Because when we criticize Israel, we are immediately labeled anti-Semites! When Germans say anything about—"

Only Germans? What happens if the French say—

"The French too!"

Then why did you use the word "Germans"?

I have no clue what she says from this point on. She keeps on talking about Israelis and Palestinians and Gaza, and all I want to do is take the next plane to Gaza and leave all Germans alone. Really; I've had it up to my skull. My initial instinct to go to Gaza, as I see clearly now, was right. I'd have had much more fun there.

But I say nothing to her. I just sit. And listen. Try to interject here and there, but I'm not really into it.

I think to myself.

I remember a while ago when a German actor said to me, "What we did to the Jews in World War II is horrible, those Jews were very nice and we should have never sent them to Auschwitz. But the Jews today? All of you, to Auschwitz!"

I smile. I don't know if that actor meant it as a joke or if he was serious. But I laughed.

The people here, the singers and the musicians of Yiddish memory, fit that description pretty well. They celebrate the dead

Jews but are one-minded in their criticism of living Jews. For whatever reason, they seem to think that this planet will be paradise if only the Israelis were less aggressive.

I wish they were right. Sadly, they're not. For even if Israel is guilty of every crime it's accused of, a man must be either totally naïve or extremely anti-Semitic to think that the root of humanity's misfortunes lies with that tiny state.

So unlucky are the Jews that even those who celebrate their culture are certified idiots and incurable racists.

I need a zoo. A zoo, with a couple of brown bears, would be really nice now.

It's late at night. I sit by myself next to the Weimar Rathaus. Young Germans are walking by. Some of them are so beautiful! But I don't want to start a conversation with any of them. It's after two in the morning and I don't want to have nightmares.

A thought comes to me: The Germans, and sorry for generalizing, will do everything and anything to look good, to appear beautiful, to sound smart. But who are they, really? They are the most narcissistic nation on the planet. They think the world of themselves, and they want everyone to agree with them.

They do their stupid theater, breaking the most beautiful plays into pieces, because they think that this way they'll look "high culture." They are against Israel because they think that by being so they can create an image of themselves as "human-rights lovers." If some Brits are against Israel, the Germans would like to be even more anti. It'll look better. And if they lose an eye in the process, like Daniel, so be it. They will go on, because they want to look good. Peace lovers. Like Gitti. Like WDR. The Germans care about the Palestinians as much as they care about the Iranians. Nada. Ziltch. But they do beautiful designs, the Germans, because they want so desperately to LOOK nice. And they are geniuses at this, no question. More than any other nation in the world, the Germans concentrate deeply on visual beauty—and they get results. But they don't stop there. Subconsciously the Germans think that if they occupy themselves with the Palestinians of Gaza they will erase from memory the Brown Bears of Buchenwald—and will look beautiful in the eyes of the world.

# I Sleep in Hitler's Room

Germany is one of the richest countries on the planet, but they complain as if it were the poorest. Better is not enough, best is not enough; they want more. Always more. They are anti-Semitic and supremacist to the core of their being, but they cover it with huge masks, declarations of love and public hugging of the other. Any issue that seems hip, they immediately jump on the bandwagon and go for the ride. They want to look cool. They love to give those huge introductions before they give an answer to any question you ask them, because they have no clue to any real answer but still want to look brainy. They love brainy. They are, in short, the most self-deluded and self-righteous people in the world.

These thoughts make me feel very bad. Because somewhere inside me, buried deep in my very being, I love the Germans.

Let me go and sleep, dream of nice.

Tomorrow will be a great day.

Sleep well, Gaza.

G'night. I'm in bed. Hi Adolfy, can you hear me? You have a nice bed. I like it.

•••

## Chapter 22

**Fact: The Israelis Are Nazis**


The first Nazi ministers in history were installed in Weimar in 1930, a woman tells me the next day. And the first *Parteitag* (party congress), after the refounding of the party, took place in Weimar. That was in July of 1926.

Enough. Really. I want to have a day without Jews, Nazis, or Palestinians. Germany. I want Germany! Just that, pure and simple.

Anja, who works for the tourist information office, drives me to Panorama Museum in Bad Frankenhausen, to witness firsthand Werner Tübke's monumental work. Anja was born in the east of Germany, she knew the GDR firsthand, and she's happy the Wall came tumbling down.

What was your first impression of the West?

"I went to the supermarket and couldn't understand it: Why do you need twenty different kinds of mustard?"

That's it?

"I went to McDonald's and I couldn't stand the smell. Smell of unnatural food. And what a terrible taste! To this day I can't eat there!"

Anja has many stories to tell, I am sure, but we have arrived at Werner's *Early Bourgeois Revolution in Germany*. This is an amazing work, 14 x 123 m in size, and since it's a rotunda painting it has no beginning and no end. It's divided into the seasons of the year, with background colors indicating an approximate time of year, but you can start and finish at any part of the painting you wish. The GDR commissioned the artist to paint the German Peasants' War of 1525, which was fought for freedom from feudal lords. But Werner went beyond a depiction of the literal scene. In his painting he presents the tales of the rich and the poor, of justice and lawlessness, and he draws heavily on biblical stories, taken from both the Old and the New Testaments. And so he opened his world to a wider audience.

The painting can give you nightmares. Its practical message, summed up, is this: There are bad people out there, and always will be, no matter what you do. This is disturbing, even if true. Still, it doesn't detract from the beauty of the piece.

This museum was designed to be a one-painting museum, a museum dedicated to only one picture. And I am told that this is how it was in the GDR. That's what it was designed to be, but that's not what it is now. Today in the halls leading to Werner's work are many other paintings. Here is one of a person wearing the yellow patch. Yes, that famous "Jude" of the Nazi era.

How did the Jew sneak in *here*!

I'm leaving. I go back to Weimar, say goodbye to Hitler, Schiller, Goethe, and mount the train to Leipzig.

•••

In Leipzig I meet Birgit, a funny creature. She asks if I want to visit the American embassy. Why would I? Well, she says, "it's just across the street." I look and can't see it. The only thing to my back is McDonald's.

Yeah. How stupid I am! That's the "American embassy"!

Brigit cried when the Wall fell, she tells me. She crossed west, and she bought a banana.

A banana?

"In the GDR we had bananas only at Christmas."

Brigit has something to say, she wants to share what's in her heart. She talks as we walk: "West Germans stole from us. After the Wall fell, they crossed the border, our sisters and brothers, and stole from us. They sold us garbage, and charged for it. They bought factories from the government, for as cheap as one deutsche mark, because they promised the government they would develop the area. They didn't. They closed down the factories, sold the parts, tools, and land and created high unemployment. People don't know. Look here, here's a memorial for Felix Mendelssohn. He was Christian, but the Jews think he's a Jew. Israeli tourists told me that a Jew is always a Jew, no matter what."

Birgit is in a relationship with a foreigner, an English man, who calls her a Nazi on occasion. But Brigit is a nice lady. She supports Human Rights Watch. And she stopped smoking when the German government raised the tax on cigarettes.

"They raised the tax because they needed money for the war in Afghanistan. I am not supporting that war!"

Once Brigit departs, I go to see Tobias Hollitzer, director of the Museum in der Runden Ecke, the Stasi Museum, a museum housed at the former Stasi headquargters. He tells me that "probably every second citizen had a file in the Stasi."

At the time, Tobias belonged to an environmental group. It wrote a report about the environmental risks, for example, of emissions from factories. The Stasi file suggests that the report was written for the purpose of challenging the authorities. Then, in a paragraph at the bottom of the page, the Stasi author of the file notes that the report is wrong. Reason? The actual risks to the environment were much higher . . .

This is funny. I love it!

•••

On the next day I sit down for a talk with the Reverend Christian Führer, one of the leading personalities behind Leipzig's famous *Montagsdemonstrationen* (Monday Demonstrations), in and around St. Nikolai Church in Leipzig, that started in 1989.

Does he believe that the demonstrations brought down the GDR?

"Yes. And the church did it, did the right thing."

And ever since those days he dedicates himself to spreading the message of *Keine Gewalt* (literally, "small power," or nonviolence and peaceful revolution) the world over.

Does he think that, after all these years, *Keine Gewalt* demos can change policies, regimes?

"Yes. We did it!"

Let me understand: Twelve years of the Reich. How come this system didn't work then?

"People were executed."

Does it mean that peaceful revolution works only against weak regimes?

"No. The message of Jesus worked here even though the GDR was a powerful regime."

If the Nazis come to power in Germany again, let's say tomorrow, will a *Keine Gewalt* demo help?

"No."

Adolf, obviously, is stronger than Jesus.

I walk through the streets of Leipzig, away from the touristy center, and find them appealing. Here's a store called Licht Design. An item in the window: A Leipziger traffic light, turned red, and around it, in English: "Don't stop now!" It's really cute, I like it. A few feet later, a sign on the wall: "Sorry. We are open." Sweet.

Later I get on the first tram that comes my way and have it take me to the last stop. And there I get off. Where am I? I stand next to a traffic light. There's a poster on it, a colored poster, which explains what I should do once I get to this very point. The red, it says, means that I have to STEH (stand). The green, it says, means GEH (go). As in the Neue Pinakothek museum in Munich, the authorities here are sure we're all retarded. Where am I? Is there a museum nearby? A passerby tells me that I'm in Wahren. Heard of it before? Neither have I. I walk into a *Kneipe* (pub), or whatever they call it. I have no idea who the people here are. Except that they all drink beer. I sit down and ask: Is it good that the GDR is over? Three people in the pub, drinking beer and liquor, and they respond:

"The GDR was much better. We all worked. We all had health insurance."

They talk more, one after the other, and the other after the one:

"It's not true what they say about the Stasi. Life was good. All they wanted is that people wouldn't leave. Yes, if you talked against the government they did something to you. But now it's the same. Talk against the system and you'll pay for it."

"In GDR times, we were all together, all the people, and we cared for each other. Today it's not like that. The western Germans are individualistic. They come here, to our neighborhood, and immediately build a fence around their houses. They don't want to have anything to do with us."

"In this neighborhood, half the people don't work. They can't find a job. The Wall fell down, and what happened? Go and see. People eat from garbage cans. During the GDR, all people had the right to work, smart or not. Not today. They say that during the GDR era we had a dictatorship. Look what we have today: Democracy with criminals. Crime all over."

"I've been married thirty-five years. My wife has worked for the same company for thirty-nine years. And after all that time she earns 620 euros a month, *netto* [net]. That's for 170 hours. *Brutto* [gross], that's 5.62 euro an hour. She's a florist. How can we live on this? Ask Frau Merkel."

"There are two Germanys, one in the west and the other in the east. We have the same roots, but we're different people. The western people are arrogant and they treat us like trash. We're people who live together. We've had better times. The Wall fell, and we pay for it. The west Germans got richer, and we're poorer.

"Are you writing this? Good. It's time people know this, it's time people know the truth."

"After the wall fell down I signed a contract for a savings account with an office in the west. That was 30,000 DM that I gave them. The first year I got something from them, like interest, and then the company said that they went bankrupt and all my money evaporated. I hired a lawyer, but all I got from it was more expenses. I should have kept my money under the mattress."

"What is this machine you carry? Is this a secret camera?"

A new customer, who came here just to have a hot tea, explains: "This country used to be a prison with a wall. Now it's a prison with money."

Says another: "Businessmen are people who know how to cheat better than others."

"It's better to be the first man in a little village than the second man in Rome," philosophizes another man.

Another man comes in. Was the GDR time better? I ask him.

"Much better," he answers.

No one here likes the German government's interior policies. What do they think of Germany's foreign policy? Yes, they do have opinions about that too. Strong opinions.

"Get out of Afghanistan! Build a wall around them and leave!"

"Israel should get tough treatment. We have to tell them to stop!"

"The Israelis are Nazis."

"They do to the Palestinians what we did to them."
Do you like Gregor Gysi?
"Yes!"
Is Gregor Gysi Jewish?
"No."
"Can't be," says another.
Why not?
"Can't! Impossible!" says a blond lady.

Yes, of course. They like Gregor so much that he obviously can't be a Jew. No wonder he didn't want to discuss his Jewishness. What a world!

Outside, rotten buildings stand empty with for-sale signs, and all around on dilapidated buildings is an abundance of posters celebrating Elvis Presley and Michael Jackson. Some new construction is also visible in the area, with signs that read "Luxury Apartments." At the edges of the neighborhood you can spot new housing units, with fences built around them to protect the newcomers from the "dreck" on all sides. A magnificent landscape soon reveals itself to the visitor: flowing water and gorgeous greenery.

Between them is a *Kleingartenverein*, the Small Gardens *Verein*. This *Verein* consists of urbanites who cultivate small gardens next to cute tiny mini-houses. It's on this piece of land, some distance from their real homes, that they grow flowers, fruits, or vegetables. In their spare time they come here, work the land, drink beer, eat in "nature" and chat. I've seen quite a few of them before, but this is my first in the east.

And I have never seen any that are nicer or more picturesque.

Welcome to Kleingartenverein Wettinbrücker e.v. Two men, who answer to the names of Stefan and Uwe, discuss a major issue: The Rat Train from Germany to Rome.

Rat Train?

"Yes. That's what we call it, because the Nazis used it to flee to Argentina."

On this beautiful, somehow cool but sun-filled Saturday afternoon, these people have apparently nothing better to talk about than Nazis. Are they out of their minds?

Stefan invites me in. "We are the shadow Germans, in the shadow of the Wall," says his next-door neighbor Uwe, referring to eastern Germans. "You can also call us 'The *Dunkeldeutschen*' [dark Germans]."

Is there a difference between east and west Germans?

Both agree that there is.

"If I were a western German," Stefan offers, by way of illustration, "I wouldn't invite you in."

On reflection, he adds: "It was better under the GDR. We had a better life. We learned how to trust each other, and we made many friends. If I left my house tomorrow, ten to fifteen people would be there helping me. That would never happen in the west. We are two nations, two worlds. We [the eastern Germans] have many friends, and that's because of the GDR."

I tease him: Friends like the Stasi . . .?

"Oh," says Gabi, Stefan's wife, "that's a big book by itself."

Did you ask for your Stasi files?

"No!" says Stefan.

Why not?

"I have many friends, and I'm afraid that if I look at the file I'd cut off my relationship with quite a few of them. I don't want to. I don't want to know."

Eastern Germany. A world unto itself.

•••

A few hours later comes the sudden news of a stampede during the techno Love Parade festival in Duisburg. Nineteen are said to have been killed. Nearly a million and a half people showed up, according to some estimates, and Adolf Sauerland orders an investigation. The funny man I met in Duisburg isn't laughing today.

German chancellor Angela Merkel has demanded an "intensive" investigation into the incident, reports the BBC. She is quoted as saying that she was "appalled" by the tragedy.

The BBC goes on to report: Pope Benedict XVI, who is German, expressed "deep sorrow" over the deaths. "I remember in my prayers the young people who lost their lives," he said.

•••

The next day I take a tram and land in the part of town known as Grünau. Many buildings, huge blocks, but little pedestrian traffic. It's a bit strange, as there must be thousands of people in the area. Here's a mom, dressed in hijab, walking and carrying a baby. Which reminds me that I haven't seen much hijab in Leipzig. Interesting. I continue walking for about ten minutes, until I finally see more people, some standing and talking and others sitting on the other side of a Kurdish bistro.

It's a hot day today and I put on a hat I bought a few days ago at Jack Wolfskin. It's a funny *Sonnenhut* (sun hat), made of a Supplex material. It has a 360-degree brim to it and it covers my forehead, the top of my eyes, my ears, and some more. Basically, a third of my head. And as I walk toward the bistro, a man sitting outside catches sight of me. He says something to his friends, and they all turn their heads toward me. They examine me, intensely following every step I make. When I get close and say hello, they refuse to answer. I take off the hat and they warm up.

Slowly. Yep. My hat, I guess, made them suspicious . . .

About fifteen minutes later, they're talking nonstop, about life. Their voices intermingle with one another.

"After the Wall fell, we could travel. That's good, but who has money to travel? Everything else was better under the GDR."

"Under the GDR you could have children, because the government took care of them. There was school, education, and food. Today you can't bring children to the world if you don't have money. This is the way of Merkel. She doesn't have children and she doesn't want anybody else to have them."

"They should have made the Wall twice as high than they did."

"They should build it again, twice as high!"

"I voted for Die Linke, but most people here vote for the NPD."

"Too many foreigners here. One thousand percent more than should be."

"I won't tell you what I think of Merkel. I won't answer this question."

"Germany for the Germans!"

"I don't know if there is a God or not. But I know one thing: There is no God who helps me."

"If my wife lets me in tonight, then there is a God."

The owner of the bistro is an Iraqi. He tells me: "Last night, at 23:00, young German kids were sitting here, right next to my bistro. They were ten-year-olds. They were drinking beer and smoking cigarettes. The parents are nowhere to be seen, because they're all drunk. Here you have girls who are pregnant at thirteen. Two years ago a girl of fifteen came over. She wore a bikini and she had a baby in one arm and a bottle in the other. The police came and hauled them off. I saw this girl recently walking alone, and I asked her, 'Where is your baby?' She said, 'What baby?'"

A German man from the neighborhood says to me: "The GDR made one mistake: They closed the doors. They should have kept them open. All those who would leave,would come back. Life was better and easier in the GDR."

I don't know. I wasn't here when the GDR ruled this part of the country. Perhaps I should roam the east a little more, see other cities.

Where next? Dresden sounds interesting. A city that knew much death, bombed almost to the ground during World War II, and is now alive and well. Or so I hear.

# I Sleep in Hitler's Room

Let's check it out.

...

## Chapter 23

**Who Invented the Bra? How Was Your First Sex? Can You Afford 100,000 Euros for a Vase? What Should We Do Because We Killed the Jews? And: How Far Will a Jew go if He Wants to Swim?**

In Dresden I am, a city once known as "Florence on the Elbe."

What is Dresden? Who lives in Dresden?

Many empty stores in the center with *Zu Vermieten* (for rent), signs, next to construction sites of new buildings and shops. What is the logic of this?

I go to see Dr. Bettina Bunge, managing director of Dresden Marketing GmbH. I ask her to explain Dresden to me. She does: "In Leipzig they trade, in Chemnitz they work, and in Dresden they spend their money. . . and enjoy life."

What is Dresden famous for?

"We invented the bra. And the tea bag. And a lot of culture as well."

Do you know who invented the bikini?

The doctor looks at me, not sure how to answer this.

You know, I tell her, if you find out which city invented the bikini, maybe your two cities should become Twin Cities.

The doctor, a lady full of life, asks her assistant to provide me with the necessary data. I think she feels I'm making fun of her, which I'm really not.

The assistant comes back with the information. Here it is: On September 5, 1899, a Dresden lady named Christine Hardt appeared at the patent office and requested to patent the bra, which she defined as "Frauenleibchen als Brustträger" (breast-holders as women's underwear).

That settled, the doctor goes on to tell me about the almost total destruction this city suffered in World War II. She talks about the Women of the Rubble, the German women who worked to reconstruct the city piece by piece, stone by stone. "There were no men to do it, they were dead," she explains.

After this cheerful introduction I go out, board a Dresden double-decker, and get off in a place with a sign that reads

"Loschwitz." And everything I ever thought about Dresden immediately evaporates. Before coming here I thought this would be a poor eastern specimens of urban decay. What a surprise! Loschwitz looks like one of those picturesque cities in Switzerland. What a beauty!

I meet a couple, Mr. and Mrs. Schmidt. He's originally from Dresden, she from Köln. They live next to Köln and they came here on their vacation. Why here? To show Papa's origin to the kids, who play nearby. Does he miss the city? Yes, he does. Would he like to move back? He wishes he could, but he has a job in Köln and he'd lose it if he left. What kind of job? He works for WDR.

I look at him. No, he's not the one who collaborates with Herrmann of the Köln Wailing Wall. No. I don't think so.

We both look at the landscape, admiring it, and he tells me what he's looking at.

Saxony's Swiss Alps. Yep, that's what they call the area on the horizon.

This man could be a child of a Rubble Woman, or so the thought runs through my head.

What a heavy history this country must constantly deal with.

•••

On German TV and in the press they keep on talking about the Love Parade in Duisburg. The number of injured people rises to more than five hundred. And the international media get busy on this story as well.

The *Telegraph* reports: Mayor of Love Parade city mobbed as he visits site.

"You greedy idiot!" yelled one. "Resign, you coward," yelled another. One man hurled rubbish at him from a street bin.

Adolf Sauerland is one of the funniest and most capable men I met during this journey. He works hard to please every segment of the population in Duisburg. But now he appears to be one of the most hated men there. How the fortunes of a man can turn so quickly!

The German media, as far as I read, calls for his ouster.

Maybe they're right. But isn't it too early to judge? Why jump to conclusions when the facts are so few? Couldn't it be that the techno lovers, not known for their quiet manners, are responsible for what happened? Or, at the least, should share the blame? Weren't they the ones who stepped over the others, crushing the weaker bodies to death?

That's what really happened, isn't it?

Were any of these people arrested? Interrogated for manslaughter? Not that I can tell.

Nobody in the media points an accusing finger at the actual people involved, the festivalgoers who smashed to death their fellow revelers. They don't get their fair share of blame. They're the victims, seems to be the overriding assumption of journalists, people who are not supposed to be judges to begin with.

Why can no one point a finger at the festivalgoers? Are they above blame just because they're not officials?

I am never wrong, seems to be the motto, as long as I am just a citizen. It's always the government. The authorities.

The leaders.

And the German media are dancing along.

I should ask Paul Adenauer for his thoughts on this.

•••

Yesterday I skipped breakfast at the hotel I stayed at. It was a three-star hotel. I can't eat that food. I got used to the food of the five-star Excelsior and Elephant. Food I deserve, like Adolfy. But the food yesterday was horrible. Good enough for third-class people, perhaps, but not for nobles like me. Today, in Dresden, I 'm in a four-star hotel. Let's see if it's worthy for humans. I mean, real humans. The Select. The superhuman. The chosen.

Well, it's OK. I mean, it's edible. Not highly, though. Maybe I should have some fruit.

I should be a king. Kings have good food. Or a politician. I am sure Obama eats well. Merkel too. I'd love to be Ludwig, that king.

While thinking it over, how to establish my kingdom in Dresden, I decide I should start by practicing. No work today. No interviews. Just walking about town and being served. Why not?

And so I walk the streets of Dresden. To get a feeling for my people, the folks who will pay me taxes.

As I walk, analyzing my citizens, I check them out. Here are some beautiful girls who soon will be my maids, and there are some finely dressed men, soon my slaves.

And to my right, believe it or not, is the Hygiene Museum.

Who the heck invented that?

I enter, King Tuvia the First.

I thought, forgive my ignorance, that I'd find here a whole panoply of shampoos, soaps, toothpastes, and maybe a lemon or two.

But no. The first things I notice are kiosks. Yes. Computers abound in this museum.

Let me read what's on the mind of my taxpaying people: "Per kiss, 12–18 calories are burned and 300 bacteria are exchanged." "There is life after death for those who believe and for their relatives." "Blue—the color of peace." Is this scholarly research or the imagination of a sick of mind? Let me read more.

To promote one's health: "A stable sense of self-worth." "A positive relationship with one's own body . . ." I can't read anymore. After only half a normal breakfast, I can't work my brain too hard. Any movies here? Oh yes. Here's one about birth. A woman is giving birth. From *A* to *Z*, all the details. And all the blood. And the umbilical cord too. Just like this, and then the baby comes out. I have never seen anything like it.

And here is a big board with one question and many answers. About sex.

Question: Wie war dein erster sex? (How was your first sexual experience?)

"Scheiße," says one. "Wie meine erste Fahrstunde" (Like my first driving lesson), says another. "Peinlich" (Embarrassing), says a third.

One room here has models of three naked women. In the next room: a man with a penis that's almost as big as the rest of his body. Note: Kai Diekmann's is bigger.

Moving along: There's an exhibition about aging and death. Thank you.

In between, in case you have an inquiring mind, you can see here all kinds of body parts, cells, and DNA. If you ever wanted to see how your kidneys look, come here.

I leave this museum and go to my castle, in the center of town.

I stop at the Frauenkirche on the way. If I am to be a king, let me play a good Christian.

Everything in this church is beautiful. And clean. Great hygiene is practiced here, and I mean real hygiene.

This church might look like the church of ages ago, but it's obviously new. Reconstructed.

Old churches convey a sense of glory and power that comes with age, but this church conveys beauty and youthfulness. The old churches, it would be fair to assume, radiated the same senses when originally built.

I go to the Zwinger, to see some *Alte Meister* (Old Masters).

Here's The Trinity, by Lucas Cranach, 1516/18.

This one is a small painting, but it captures the idea of the Trinity precisely because it's so small. Old Papa with a long beard, that's God, having His son Jesus on one side and a dove, the Holy Ghost, on the other. The whole idea of Christianity in one striking visual image. A story: Papa, son, dove. End of story—and the start of faith.

And for this, millions upon millions died and will most likely continue to die. Striking!

You wouldn't believe anybody would be killed for the images in this painting.

But you'd be wrong.

Beautiful.

Outside, a group of Israeli tourists pass by. I catch a conversation, held pretty loud, between a man and a woman.

He, pointing at the Zwinger: "This is the castle of the king."

She: "You mean, like King Solomon?"

Funny, no one in this group finds this little dialogue absurd.

I check the news, as I have nothing better to do. Calls for Adolf Sauerland to resign increase, according to media reports.

It's not so easy to be a king nowadays, the thought comes to me.

I think about my kingdom with fresh eyes and decide right here and now that I don't want to be a king anymore. Unlike King Solomon, I would not be able to hoard concubines in the Zwinger if I were appointed king today. Imagine if they put my picture, next to my 999 women, in all the papers and blogs. All Germany would call for my immediate resignation.

I officially give up the idea of moving into the Zwinger.

Instead I take the tram, one of them, and take it to the last stop.

I am in Hellerau now. God knows what this place is all about. Small and medium-sized houses are all over, and no soul walking the streets and gardens. But wait, here's a man and his dog. He speaks unto me: "This area was founded by Nazi Party members before the war. They used their money to invest after the rise of Hitler. They were sure that life would be good. They survived the bombardments of 1945, because they weren't in the city. After the war, these Nazi officials fled to the west of Germany. To Frankfurt and other places. The houses they left behind were seized by the government and given to people who had lost their homes during the bombardment of Dresden in 1945. After the Wall came down, the government returned the houses to the original owners, or their families, if they could prove that they, or their families, owned them before the seizure. Of those, some came to live here and others sold their properties. My family, I am lucky, didn't have to leave our house. Nobody asked for it, and the government offered the house to us to buy at a very cheap rate. My grandmother was a minister, from the Communist Party, before the war."

Oh God, these people have a very complicated history. I board the tram again and take it back into the city of Dresden.

•••

"Germans don't enjoy life," Peter Förster, artistic director of Sommer Theater Dresden, tells me. "Our parents teach us to be good at our work, to have a good education and to work hard. But nobody told us to sit down in the sun, drink good wine, and enjoy life."

What's the problem with the Germans? Why are the parents like this?

"They think it's not important in life. They think life is about having enough money in the bank and about ensuring financial security in the future. They're not like the Italians, who take off in the middle of the day to eat and drink."

Why aren't they like the Italians?

"Germans don't know how to laugh. Looking at myself, I realize I learned to laugh only six years ago. It was very hard for me. What happened was that I had cancer and it was then that I learned to laugh. It was after the operation, for my cancer. I didn't eat for three days, and then I was told I could eat. It took me ten minutes to walk from my bed to the table. A nurse came by and she took the shit from a patient in a bed next to me, just as I tried to put the food in my mouth. The smell was so horrible that I lost my appetite. And suddenly I burst into laughter. That's when I learned to laugh. And I started writing comedies. That was the breakthrough. I became free. On the next day, I was very hungry. The nurse came and gave me my food. And then she took the shit from that man again. But I ate! I was laughing so hard, but I ate!

"That was my total deliverance!"

Does Germany need cancer, to learn how to laugh . . .?

"Could be . . ."

World War II was not enough?

"I didn't do anything to deserve the cancer, but the German nation did. One actor I know, his grandfather was the man who constructed the crematoriums in the KZ. When I learned of it, at that moment the story of World War II became a personal story to me. In my parents' generation they tried to shove these stories under the rug, and what they did is work hard at being perfect in their work and at their jobs. The result of this was that they were detached from their feelings. The effects of that behavior still haunt the younger generation of Germany today. Life, this system of thought says, cannot be beautiful. Not really."

But there are beautiful places, like Meißen.

•••

Do you know Meißen? I didn't either, but now I am in Meißen.

An elderly couple stands at the window of their apartment on the second floor. They look out at the people below, me included, and they talk. Did they demonstrate against the GDR? I ask them. Yes, they participated in demonstrations for freedom during the GDR era, but "now we have freedom. Old people with freedom. If we didn't demonstrate we might not have 'freedom,' but we would have good health care. We made a mistake, we didn't know. They were better, those days."

Of course, not everyone in Meißen has such a bleak outlook on life. Take, for example, Gottfried Herrlich, owner of Vincenz Richter here in town.

My psyche or, more precisely, my stomach demands good food, the five-star variety. If I don't get it I might collapse. Yes. I was born to be rich, seriously.

"On Sunday afternoon," Gottfried preaches, "when God was relaxed and felt very good, He created the Vincenz Richter restaurant."

If you really want to know Germany, you have to go to a wine restaurant, like Vincenz Richter, and there you will find the German soul.

"I am an old, stupid German, but there are things I know. The Germans unite the five senses, all at the same time, when they drink wine: Touch the glass. Look at the color. Smell the wine. Drink it. Hear the wine."

Thus Gottfried holds forth.

HEAR the wine?

Instead of answering me, Gottfried has his waiters prepare three different wines in three identical glasses. Then he delivers his Sermon on the Table for me:

"The father of all wines is Burgunder, a pure wine, which is identical with Bach—Father of Music.

"Riesling, the king of German wine, is identical with Mozart—King of Music.

"Traminer, wine full of power, is identical with Beethoven—Father of Gods."

Every glass is drunk to a different music. That's how we "hear" the wine.

He concludes his Teaching by saying, "To think in a deep way, to dig to the bottom, that's German."

You don't believe it's true? Think again. Here is what Gottfried inscribed on the front side of this establishment, right above this fabled restaurant's name:

"Schöne Frauen, die macht der Herrgott allein, schöne Häuser aber und Wein müssen von Menschenhand geschaffen sein" (Beautiful women are made by God, but nice houses and good wine must be created by man).

As I eat a delicious dinner in this five-hundred-year-old house, Gottfried draws a number of circles on a piece of paper. The circle in the middle, he explains, is Germany. In his words: "We are in the middle. Not hot like the south, not cold like the north. Middle. Bach could come only from us. We, the Middle Europe people, have controlled manners. That's German."

Meißen's got a Meißen, the famed porcelain company. They don't think of women and wine, like Gottfried. They think PC. There is this big sign at the entry, announcing to the world that "All Nations are Welcome." A little note on top: "Restaurant Meissen, täglich geöffnet ab 11.00 Uhr" (opened daily from 11:00 AM).

Once inside, and once you feel welcomed, you can buy stuff. Items sold here are between 39 to 100,000 euros. Whatever your nationality, they'll accept your 100,000 euro.

It's a beautiful store, granted. The riches here shout loud and proud.

Too many opposites in Saxony. Can anybody explain to me this Saxony?

•••

Maybe Stanislaw Tillich, Saxony's prime minister. I go to meet him. But before I get to see His Highness, members of his staff have a chat with me. They tell me, though I never asked, that PM Tillich visited Israel just a few weeks ago.

Israel again? How do these Jews sneak in always, especially when least expected?

When I enter the PM's chambers I ask him why he went to Israel and why now. He couldn't do it before, he says, because "I was in the European Parliament for ten years, I was on the budget committee, and there people save money, they don't spend it . . ." This man, obviously, has a healthy sense of humor.

Why Israel? I ask.

"We have a long, long relationship with Israel. You know, I was born in the eastern part of Germany. We've learned a lot of things about Israel, but not the truth. We have learned two things, two definitions that the GDR used: There are two aggressors in the world. One is the US and the other is Israel. This is what I learned in the first years of my life. So I started reading about Israel, I read articles and books, and now that I am a PM it's important to me to continue a relationship with Israel. And it was important for me to get my own impressions of Israel. For me it was really interesting because on my first evening, on the Mount of Olives, we met Germans working there to achieve better understanding between the West Bank and Israel."

He goes on.

"For me, as a Christian, I didn't understand why they have a wall in the only democracy in the Mideast. Why they use this instrument. I said to my partners from the Israeli side, You have to allow the Palestinians a chance to develop their own economy and to give them free movement. There should be, for the future, a better relationship between both sides."

So, you're a critic of the wall?

"I could understand, for security reasons, that the wall is OK. But, on the other hand, a wall does limit free movement."

This goes without saying. I mean—

"I have seen different lines, which were agreed to by the Palestinian side, by international organizations, and by Israel. But now they develop different plans, how they build the wall. There are now islands in the West Bank, making it very difficult to go from one island to another island. For me it was understandable the first plan that I saw, to make a wall around the whole area. But now they start to make islands too, they make corridors because they go to the beach in the Dead Sea. Of this I am critical."

The Israelis, perhaps you weren't aware, strangle the poor Palestinians, deprive them of freedom, deny them the chance for economic viability, only because they feel like swimming in the Dead Sea.

Stanislaw is not the only one attending this very deep conversation. His press person is here as well. And, as the saying goes, he smells a rat. He's paid to make sure his boss doesn't make any mistakes. And right here, right now, he interjects. "Our issue today is a different one. I didn't mean to interfere, but maybe we should go to—"

Reasonably enough, he wants to run away from the "Jewish" issue as one would from a blazing fire. We agreed beforehand that we'd be talking about Germany and Sorbs. But I tell him that no-Sorbs is actually more reasonable. I explain: If you go to the market to buy a banana and on the way you meet a beautiful girl, wouldn't you go for the girl?

Stanislaw is laughing, he digs it. His press person, on the other hand, sees more red lights. Problem is, he's not the boss. Sorry.

Why are Germans so obsessed with the Mideast?

"We live with our history. Normally we are friends of the Jewish people, because of the Holocaust. That's why, on one hand I say, the state of Israel is our partner and our friend. But on the other hand we say, Why don't they find a way to solve this long-existing problem? That's two points. The third, I'd say, is that

Israel is a key element in the Arab world, key for the future development of this region. We say, why don't they find better ways to deal with it? Then, Israel is in the Arab world, which is very important. Israel is a key element. Each action that Israel takes against, for example, I don't know—the Palestinians, Lebanon, Syria—will always influence the balance of power in the world. Israel is a key element."

He and Helge Schneider, I believe, should be sent to the Middle East to solve this conflict once and for all. Stanislaw will get the Israelis off the beach, Helge will give the Arabs and the Jews 20 euros an hour and, boom, peace will take effect immediately. Then we could even transfer the Rose Garden from Marxloh to Jerusalem, raise up two fingers, peace and love, and the German people would finally stop worrying about the Palestinians and everybody would have a good night's sleep.

Stanislaw goes on and on. His press person can't stop him. That's it, the boss wants to talk. It's almost half an hour since we began, and Stanislaw is on the ride of his life. The man talks. He's on automatic. He tells me about a book he read, he explains to me intricate political ideas, and he seems to be very proud of himself. He's proud and I'm happy. Yes, really. I am happy that a German PM tells me that he has no choice but to love me, the Jew, because his family killed my family. That's real love. I feel embraced. Desired. Maybe the whole Holocaust was actually worth it. I wouldn't get this love otherwise. Things are going well for me. I think I'm going to get a tattoo on my forehead. It will consist of one word: *Jew*. Maybe a little yellow patch on my shirt as well. I'll walk the streets of Germany and everybody will love me. Young men will shower me with gifts, young ladies with kisses. My grandpa, let me tell you in confidence, was Jewish. Honest. I feel so German suddenly.

The PM talks on and on and I'm dreaming and dreaming. And when I dream of the German masses kissing me, all of a sudden Duisburg enters my mind. Adolf Sauerland!

Should Sauerland resign? I ask His Highness.

"Mr. Sauer, Sauermal, Sauerland," says Mr. Highness, "gave the right answer. He said that if he goes now it would be a failure of responsibility."

Stanislaw's p.r. man looks at his watch, constantly. The interview time was set at thirty minutes, time long gone. I have pity on this man and move on to ask the questions I said I'd ask.

What does it mean to be German?

"The German is curious. You'll see it, because the Germans are world champions in traveling. On the other hand, in technology, for example in genetics, they are also curious but they are not willing to take risks. Oh, they say, this could hurt my eyes . . ."

Stanislaw illustrates what Germans are: They take the plane and they ask the pilot, Is it true that it's taking off? Will it land as well? They want to cross the river from one bank to the other but without leaving the first bank. That's the Germans.

"They are constantly worried."

At this Stanislaw points to the chandelier in the room: "We changed to energy-saving bulbs, but now we're discussing if the material in the bulb might hurt the environment . . ."

On the bright side, he says, Germans are good in engineering, and "I think that they are proud of their history too. The Germans really like classical music," for example. Then he points at another Good Quality of the Germans and relates what usually happens in book fairs, how thousands come to listen to authors reading their new books.

Stanislaw, a man with a foxy smile, is a Sorb. I never met a Sorb, at least not knowingly, and I ask him to explain to me who the Sorbs are.

But before he talks about Sorbs he wants to tell me something about . . . Israel. Again. I thought we'd done with that, that we already said good-bye to that part of the conversation. But no. He learned something in Israel, he says, and he's got to share it. What is it? What's the Emergency? Well, before going to the Middle East he didn't think that the absence of peace was the fault of the Israelis. Good. But what new thing did he learn? That as long as Israel has the Islands, as he calls them, there won't be peace.

Never occurred to me that the Sorbs, too, are obsessed with Israel and the Jews. But I've really had enough of the Jews. Let's move on!

Tell me, I beg of him, about the people of Saxony and about the Sorbs.

Saxons, he says, are more open-minded and greater risk takers. Saxons "are proud of each stone outside their home, river, or lake."

And the Sorbs?

"We've been living together with the people of Saxony for more than a thousand years. There are a lot of differences. The main difference is that Sorbs don't know the word *enemy*. It doesn't exist in our language."

As we depart, I tell him that I'm thinking of going to Görlitz. He tells me that I should. Visit the Holy Grave, he says. It is the exact copy of the one in Jerusalem.

Israel again . . .

•••

Before going to Görlitz, I check to see what's going on in this world, Germany.

"German rage over festival deaths focuses on mayor," says the AP.

Under the headline "Deadly German Stampede Gets Its Villain," the *New York Times* reports that "politicians around the country, newspaper and television commentators and many citizens of Duisburg are calling for Mr. Sauerland to resign."

The *Deutsche Welle* reports that "Hannelore Kraft, state premier of NRW, has called on the lord mayor of the western German city of Duisburg to accept moral responsibility."

I take time to reflect on Germany and the Germans.

I don't know if this Adolf is guilty or not. Nor do I care. But the animosity, reaching a level of boiling bloodthirstiness, coupled with the vicious onslaught by the media, is strange to me. Convicting a man before all the facts are known is not the way of democracy, nor should it be. Why is it happening here?

A thought recurs to me: People in this society, contrary to what many of them claim, feel a deep need for an authority to follow. Not so unlike the last century, when they blindly followed Hitler. It's in them to worship authority and to totally rely on it. This perception of the Germans, at least at this stage of my journey, is the only way for me to explain why they're so keen for the blood of Adolf. It makes sense to me that a strong and faithful believer, one who has put all his faith in another and has deemed that other to be the utmost protector, can in his disappointment become so venomous when, as he feels, that authority has failed him. It's this huge disappointment that turns blind obedience into an uncontrolled need for slaughter.

A thought. Just a thought. An impression. A "first impression."

One more thought: The need to worship authority is, at least in part, a need to not think on your own but have someone else do it for you. This way, you never have to take personal responsibility. That "someone else" can be the God of the Bible, a Prophet from America, or the Collective. That last one is especially powerful these days. Germans whom I met attach almost a sacred meaning to the collective, which is basically a group that they're part of. If you're a member of a group—a *Verein*, of course—the group thinks for you. And if the group decides it doesn't matter whether its decisions are right or wrong, you, the individual, just follow the group. Size doesn't matter. The group can be as big as the UN or as small as a WG.

In practice, this is the way it works: If you fancy yourself a radical leftist, you throw broken glass at the faces of police officers. If you delight in being called Christian, you stand on line to get a blessing from an American prophet. If you love being peace and love and you flash two fingers two thousand times a day, the sweet dream of killing everyone who's not like you makes you feel safe. If you believe yourself to be an intellectual, you must be pro-Palestine. If you view yourself as a soccer fan, you raise the flag as high as stupidly possible. And if the group you belong to is the media, you desperately want the head of a little mayor. If this is true, it does neatly explain much of what I've seen so far during my time here. Also, if this is true, there's not much of a difference between worshipping the "group" or worshipping an individual. Group is a name. Hitler is a name. Both connote the same idea: I don't think for myself and I'm not responsible.

Why are the Germans like this, if they are? Because they are babies. They have a Chocolate Museum. I shiver when I write this, but it seems to be the truth.

There's one more place I must see before I move to Görlitz.

Do you want to know what it is? Join me for the ride.

•••

Wow! This is a beauty. Have you ever been here? Have you ever been to Asisi Panometer? You must experience it at least once in your life. More important than going to Mecca.

Here you experience Baroque architecture head-on. In this awe-inspiring work, Asisi gives us Dresden and its Baroque art as it was hundreds of years ago. Housed in an old gasometer, the panometer, whose name is a hybrid of the words *gasometer* and *panorama*, will make you fall in love with Baroque and classical painting. Go up the stairs in the middle of this museum—yes, there's a staircase here—and you'll be transported back in time, as this painting has a 3-D quality to it. It's alive. It moves with you as you move from point to point at the top of the staircase. Stick around and experience the light scheme employed here. The time of day moves from night to day and, as it does, you feel as if all of this were real. House, churches, grass, water, people: All "real."

Just amazing!
This is Dresden. This is Germany. Land of masters, visual masters. Geniuses. And when you experience this, you'll thank God that Germany exists.

Now, finally, I can safely go on to Görlitz.

•••

Have you ever been to Görlitz? What a gorgeous little place!

Görlitz, a beautiful German city across the river Lausitzer Neiße from the Polish city of Zgorzelec.

The two cities used to be one, all Görlitz, but the war separated them.

As the locals tell it, the German citizens on the other side of the river were forced to flee in 1945, making room for Polish citizens who were forced to flee from their homes on the Ukrainian border. Double refugees here. But when the various nations agreed in 1990 to Germany reunification ("The Treaty on the Final Settlement with Respect to Germany"), they stipulated that all German claims to ownership of previous areas had to be abolished. Tough luck.

The good news is that the people did not elect to be refugees forever and to stew in their own miseries for eternity. On the contrary: They did everything and anything in their power to move ahead in life. And whatever German borders took shape in the end, they did their part to rebuild what was left in their hands.

Görlitz, a city left almost intact following the Allied bombardments of Germany in World War II, was left to rot during the GDR era. After the Wall fell, some thought that most of the buildings in the city would have to be demolished. But the people of Görlitz instead decided to fix and reconstruct. A wise decision indeed. Today Görlitz is a beautiful city, ancient and new. Walking its streets is a pleasure both to the eye and to the spirit. It's as beautiful a city as you can imagine. And it's full of history.

Take, for instance, the Holy Tomb. Yes, that of Jesus. Really. PM Tillich was right. How did Jesus get here? A cute story: The mayor of the town long ago in the fifteenth century, was involved in a sexual relationship with a married woman. It was good and hot and sweet, but he regretted it afterward. Nobody knows exactly why. There was no Google in those days, no YouTube, no iPad, and no Facebook. He regretted it, and he went to Jerusalem to visit the Holy Sepulcher. How he made the turn from hot love to a cold grave is something that's still murky. But it happened. Truth be told, even today, as we speak, all kinds of strange stories are set in Jerusalem, a city of angelic Messiahs and flying Messengers. And that's not all. It turns out that our German mayor went the extra mile: the measurements of the Holy Tomb. He brought them with him and commissioned a replica of it to be built here.

Yes. And for one euro and fifty cents you can visit the place. Cheaper than a flight to Israel. But please pay attention to your surroundings: Adam's grave is here as well. Yes, really, the one from the Bible. That first man. How do I know? It says so in the brochure that I was handed at the entrance to the Holy Tomb.

Jesus, I am delighted to inform you, is not here. He rose. That's the whole trick. And, what else, this Holy Tomb, the caretakers here say, is more exact than the one in Jerusalem today. That one, you'll be informed on entering this holy site, itself is a reconstruction of the original, which was set ablaze a few hundred years ago.

Don't misunderstand. What all this means is that the Holy Tomb in Görlitz, built five hundred years ago, is more exact than the one in Jerusalem.

I wonder what happened to that woman, the object of the mayor's desire, and if anybody has a picture of her. She must have been very sexy.

To me today, what's most fascinating about Görlitz is that it's the end of one country and culture and the beginning of another. Totally different. Poland, that is. A word of caution here: When you cross the bridge to Poland, a two-minute walk, try not to pay attention to the graffiti on the German side. Ignore the "Sieg Heil" next to a swastika and the "Nationaler Sozialismus Jetzt!" (National Socialism now!), as you might lose your appetite before you even get to try the Polish food, which is delicious. That would be really bad.

Join me. I'm in the restaurant, across the waters, in Zgorzelec, Poland. Just to have a little Polish cake. I get into a conversation with the waitress. About the English language, no less. After several minutes, I notice that I have my hands on her, the way I would touch a close friend. She does the same, by the way. As if we were very close friends. And I don't even know her name.

This never happened to me on the other side of the river.

This closeness between people, this friendliness, this borderless and immediate affection, this humanness, belongs here but not there.

Back in Görlitz, I walk its streets one more time, wandering in corners tourists don't frequent. So many empty buildings, it's hard to look at them. Once upon a time families were formed and raised here; now only dust.

Imagine if Germany had never waged war. Imagine if the War hadn't happened.

Imagine if the Weimar Republic had endured.

Imagine if Germany hadn't tried to grab more land.

Imagine if Germany were much bigger than it already is.

Imagine.

Imagine if Germany didn't follow.
Imagine if instead Germany led.

There is a big synagogue in town. Its gates have been closed for about eighty years. It's more of a monument today than anything else. To the people who were there and died, and to the hands that killed them.

But why should we think about it? It's not my history.

My history is my mom, who had some tough nights with Russian soldiers...

•••

## Chapter 24

**Fact: Ahmadinejad Is a Jew**

I board the train due north, back to Hamburg, my base while in Germany.

A lovely couple sits in my compartment. He's doing his doctorate in biotechnology, she's an undergraduate in the same field. He used to be her teacher, she tells me. Now he's her husband. They both study in Germany, and both are Persian. He introduces himself as Amir and says something similar to what Farah told me: that the Western world knows nothing about Iran. But he has more detail to share: It's not the president, Ahmadinejad, who controls the government. How does Amir know this? Very simple: "Everybody knows this." Everybody? How come I don't? Well, I'm not Persian. The Persians, so Amir says, know that the person who stands in front, the man who goes on TV, the man who is forever in the news, has not a scintilla of power.

Is this some quirk of the Persian people?

"No. It's the same in the US. It's not the American president or the American Congress that decides things. They're just the public faces of the real power."

Who's the real power?

"The Jews."

Amir's wife, Maryam, totally agrees. In Iran, she says, she would be "arrested and flogged if caught sitting in a train the way I am now." No hijab. And that's not all: Her flowing long hair is showing in all its majesty, her hands as well, and even a little cleavage where men, may Allah save us, can see, Allah forbid, part of her tempting breasts.

Of course, if a man were tempted and she agreed to his advances, she would be "stoned to death. A man can have at least four wives but I cannot have even two husbands."

But, that said, not everything is the way it looks in Iran. "Ahmadinejad," says Amir, and Maryam agrees, "is a good friend of the Jews."

Good friend?

"Yes."

How come?

"Ahmadinejad denies the Holocaust. Why does he do that? Doesn't he know that it really happened? Everybody knows. But because there are many Holocaust deniers out there, Ahmadinejad wants to make sure people don't forget. And that's why he keeps bringing the issue to the forefront. His supposed denial of the Holocaust forces people to prove it again and again. Is there a better way to keep alive the memory of the Jewish Holocaust? There is not."

Ahmadinejad loves the Jews. Maybe he's even a Jew himself.

"Why is it," asks the soon-to-be PhD, "that every country sends a flotilla to Gaza except for Iran?" The man has proved his point. Life is so simple, and I never knew.

•••

I also never knew the story of Ulrich, the man who sells kosher wine in Hamburg. He's a rare sight in Hamburg, a Jew with a big skullcap. Would you like to drink something? he asks.

I sit with Ulrich and listen to him. Germany is good, he says. He's never encountered any form of anti-Semitism in this country. It's a good land for the Jews, really good. Is he from Hamburg? Yes, born here. His parents too? Yes, them as well. He's also a dentist, he tells me. His father too. Not only that: His father was also an insect specialist. He knew beetles inside out, and he collected them. Even during wartime. Life is good in Hamburg. So good, that his papa even survived the war.

How did he do it?

"They forgot to take him."

Forgot?

"Yes."

How come?

It's a complex and complicated story. Ulrich, you see, is a convert. Was German, now is a Jew. His mom was not Jewish, his pop was. Papa even wrote a diary during the war, documenting what happened. What happened? He collected beetles. Papa "wrote about insects" but never about the other stuff. Didn't. Life is good.

Hamburg is good for the Jews. But mama, not a Jew, "lost her mind after the war." She became a mental case.

Why?

"She was treated worse than a whore" by the regime.

I understand Ulrich. Not because he makes sense. He doesn't. But I hardly notice it: Somewhere along the tracks of my journey, sense had lost its value. The idea that Germany is not good for the gentiles but good for the Jews seems plausible to me at this stage. Why not?

Insects. He wrote about insects.

And then Ulrich says: "I asked them. They told me they knew. They told me that everybody knew everything. The Jews being killed. Everybody knew."

To understand an insect isn't always easy. To understand humans is close to impossible. I light up a cigarette and stare at the smoke coming out. My own little ash cloud.

It was with an ash cloud that I came here. It is with an ash cloud that I end my journey.

My job done. Journey over.

Now that the book has been written, I need a vacation.

Next to a border, just in case.

•••

## Chapter 25

## Sylt: Where the Rich of Germany Eat Gold

*Everything from now on is a Bonus. Awarded to you free of charge, because you've recommended this book to all your friends. If you haven't, stop reading here! Now.*

Sylt, across the border from Denmark, is where I go.

But this is a vacation. I'm not interviewing people anymore. Whoever has something to say about Nazis, Jews, Arabs, or anybody else, let them keep it to themselves. I'm not interested. I've done my part. Sorry. Anybody who wants to fight, a reminder: Without me. The only issues I'm willing to discuss are: money, food, sex. Nothing else. I am on vacation.

First I'm going to Kampen, a little town in Sylt, with big-name designer stores and moneyed shoppers.

This will cover, I hope, the money part of my Personal Trinity.

It's early afternoon in Kampen. Comfy cafés on the sidewalks. People sit and drink mineral water, not beer. Some, who splurge, have a helping of small fruit juice. Got to keep the weight down. Most of the ladies have the same breast size, more or less. It's summer, vacation time, time to wear simple clothes, like T-shirts. Only that the T-shirts I see here aren't coming from the 99-cent stores. They cost. I go to a little store and try out a sweater. Only 1,195 euros. It's too tight on me. The saleslady says I have to take off some weight. She's right. I am the fattest man in Sylt.

In the tourist information office, I am greeted by two blond models. Everybody in Kampen is a model. I look at them, such a nice sight, and then I leave. I need a cake. I want to see if Kampen has better cakes than Zgorzelec.

The waitress serving me is more of a model than a waitress. I didn't see the chef, probably a model too. Not a great cook, sad to say. In Zgorzelec the cake was better, hands down.

A ninety-year-old skinny beauty, with her hubby and friend, sit by me.

He puts sugar in his latte. He used to be a sugar commodity trader and he would like to keep the sugar value high, he jokes with me, but he seems to be pretty serious. Funny. I don't know why, but I'm the only one sitting and laughing. The other people here, the skinny and sexy, have this bitter look on their faces.

Cakes done, it's time for food, the second part of my personal Trinity. Johannes King is my man today. He is the chef of Söl'ring Hof, Sylt, hotel and restaurant. He tells me of his assets: five suites, ten rooms. At the hotel, an average of 500 euros a night for two includes breakfast, bicycles, wellness, and drinks. Top price: 1,000 euros a night..

"Rudolph Moshammer [the late German design guru] wanted a room the other day but was declined because he wanted to bring his dog, Daisy, with him."

A Rolls-Royce, from Monaco, leaves the premises as we speak. Who is that?

"He wanted a room for August next year, but they're booked."

Rolls-Royce, by the way, has an agreement with this establishment: They give a car to Johannes for use by his guests. Free of charge. The idea is simple: Let the rich enjoy the car, desire it, and eventually buy one.

Average dinner in this place: 300 euros per person.

"For the restaurant, people reserve four weeks in advance. We teach people how to spend their money."

So far, the people I saw in Sylt are bitter-looking. Any reason?

"That's typical German. The joy of life does not express itself automatically on the German's face. The wallet is important, the auto, and the watch. They are very tense. There can be no scratch on the car, the neighbor should not have a better watch, and they have at least one platinum card. Given those three requirements, how can you find joy in life?"

A few elegant women pass by, perfect breast size, skinny like a candle.

Johannes comes back to the Bitter Look issue. He has something to add.

"Look at the eyes of the women and you will understand why the men are bitter."

As Johannes says this I think of that man from Autostadt who told me that his wife is better than the car because "she is softer." What would he say to these bone ladies?

Are you happy, Johannes? Are you married?

He is, but "I am rarely home."

"A happy cook is a better cook. He is more spontaneous. The serious cook looks at one pan. The happy cook looks all over. The serious cook does not taste, the happy cook tastes."

Time to eat. Dinner today: Black caviar. Each tiny spoon: 38 euros. Appetizers, a selection of, 36 euros. Meat of deer with truffles, 55 euros. Wine: € limitless.

Christina is my waitress, very charming girl. Would she like to marry any of the people here?

"No. They're snobbish."

Glasses are poured. Red, white, whatever. Every glass has a different shape.

Why are the shapes different? I ask my wine waitress, Bärbel.

She's also very charming. Every waitress and waiter here is charming. Part of the experience. Johannes knows how to spoil his rich clients.

"Every wine needs a different glass to bring out the taste," Bärbel says.

Will the same wine taste different in different glasses?

"Certainly."

Can we do a test? I'll blindfold you, so you don't see the glasses, and then I'll hold the glasses to your mouth—

"Now?"

Yes.

She blushes. "I'm busy . . . Maybe later." I can't believe I said to her what I did. But who cares? I'm rich and everything I say is holy.

The food here, this food critic declares, is worth every penny if you can afford it. Your body will thank you, every limb and organ.

Johannes tells me that I can use the Rolls-Royce if I so desire.

Yes, I knew it all along: I was born to be rich.

Whoever believed that I would leave this country in a Rolls-Royce?! Good to be an Unwilling Capitalist. I convert. Then go to sleep a new man. Thank you, Deutschland. I finally found my purpose in life. I have faith. New faith. Something to die for. G'night. My Rolls-Royce will be waiting for me in the morning. Life is good.

On the morning that follows I wake up to the glorious skies of Sylt and am faced with a hard choice: Should I call Johannes and get my Rolls-Royce, or am I to forget my Rolls-Royce and instead go to the nude beach? Yes, I hear that there is a nude colony here and I, from childhood on, don't ask me why, love nude people.

This is a tough choice. For the first time in this his life of faith, this new man with the new religion is faced with a choice: Forgo his Rolls-Royce so he can sinfully go to the nude beach, or do good and run for the big car?

Satan makes me do this, as is always the case, and I commit the first sin: I go for the nude.

Well, at least I accomplish the third of my personal Trinity: Sex.

Yes, I know it's not PC to say this, but I love the sight of young women in their natural form. Love the shape. Love the feel. Love the spirituality of it. To the nude shrine I go.

Yes, my first sin. I feel like Adam. Hope no snake comes my way.

But, as in all religions, sin in this case doesn't pay off.

I'm at the nude beach of Sylt.

Most of the nudes here are old males or little babies.

The young babes, as we call it in the male chauvinist world, cover their treasures.

Why are these old men so happy to walk in the nude?

Here comes a beautiful lady walking by. She's almost totally dressed.

O Satan! I am going to get you one day and slaughter you! Yes, I will join the Children of Abraham on Judgment Day and personally kill you with my sword!

Promise!

I could have had such a nice day today! Imagine me and my Rolls-Royce in Sylt! The beautiful and skinny ladies would run after me, so eagerly sharing their beautiful selves with my Royce! Why didn't I think of it! I could have had a nudist colony inside my Royce.

But no, I had to succumb to Satan's persuasions. What a fool I am!

Instead of enjoying Royce and the babes, I stand here like a beggar, staring at old men's wrinkles!

I must ask for forgiveness. Does my new religion offer salvation? Can a man repent and be forgiven?

My new God, the Almighty Euro, offers me a chance. Go to Sansibar, I can clearly hear the voice of the Lord Almighty Euro, and see if they have a Rolls-Royce for you.

Off I go, the repenting Euroist.

As you drive to Sansibar, be advised: There's no place to park. All the spots are taken. Expensive cars, with bitter-looking rich inside them, eternally wait in long queues. I check all over, but there's no Rolls-Royce for me in sight. My Lord Almighty Euro was playing with me. Just as the Lord of Israel plays with His Chosen People.

At least let me eat well. I sit down and look at the list. First: the wine list. It's huge, pages upon pages.

Here's one that catches my eye: "2001er Château Cheval Blanc, 1er Grand Cru Classé A, Imperial 6,01." Cost: 6,500 euros. Too big of a bottle? They have a normal-size bottle too, Romanée Conti, Année 2006, for only 4,000 euros.

Herbert Seckler, Mr. Sansibar, comes over to say hello. I want to know how he made it so big. I heard from a member of his staff that during the season they serve an average of four thousand people a day. That's huge. What's your secret? I ask him.

"When you come here you feel it, but I can't describe it . . ."

This Seckler talks like a Picasso. An artist, all of a sudden.

Talk to me, my man!

"I listen to my clients. When they told me that they liked this or that food, I listened. And I gave them what they wanted. And when they said they wanted T-shirts, I made T-shirts for them. My clients tell me what they want, and I give it to them. This is very important. I also listen to my wife. I never changed my wife. We've been together thirty years. Maybe that's the secret. When I started I had no idea it would get like this."

And . . .?

"I come from a very poor family. My clients are very rich. But listen to this: Not one of them has ever written me into his will. I had to work hard. I didn't get anything from anybody as a gift."

What is the typical behavior of a rich client?

"They know what is good service. They order and they don't complain, 'Where's my food?' if they don't get it immediately. They know it takes time. It is very German to say that the poor are good and the rich are bad. But it's not true. I was poor. Now I am rich."

Do you serve poor people here?

"Sylt is the most beautiful place in Germany. No poor people come to this island. My clients are rich, very rich."

What makes Good Taste?

"The difference between good and perfect food is very, very small. I have the talent to understand taste, but I cannot explain it in words."

What do you think of Johannes King? Do you visit his restaurant?

"In the last fifteen years I haven't visited any other restaurants. Maybe McDonald's. My children like it."

How long do you plan to still be working?

"When I walk out of here, it will be to the cemetery."

What do you think of the German people?

"Germans should not be allowed to wear uniform. You put a uniform on a German, and he changes for the worst. We had a man at the beach here. You know, the man who takes the entrance fee for the beach. For years he worked here. Such a nice man! Then, one day they decided to give him a uniform. He got a hat that had 'Guard' on it. From the moment he put that on his head, he changed. He became rude, aggressive, and he chased people. He changed. Totally. They should never have given him the hat. You couldn't talk to him anymore. He used to be a nice man and now he became a rude man. This is 'German.' Something happens to us the moment we wear uniform. I can't explain this."

Man of no uniforms, do you have fears? Are you tortured inside?

"I have fears of being poor again, that I might lose it all. I used to have this fear every other night, now I have it every other month."

How do you deal with it?

"When it happens, when I get a panic attack at night, I get up from my bed and I go to my computer. I look at the numbers and I feel better . . .!"

This Mr. Sansibar knows how to live life and how to enjoy it. He smokes two to three packs of no-filter Gauloises cigarettes daily, is a heavy drinker of Cola Light, and loves bread. He's overweight, jolly-looking, wears a constant smile, and is a perfect candidate for Macy's Santa Claus.

Goldflocken
Echtes Blattgold – 22 Karat
E175   0,3 Gramm   Trocken lagern

L060357 Mindestens haltbar bis: 12/2011

J. G. Eytzinger GmbH   Hansastrasse 15
91126 Schwabach GERMANY
Telefon: 09122-97 65-0   Fax: 09122-7 30 30

He invites me to try his food. I go for the Nordseesteinbutt, a fish portion the size of a tractor. I think I need a bottle of Romanée Conti to go with it. Being the Capitalist that I am.

Herbert gets me a gift before I leave, a nice sweater. Fits, my size. Great.

It takes about ten minutes by car to get from Sansibar to the local supermarket. Worth the trouble. Definitely.

In the spice section you can get a very special spice, yellowish in color. Or, more precisely, goldish. Or, to be totally precise, gold. And to be even more precise, 22-karat gold. Yeah. Here's what it says on the jar: "Gold Flakes. Real Gold Sheets—22 karat. Store dry." You can buy a small jar for 25 euros, or the bigger one for 99.

People here, it turns out, eat gold.

Two hundred of the smaller jars were sold the last few months here, a store staffer says. A shopper, passing by, says she would sprinkle the gold on the dessert cake.

It takes an Unwilling Capitalist, as far as I can see, to finish a great meal by swallowing gold. Decadence might be a good word to describe this behavior, but let's not get political.

Don't ask me why, but I buy myself a liquor with gold. It's called, what else, Goldwasser. My little souvenir.

Sylt, Germany.

The most beautiful thing in Sylt is nature. A visual miracle to behold.

Here you can fully experience low tide and high tide. The sea changes every six hours. When the tide is low and the sea retreats, you must walk down there. You will be on dry ground, or almost dry ground, yet in reality you're in the middle of the ocean. Stand there and look around yourself. Start by looking up. The sky is yours. Heaven is yours. You see all 360 degrees of the sky above, and you're in the middle of it. It's an amazing experience. You feel you see the whole world, and you've never seen the sky so gorgeous. Clear, shining blue, like a bubble, a circular gem, a sapphire above you, a fascinating globe with a diamond in the shape of a sun—and it's yours for the asking.

That's Sylt. Heaven on earth.

But don't get lost in thought and dream. The tide will return in a matter of hours. And if you don't run for your life, you'll drown in your dream.

Sylt is beautiful, but it can get dangerous pretty quickly. And so is Germany. A shining gem on the planet, a diamond to behold. With the most beautiful music. Yet such dangerous thought.

Will Germany save itself from its raging seas and run to safe ground when danger approaches? Only Germany can answer that question. Only the Germans can save themselves from the clichés and stereotypes that, sadly, do reflect their true color. But the Germans, people who have proven beyond doubt that they can so faithfully restore every stone of their history to its former detail in all its glory, also have the ability to restore to human honor their dignity, create from nothing a strong backbone for themselves, and turn a corner for the better.

If anybody can do it, it's the Germans.

Move away from forced PC. Move away from "we decide together." Move away from group thinking. Move away from "intellectual thinking." And from thinking about The Jew, for better or worse. Let the Jews alone. It's time for the Germans to think for themselves, of themselves.

And do this before the tide changes.

As for me, it's time to end my journey. Denmark is across the water, and in ten minutes' time I am to board the boat that will take me there.

I will leave behind this book, the book that contains the sights and sounds of contemporary Germany that my eyes saw and my ears heard. This book, if it could speak, would say: "I am Germany." And though it contains the thoughts of this writer as well, they reflect only the first impressions made on him by the people and places of Germany.

I am on the boat. As it makes its way through the water, I look at the land I spent the last few months in. I think of the questions I asked when I started out: Who are the Germans? Is there something "German" beyond mere possession of the passport? Is Germany one nation? Two, three?

Yes, definitely. There is something "German," many things "German." The Germans I met, east and west, center, north and south, share these qualities, the ones I call German: Love of technology, self-righteousness, innate anti-Semitism, cultural curiosity, stubbornness, visual genius, emulation of America, legalism, brainy stupidity, and, the worst of all: childish extremism.

While in Berlin, I met one of the finest intellectuals crossing my path these days, the famous journalist and author Peter Scholl-Latour. We spoke for quite some time, and when I left his penthouse he said to me, "As a German, I beg you not to think that most Germans are anti-Semitic."

Well, yes and no. The anti-Semitism I encountered in Germany is probably more subconscious than conscious. Perhaps it has to do more with the psychological history of the German than with thought-out anti-Semitism. It is, maybe, in the line of: I have to blame the one I killed. It's not the same anti-Semitism that I encountered, say, in Poland. Polish anti-Semitism, as far as I can tell, is grounded in religion. Germany's is grounded in psychology and narcissism. Grandpa and grandma built entertainment centers, such as the zoo-plus-crematoriums, and I can't live with it. For them it was double the pleasure for one ticket, but for their grandchildren it's double the horror. The fastest and most childish way to ease the weight of such baggage is to blame "the Jews." They are the real Nazis; not grandpa, never grandma.

A few days ago I had an interesting talk with Giovanni di Lorenzo, the Half and Half of this book. He wanted to remind me of a big change taking place in Germany, the realization that it's an immigrant society. Well, the question is: Who are these immigrants? I met some of them, mentioned in the book, and they're as anti-Semitic as any German German. There are others I didn't mention, like that student in Hamburg who raised his glass of Coke in my honor, in memory of my family "that will soon die, Allah willing." It was not funny.

But a word of caution is in order here: German anti-Semitism is worlds apart from Islamic anti-Semitism, either that of Gaza or that of Duisburg. I had a great time with the Turkish people of Marxloh, despite the lamentable anti-Semitism I encountered there. But no matter how we differed in thought, we still enjoyed each other's company greatly. I think they're racist, they think I'm racist, but we felt perfect together. We share "racism" in common, and we go to eat together, laugh till the wee hours of the morning, and have the time of our life. Never so with the German. Children don't play with "bad" people. Islamic anti-Semitism is grounded in politics, or in religion, but German anti-Semitism runs far deeper.

It will be much easier to make peace between Israelis and Palestinians, and between Arabs and Jews in general, than to uproot the Jew hate of the German. The first two are on the table, no surprises; the third is wrapped in heavy brainy arguments and eye-blinding magical color shows in addition to being hidden behind the many masks so common to our present-day Western culture.

Do I generalize? Yes, I do. I'm sorry, but this is what I saw.

"You Americans always generalize."

As these thoughts fill my head, there is only one emotion left in me: I want to cry. The dream I once had of buying a little house in

Berlin is over at this point. I don't think I'll ever do it, not in this lifetime.

•••

Germany gets smaller and smaller the closer I get to Denmark. I look at it from afar and I imagine it to be a teakettle. A boiling teakettle.

Time passes, the boat sails, and then there's no more Germany. I disembark in Denmark, a land that impresses me as a quiet place. Might be a teakettle too, if looked at from afar, but this is not a boiling teakettle. Just a teakettle. In Denmark, it seems, the tea has already been prepared and its people are relaxing and drinking it. Will it be boring here?

In an hour's time I miss Germany, the boiling teakettle that might never cool down.

I have the Gold Liquor with me, my souvenir from Germany. The gold particles have settled to the bottom, like the gold on the German flag, but there's no black on top. It takes a little shaking to bring the gold up, to shine in its fullness. Perhaps a little shaking of the Fatherland will move its gold to the top as well.

Shake it, baby! I love you, child.

•